1/94

op.
1st d. 22⁵⁰

D0046295

High West

Other Books by Bill Ballantine

WILD TIGERS & TAME FLEAS

HORSES & THEIR BOSSES

NOBODY LOVES A COCKROACH

by Bill Ballantine
Photographs by the Author

HIGH WEST

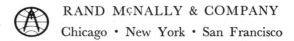
RAND McNALLY & COMPANY
Chicago · New York · San Francisco

This trip through the High West was made in a *Goldline* pickup camper, Model 220, manufactured by Travel Industries Inc., Oswego, Kansas, and mounted on a Ford Motor Co. *Camper Special.*

Copyright © 1969 by Bill Ballantine
Copyright 1969 under International Copyright Union
by Bill Ballantine • all rights reserved
Library of Congress Catalog Card Number: 75-87259
Printed in the United States of America by Rand McNally & Company
First Printing, September, 1969

*"The frontiers are not east or west,
north or south; but wherever
man fronts a fact."*

THOREAU

Contents

Illustrations

Sheep-watering hole, Monument Valley, Arizona / Stone-pocked petroglyphs, Monument Valley / Windows in ancient cliff dwellings, Mesa Verde, Colorado

Artist Peter Hurd, San Patricio ranch, New Mexico

Artist Georgia O'Keeffe, Ghost Ranch, New Mexico / A poor man's piece of land, New Mexico

Billy the Kid Museum, Fort Sumner, New Mexico / Reies Lopez Tijerina, champion of Spanish land-grant claimants

Old Indian man, keeper of the kiva, Taos Pueblo, New Mexico / Resurfacing an adobe wall, Taos Pueblo / Back entrances to "apartments" in Taos Pueblo

High West

Cowboys & Indians

The Big Doin's

By the time we hit town, the "big doin's" of Frontier Days were well under way. The Royal Coronation Ball had taken place; Miss Frontier was reigning with her lady-in-waiting. The big rodeo—said to be "The Daddy of 'Em All"—was on, with some 600 cowboys competing for over $100,000 in prize money. A carnival rattled along, fleecing willing suckers. There'd been a couple of free open-air chuck-wagon breakfasts downtown and dancing nightly at the rodeo grounds' Pavilion—three folk-rock groups and a Mexican Brass for what cowboys call push dancing (when couples dance).

This big civic celebration has been held annually at Cheyenne, Wyoming, since 1897 without having missed a single performance, even during wartimes. Because there would be plenty of cowboys and Indians there at the time, my wife and I chose Cheyenne as the jump-off point of our summertime tour of eight Rocky Mountain states—the High West —made with three of our five children by pickup truck-camper.

We'd decided to ease into camper life by degrees, so for these first few days we holed up in the Little America, an extraordinary $5-million motel, well out of the downtown hoopla and confusion. My wife, who'd complained of fleas all the way out on the plane, discovered upon showering that evening that her problem was merely thrips from a rose which, on leaving home for a long nomadic summer, she'd impulsively plucked from the border along our driveway and stuck in the cleavage of her bosom.

We didn't get into the heart of the city until the following morning—Saturday—to see the big parade, a boisterous, extravagant, oldfangled procession of the sort that has all but passed from our land. Lots of bands and drum-and-bugle corps . . . glockenspiels, snaredrums, trombones . . . tubas catching the panoply in their shiny brass bells . . . a Polaris missile model . . . Mrs. Wyoming pulling leather . . . square dancers . . . drill teams . . . a pregnant, lactating Arabian mare . . . pseudocowboys and mountain men shooting off blank pistols . . . a gilded "Pioneer Family" frozen in statuesque tableau . . . a tribe of plump Indians in full regalia, including wristwatches and sunglasses . . . a disreputable greasy-faced clown on roller skates . . . pom-pommed and screeching collegiate majorettes . . . runty, marching Mexican orphans . . . cancan dancers flipping lacy petticoats . . . "Abraham Lincoln, Father of the Union Pacific" riding nobly and wobbly on a float and looking hung over.

Vendors walked along the curb, offering hot corn on the cob and inflated rubber-horse toys, pinching them to make them buck and whinny. Boys and girls sitting on the curbstone wore Indian feathered bonnets advertising a local Laundromat. When lollipops were tossed from a float, kids jumped up, ran into the street, and snagged them gingerly from among the horse droppings.

Horses are this parade's big attraction—at least 500 in the line of march and about 100 old-time horse-drawn vehicles, all owned by the Frontier Days' committee and occupied by townsfolk decked out in family-heirloom costumes. A splendid parade!

"Wonder how the street cleaners feel about it," said Lulu, our youngest, aged 12. She'd been put in charge of laundry, transferring baggage, and keeping the log. Her big sister, Tia, 15, was our navigator and cook's helper. Tim, 13, would be our camper handyman and fresh-fish furnisher.

In the office of the Wyoming Travel Commission, a hop-skip from our parade vantage point up near the state capitol, we were introduced to Chief Iron Shell, in beaded buckskins and full-feathered headdress. He said he was sorry we couldn't meet Princess Blue Water, but after 17 years of perfect attendance at this festival, she'd decided this year to stay back on the reservation. "Can't really blame her. She's getting on—just past ninety-three."

At lunch that day, with the chairman of the Frontier Days' nine-member committee and another man who is in charge of the Indians, I learned of the enormous amount of planning and labor that goes into this once-a-year, nonprofit community affair, which brings to Cheyenne between three and four million dollars' worth of business—an amount comparable to the yearly payroll of an industry employing 300 people.

I asked about Frontier Days' Indians and was told, "We hire fifty-five, mostly Oglala Sioux from the Pine Ridge and Rosebud reservations in South Dakota. We've had different ones in charge: Wallace Littlefinger, Albert White Horse, Albert Jumping Bull. For the past two seasons we've been dealing with Iron Shell—Norman Knox.

"Mostly the same Indians come back year after year. The daughter of Matthew Two Bulls has been coming here since she was three days old. We pay the men three-fifty a day and their grub. We furnish the tepees, electric light, and cooking fuel. The women get three dollars a day, same food deal. Then there's what we call the 'dance dollar,' an extra buck per performance for each one that dances."

My wife remarked on the beautiful regalia worn by the Indians. "Most of it belongs to the Committee. We found that they were selling their original costumes, so we stepped in and bought up all we could. Now we loan it out to them for free, and we're sure always to have the authentic stuff we need to put on the show."

Was there ever any trouble with the Indians?

"Closest we ever came to it was once when Casey Tibbs wanted to do something nice for his South Dakota Indians—he comes from there, you know. He proposed to us that he could send around ten cases of beer, but we managed to talk him out of it and instead he sent a truckload of chocolate-covered nuts."

The two men smiled and shook their heads. "Ten cases of beer," one of them said, "that's about all we'd've needed for some *real* war dances."

Rowdy Rodeo

We got to the rodeo grounds, Frontier Park, early enough to look around the tepee village. Eight of the tepees were purchased by the committee from the Shoshones; an additional eight were copied in canvas by a local awning maker.

We made a brief tour with Chief Iron Shell as guide. Aside from my addressing him once as Chief Blue Shield, everything went smoothly. These professional Indians were sleeping on innerspring mattresses; we noticed an electric blanket. There were several electric frying pans and irons; most of the kids had bicycles. We met Calvin Jumping Bull, great-grandson of Sitting Bull. The White Horse family was pointed out: Nancy, Sam, Albert, Benny, Bernie, and Marlene. We spoke to Donna Red Ear Horse, Carmelita Pawnee Leggings, Nellie Two Bulls, Charlie Hard Heart, Phyllis and Darryl Tobacco.

The big show opened with a soprano shrilling through the "Star Spangled Banner," and when she hit the high notes the horses whinnied along with her. At the part about the rocket's red glare, an actual rocket burst high in the sky over the grandstand and released a silken American flag which fluttered down slowly by small parachute. The kids were impressed.

The Mayor of Cheyenne began his speech of welcome. "I know you're gonna—*going to*—enjoy the show this afternoon," he said—and so on. The kids were not so impressed. Then the arena gradually filled with the opening serpentine of horses, and the announcer gave the license-plate census in the parking lots.

The kids had never been to a big-time rodeo; my wife hadn't ever seen that of Frontier Days. It's one of the so-called Big Four, the others being Pendleton Roundup, Calgary Stampede, and California Rodeo at Salinas.

The rodeo was everything I'd told them it would be. We were fortunate to see a cowboy named Mel Holland make what rodeo authorities later said was likely the finest saddle bronc ride ever made in the long history of the sport. The bulls were properly ferocious. The steer bull-dogging stood all our hair on end. The scramble of the wild-horse race brought our kids excitedly to their feet. The clowning was different from the kind they see at the circus. Lulu's favorite event was one in which colts are separated from their mothers and then released to race down the track for a joyful reunion.

This was the first time I'd sat through a rodeo formally in the main grandstand. My usual haunt is at the chutes, the starting stalls of the bucking horses and bulls set up directly in front of the judges' pavilion.

As "working press"—writing for magazines—I've been privileged to stay loose around that area. I prefer being part of the ebb and flow of the cowboys as they shuffle about, hunker over their equipment bags, and gather in quiet knots drinking coffee or beer and comparing notes.

At the Cheyenne chutes, the contesting cowboys gather in a saltbox-shaped space, roughly 12 by 30 feet, enclosed by chicken wire, beneath the judges' stand. This is where they park their well-used saddles, bull ropes, bareback bronc riggings, contesting boots, and their tired bony behinds while awaiting their go-rounds. They loll about, chatting, smoking, and reading *Rodeo Sports News,* which is the Bible and *Wall Street Journal* of the business.

The only place to sit is on the equipment or on the floor, and there you run the risk of an encounter with tobacco juice splatter. There is a continual shuffle in the enclosure as cowboys come and go. When the bucking bulls are in the chutes, you hear the mournful clank-clunk of cowbells being dragged through the dust. You catch the pungent stench from those nervous monsters backed up against the sliding ends of the narrow enclosures.

At the chutes you smell the horses as well as the sweating cowboys. From the arena can be heard the straining rhythmic creak-squeak-creak of the saddle as a bucking horse tries to unseat its rider, the rowels' silvery spin as the spurs are raked across the animal's flanks, the cowboy's grunt and thud as he hits the ground. This is where rodeo is best. You feel the power of man against animal and better understand the danger involved. The horse's kick means more when seen at close range or when heard crashing against the wooden chute wall.

Frontier Days' custom is for everyone in town to dress Western style. Some of the getups are gaudy and expensive, but it's easy to spot the true twisters, even though the cowboys' outfits are often every bit as splendiferous as those of the towners. The true cowboy walks differently, with a raunchy go-to-hell swing, and he has a distinctive hard-bitten look. He's *been* there—something no gillie in fancy boots and spotless sombrero can take away or buy in any damn emporium.

The average rodeo cowboy deeply resents the popular public image of him as hell-raiser. The physical excitement and romance of the sport inspires all sorts of licentious ruckus on its fringes, but the contestants themselves are rather gentle fellows, many happily married, having children, and traveling with their wives. They take their work seriously.

Usually there's too much at stake for them to get involved in rowdydow. Payoff money is needed to run cattle ranches back home.

True, there is a certain amount of serious drinking among rodeo cowboys, but mostly not in public. Nor do rodeo cowboys hang around bars much to pick up loose dames. As one saddle bronc man put it: "Any cowboy what's for cattin' around, he's not wastin' his time in barrooms. He buys hisself a pint, goes to his *mo*-tail, calls up a woman, tells her he's in number such-and-so, c'mon over, babe, loosen the cinch an' let's go. Rodeo cowboys don't like to mess around with pre-*lim*-inaries. They're all for saddlin' up an' gettin' on with the main event."

Night on the Town

Bending the elbow is what Cheyenne does best of all during Frontier Days' week. After 5:00 P.M. it is doubtful that any adult male in town draws a strictly sober breath—excepting ministers of the gospel, bar owners, and cops—and maybe even they need an occasional bracer against the nightly bash. Two-fisted drinking in the city's 26 bars is the norm; there is heavy consumption of alcoholic bottle goods toted home from 22 legal purveyors.

For the young hellions of Frontier Days, Saturday night is the night to howl—*the* big one. When I told a rodeo official that I planned to go downtown, he said, "What do you want to do *that* for? It's nothing but a big drunken brawl—a lot of punks busting around looking for trouble."

I'd seen the nighttime shenanigans once a few years ago. They'd been wild, raw but very convivial, and the evening had been enjoyable. I'd gone around with a native of Cheyenne who knew just about everybody in town. He was a big black-haired Scot, known to all as "Turk," because once at a civic celebration up in Montana he'd been involved in a turkey catch that went haywire. Live gobblers, tossed off a high roof, were supposed to fly down into the waiting arms of lucky people below. A great idea—except nobody on the committee remembered that only wild turkeys can fly. These domestic birds plummeted like bombs into the crowd. They knocked down kids and old ladies, dented car roofs, and tore holes in store awnings. "For sweet Jesus sake," the Scotsman would say whenever he was reminded of the disaster, "it was awful. I come near to being rid oot of toon on a rail."

It's not hard to make the rounds in Cheyenne, for the best and biggest drinking joints are all within sight of each other; the liveliest action centers around a two-square-block area. The entire downtown section is small—only nine streets from the Union Pacific Depot's dazzling stars-and-stripes trademark up to the state capitol with floodlighted dome, easily seen by barhoppers. It gives a comforting sense of security, like God or the governor is watching over—a dangerous interpretation in either case.

My wife said that she'd already seen enough drunks to last a lifetime and so declined to accompany me into the eye of Cheyenne's annual bacchanalia. I called a cab, feeling that the camper would make too delightful a target. It was a beauty—didn't look at all like a backlot garage on wheels, as most of them do. Our camper was a new type, molded of plastic—streamlined with rounded corners and graceful curves, cream-colored with seal-brown trim.

"Don't know how close I can get you to the Plains," said the cabbie. "Took me forty minutes just to go four blocks from Jack's Bar to there a little while ago."

When we got to the Plains Hotel it had closed. At the main entrance two beefy policemen—biceps bulging their short-sleeved blue shirts, heads protected by gold-and-black hard helmets, nightsticks borne at the alert—barred entrance to everyone.

"They started tearing up a few things last night," one of the cops told me, "so the Plains closed early tonight, figuring there'd be more of the same tonight."

Looking past the officers I could see that the lobby had been denuded of furnishings. A goateed young fellow wearing a sweatshirt with "FUCH'S" printed across its front in large letters, said to me, "The Plains is chicken. All it was, was a kid said he was Tarzan and swung on the electric chandelier, and some was climbin' between floors outside on fire hoses that they unreeled, and one girl got her head cut when someone dropped a glass, a bottle, or something on it from the lobby balcony. An' there was a little fistfightin', but nothin' serious."

In the street big bruisers carried girls astraddle their shoulders. Arm-in-arm drinking buddies passed bottles of beer back and forth. A stony-faced, middle-aged Indian woman strode purposefully along leading her drunken man, his eyes glazed, right hand on her left shoulder so that chivalrously he had the protective position next to the curb. Save for them, the cops, and me, there was no one abroad over 30. The mood was tense. Drunks were truculent and those accompanied by girls had challenge in their eyes.

The cop stationed at the rear entrance of the Plains was lonesome, more than willing to talk to a stranger beyond the flush of youth. He told me that, of the total force of 52, there were on duty that night 35 police, armed with "secret weapons."

"Such as?"

"Dogs, tear gas—to name a few."

From a pocket he proudly produced a pencil-shaped container. "You can't get your breath for a while," he explained, "and then your whole upper face goes dead for about half an hour and when you recover you're in jail. It's a beautiful weapon. It can shoot twenty feet. Just this week a fellow was breaking up his jail cell. The cop on duty just called him over to the peep hole—*phffft*—and put him right out of business. Beautiful! And we also got a fire extinguisher for riots that'll shoot a good hundred feet. Our chief is a Negro. He's cutting down on all this roughhousing. It's bad for Frontier Days. We only had seventeen arrests last night, and for the week so far it's only been seventy. Last year, just on Friday and Saturday alone, it was way over a hundred."

The street fronting the Mayflower Cafe had been barricaded by the police to all but pedestrians. Along one of the metal sawhorse barriers young people perched like so many crows; the long yellow strip had bent under their weight. Against the curbs were channels of glass shards two feet wide. Young huskies—loners, pals, and those with dates—lined the curbs shoulder to shoulder.

From around the corner came a beer-drinking paraplegic in a wheelchair pushed by two buddies; it careened wildly through the crowd that milled in the street. Before the cafe's dance hall the mob was thick—at its center, a noisy argument.

From behind the windows and locked glass front door of the Elks Club, members and their primped-up ladies ogled the spectacle with morbid fascination, and in the doorway of a dress shop stood a thin young mother with babe in arms. I asked how old it was.

"Ten months," she said.

"Aren't you afraid, being here with a baby?"

"Not here," she said, "but over there I'd be."

As I walked past the entrance of a shabby second-floor hotel, a bottle zinged over my head and crashed into a plate-glass window alongside, leaving a large gaping hole. I'm still not sure it wasn't aimed at me.

I ducked into the hotel enrtance and dashed up the stairs, three at a time. The night clerk, a stoop-shouldered grizzled old geezer, let me go into a sitting room just off the vestibule lobby to look out the window at the confabulation in front of the Mayflower. He then ambled down to the sidewalk for a closer view. I preferred the aerial one. That was some hole in that window.

Suddenly the mob exploded. People skittered back like startled cockroaches. A young fellow sprawled bloody in the street.

"He got cold-cocked, didn't he?" the night man gleefully called up to me. Then he trudged back upstairs and turned off the hotel's neon sign. "You know what they ought to do with 'em?" he said. "Take 'em to jail, book 'em, and then take 'em to the Warren Air Force Base and put 'em in the stockade to sleep it off, and then put 'em on bread and water for two days. That'd teach 'em. Damn young smart alecks."

An ambulance caterwauled out of the dark, red light flashing. Efficient men in white hoisted the casualty onto a stretcher, slid him into the ambulance, and it glided away, red light flashing.

The bank clock said *12:43, 60°*—time for me to get back to sanity.

There were little drunken seminars all along the sidewalk leading to the Plains Hotel. Oddly, no loiterers before the Christian Science Reading Room, but next door in the vestibule of Sopher's Child and Teen Shop two young bucks were playing golden streams against the wall. An overalled trainman heading homeward from his work at the Union Pacific walked by, looking disgustedly straight ahead. No cabs at the Plains stand, but I got one two blocks away at the bus station.

"We pulled them all out of the Plains," said the cabbie, "after they turned over a Volkswagen on its side."

"Imagine how the guy would feel to come back and find it like that," I said in commiseration.

"Yeah, sure would tee him off, wouldn't it?" The driver chortled happily.

As we rolled along, he continued. "They're not genuine drunks; they're kooks—young kids what get three, four beers in them and go wild. They shouldn't be allowed to take the bottles and glasses out into the street. But with so many people, how can you enforce it? You can't."

I ventured that if bar owners were responsible citizens they'd not oversell the drinks.

"But it's their one big time to make it," said the cabbie.

My dreams that night were strewn with broken glass.

"Where did you go last night?" Tim asked at breakfast.
"Out," I replied.
"What did you see?" asked Lulu, "Nothing?"
"No," I said. "Plenty."

Miners &
Highland Highbrows

Pikes Peak

I'd read somewhere that two good things parents can give their offspring are beauty and privacy. I made that thought the touchstone of our trip, although it didn't work out perfectly. How much privacy can five people have in a camper built for four, where when you sit in the lavatory your knees stick out into the dinette?

Our travels with camper, however, were to take us through a section of our nation where privacy and beauty are truly treasured—the land that spills off our country's granite backbone, the Continental Divide. Our route marked off on a map of the U.S.A. didn't look formidable until it was transferred to individual state maps. Then the bite of geography seemed indigestible. It would include, besides Wyoming: Colorado, South Dakota's Black Hills, Montana, Idaho, Utah, Arizona, and New Mexico.

We were heading into a wonderland of col, crevasse, butte, escarpment, precipice, peak, pinnacle, spire, talus slope, Alpine tundra, canyon, gorge—words of enchantment. It is a terrain that must be taken seriously, especially by the motorist. The roads that squirm wickedly up, down, and over the massive mountains demand a cool head.

These states embrace more than three-quarters of a million square miles (830,394), more than one-fifth of the United States. South Dakota, smallest of the lot, claims 77,047 square miles; Montana, the largest, totals 147,138. Within the area are 12 of America's 34 national parks, 89 state parks, more than half the national monuments, and close to 70 national forests. A sampling of majestic serenity such as relatively few humans ever get is offered by thousands of acres of specially designated wilderness reaches that are absolutely free of man's pollution. In those solitudes, and in a wealth of Indian ruins, the ancient past lingers, but almost everywhere are historic scars of more recent time gone by, America's frontier days—a cruder, more amateurish age of violence than the one in which we now are embroiled.

From Cheyenne, we went south to Colorado Springs. In travels through the West I'd never made it up Pikes Peak. Always thought it a corny thing to do, like going to Atlantic City, Niagara Falls, or the Statue of Liberty. (I've been to them all.) But my family wanted to, so we did— the easy way: by diesel cog-railway.

If we'd had the camper I might have been tempted to drive up the motor highway, named for Ulysses S. Grant—once free, now operated by the city of Colorado Springs as a toll road, and likely the most expensive 20 miles of highway anywhere, for about seven million cubic feet of snow must be cleared from it every spring. But the camper was at a trailer outfitter for the day for various things we felt it needed—especially an intercom between camper and truck cab.

What is perhaps our nation's most famous peak (though certainly not its highest, for in Colorado alone about 27 peaks surpass it) was discovered in the winter of 1806 by a U.S. Army lieutenant, Zebulon Montgomery Pike, who predicted in his journal that the "Great Peak" would never be scaled. He was wrong. Everybody and his brother has made it up Pikes Peak. There even is a mountaineering club that has been hiking to the summit for the past 37 years on New Year's Eve to set off a fireworks display. One year that traditional climb was made at 32 degrees below zero.

Each summer for the past 45 years there's been an auto race up Pikes Peak. The course length—12.42 miles, with a rise of 4,708 feet—has been made in a little over 12 minutes. No fatalities, and few serious injuries, have marred the history of this race.

The climb from the cog depot at Manitou Springs begins almost immediately and so steeply that the few houses alongside the tracks at the beginning all seem to be tilted, a disturbing illusion. So do the trees.

The double seats face each other, which makes for congeniality among the passengers. I sat with Tim and Lulu, facing up the mountain. Our seat partners were a young couple with two infants. The man said he was a barber from Oklahoma. "I just locked up the shop and come up to the Springs to get away for a spell," he said—an admirable idea, the sort of thing more barbers should do.

At first we were hemmed in by massive rocks and monster trees, but before long there were modest vistas of mountain meadows and limited panoramas of mountains. The sky was an unbelievable blue, and often stands of immense evergreens far below looked like so many tiny upended and closed green umbrellas. Right from the start there was an abundance of wild flowers along the right of way. Everyone remarked on the appearance of both spring and summer blooms, due to the extreme wetness of the season. "So many I've never seen before!" my wife exclaimed delightedly. She began naming each flower she recognized and the words were poetry. Aster, yucca, Indian paintbrush, wild rose, shooting star, cinqfoil, potentilla, fireweed, yarrow, wild geranium, thimbleberry.

The views began opening out to broader, more thrilling sweeps; a light drizzle in sunshine sent a gorgeous double rainbow arching behind us. Blue lakes below in the distance looked awfully cold. After we got above the timberline there were strange and lovely Alpine flowers. It began to snow, and then a light fallout of hail rattled against our picture windows. We passed a couple of young hikers sitting out the flurry, huddled together at trackside under a blanket—only the toes of their boots visible. The colors now were wonderfully muted like those of a Japanese print. Three bighorn scampered over high rocks quite close to our train.

Near the summit we had a view across miles of space to the Gold Camp Road leading into Cripple Creek, the famous bonanza town. There was no magic golden glow; the landscape looked just like any other stretch of Rocky Mountain beauty. Soon we encountered the peak's motor road, slushy and rimmed with a light snow—much better to have come the way we did. At the top it was really cold. My bare knees felt the chill and I was glad for the heavy sweater I'd brought. We didn't linger long over the awesome view. Eastward, the plains far below were a hazy sea of blue, reaching to the Kansas border. To the north and west were snowcapped giants of the Rockies; southward stretched the Sangre de Cristo Range. This panorama inspired Katherine Lee Bates to write "America the Beautiful," but I'll bet the wind wasn't blowing through her drawers like it was through my thin linen shorts.

We hustled into the Summit House to still our chattering teeth with steaming coffee and hot chocolate. In the gift shop ("Handle If You Must, But Pay If You Bust") I bought my wife a belt strung with colored beads that spelled "Pikes Peak Or Bust."

There were some intelligently conceived and well-executed displays depicting historical aspects of Pikes Peak, its geology, wildlife, and flora. From one of them we learned about a joker named John T. O'Keefe, a sergeant in charge of the U.S. Army Signal Corps observation post on the peak back in 1876. The isolation in the clouds eventually got to Sergeant O'Keefe, and he took to the bottle with a certain dedication. When in his cups he'd send reports back to headquarters concerning violent volcanic eruptions, featuring snow-melting lava and immense explosions that "shook the peak to its very foundations." The best hoax he perpetrated— or worst, depending on your viewpoint—was his tale of an attack by an army of giant, ferocious, mountain pack rats. O'Keefe claimed that they devoured a side of beef as well as his infant daughter and would have killed his wife had he not encased her in zinc roofing material. To battle the rats with a heavy club, the sergeant said he wore stovepipe on his legs and forearms, but the rats were getting the best of it until his wife threw over him a wire lasso, which she then hooked up to a powerful storage battery and thereby electrocuted the beasts. Soon after that report hit the brass, Sergeant O'Keefe was removed to more firma terra. You see, he had no wife; there was no daughter. The fact that he was Irish didn't save him.

The trip back down the peak found everyone exhausted from the altitude and sated with scenery, hamburgers, frankfurters, and hot chocolate, but it was enlivened somewhat by the sudden appearance against the skyline of a family of marmots gazing intently at the sunset as though they were really enjoying it. Evening began overlapping daylight as we descended. By the time we pulled into the depot it was dark.

We checked out of our hotel in the morning into a shipshape camper. The intercom was a real blessing; the kids loved talking over it—"passenger to pilot, over and out." And besides, we could listen in to whatever they were saying about us back there.

The children wanted to name our vehicle. Its factory-given one, GOLDLINE, displayed in large raised golden letters on the backdoor, didn't seem personal enough. The best suggestion was "Whiskers' Wagon," after my wife's odd nickname acquired when we both were troupers on the Ringling Bros and Barnum & Bailey Circus. (She was *not* the bearded lady, but a center-ring showgirl, six-foot-tall, and at that time, 20 years ago, I was a clown.) John Murray Anderson, then director of *The Greatest Show On Earth,* nicknamed my wife "Whiskers" after her Uncle Ron, who had been a professional wrestler using that pseudonym.

Whiskers vetoed the kids' proposal. She favored *"Malgré Tout,"* which is Haitian for "in spite of everything." It was the name of a bus she and I had ridden while in Haiti on our honeymoon. I knew that whatever name they gave the camper it would end up being called simply "it."

I'd never in my life driven anything as big as this camper. The friend from whom we'd borrowed the rig had advised me somewhat regarding its handling.

"Main thing is," he'd said, "don't depend too much on the decommencers—the brakes. Just leave enough white space between you and the guy ahead or behind—one car length for every ten miles of speed and double that distance when you get going over forty. At sixty, that figures to be the length of a football field. Just remember that's no playtoy you're driving. It's a truck—a powerhouse. Be sensible."

I was told to look out for old men drivers wearing hats. Give them the widest berth possible. Watch for a woman with female passenger. ("Worse'n a car full of deaf-and-dumb mutes. No broad can converse with another without looking her in the eye to see if she's lying.") I was warned not to count on the prudence of a woman driving with children, and to beware of a teen-ager alone in a beat-up car—one more dent won't matter. I was cautioned that Cadillac drivers like to show off their power by passing a whole line of cars at one clip; sports car drivers are *virtuosi* of the gears; and Volkswagen elves will hang you up on the hills.

Young Eagles, Anthropomorphism, and Modern Cavemen

I wanted the kids to have a look at the U.S. Air Force Academy, about ten miles north of Colorado Springs by freeway, and I was curious myself to see how tax money is spent. After obtaining a map of the 17,900-acre grounds (former ranchland) at the visitors' center just beyond the academy's north gate, we proceeded to the Cadet Area, where we were permitted to view from a distance the complex of Spartan buildings—

each one enormous, but dwarfed by the surrounding Rampart Mountains. From above the Court of Honor, a vast concrete floodlighted esplanade, a neophyte cadet from Iowa was identifying some of the buildings for his lady friend.

"That un' there," he said, indicating Mitchell Hall, the cantilevered dining arena (named for Billy Mitchell—the general, not the jazz saxophonist of Dizzy Gillespie's band) "is 'Mitchy's Bar and Grill.' They can feed two thousand five hundred and twelve of us—ten to a table."

The young man didn't have to point out the interfaith chapel, which contains a synagogue and Protestant and Roman Catholic naves. The unorthodox design, long a governmental sore point, makes it a standout on campus.

The chapel's lineup of 17 tepee-like spires of aluminum and colored glass, each 150 feet high, look just like a battery of missiles zeroed in on God—the architect's iconoclastic joke, perhaps. "Some of the roofs still leak," said the cadet.

Our exit from the grounds took us past Falcon Stadium (cost, $3.5 million), named for the gyrfalcon mascots of the academy (favored bird of medieval royalty and nature's most aggressive), and we skirted the Eisenhower Golf Course.

The Garden of the Gods, a hilly municipal park of 750 acres, studded with a variety of grotesque rock masses of red Morrison sandstone with a few upthrusts of gypsum, is a highly touted Colorado Springs tourist attraction. Helen Hunt Jackson, the novelist, described it as "a wonderland of red rocks of every conceivable and inconceivable size and shape ... queer, grotesque little monstrosities looking like seals, fishes, cats, and masks ... colossal monstrosities looking like elephants, like gargoyles, like giants ... all motionless and silent, with a strange look of having been stopped and held back in the very climax of some supernatural catastrophe." You have to remember that she also wrote *Ramona*. Another author, Julian Street, once called the place "a pale pink joke." To me, it is Gutzon Borglum berserk in Disneyland.

All the principal formations have been named: Winged Victory, Baked Potato, Devil's Pulpit, King Arthur on Horse, Three Graces, Santa Claus, Setting Hen, Kissing Camels, Harry Lauder, Irish Washerwoman, Abe Lincoln's Profile, Siamese Twins, Elephant Rock. To distinguish most of them requires a well-honed imagination, a guide, or a liar. But in the High Point Curio Store we did enjoy an old-fashioned viewing device, the *camera obscura,* that projects—on a round tabletop—a 360-

degree panoramic live view, six feet in diameter, of the surrounding landscape.

We drove seven miles south of town for a drive-past look at the most fantastic military-defense installation in the Colorado Springs area, and a major contributor to its flourishing economy—the nerve center of the North American Air Defense Command (NORAD), built at a cost of $142.4 million and operated jointly by the United States and Canada. It is a huge engineering marvel, a five-acre cavern blasted and carved within the base of granite Cheyenne Mountain.

In the Space Defense Center within the Cheyenne Mountain cave, there is constant radar watch of the skies and observation of all objects currently in space—about 1,000 now circle and recircle the globe. Three dozen of these are destined to remain up for at least 10,000 years. One imaginative prober of the Cheyenne Mountain installation wondered whether fertility tests are given the workers, since, in the advent of nuclear attack on the United States, they may well be the only survivors. He was told no, but was informed that at least 40 of the 900 personnel are female. Reassuring, but I'd sort of like to know just how these future mothers of the American race were selected.

Gold Camp Towns

We headed on west via Gold Camp Road, a mountain way built on the roadbed of the old Cripple Creek Shortline.

"TRUST IN GOD," said big white letters painted on a rock at roadside as we started out. "But be sure you've got a good transmission," added Whiskers, "and a rugged constitution."

This was our first mountain workout with the camper, and I was a little apprehensive. But as we climbed and climbed the rig behaved beautifully, shifting automatically from high to second to low and back again with more judgment than I would have had doing it manually.

There were bluebirds, and cattle in Alpine meadows, and pentstemon everywhere—pink, rosy, blue, scarlet—and big fleabane-type asters, and white thistly spikes, enormous black-eyed susans, and something with a powerful sweet odor. The air, marvelously sharp and clear, made breathing a pleasure.

For 36 miles, this risky devil of a dirt road skims along, tunneling through, curling, and clinging to high country six miles southwest of Pike's Peak, passing through landscape so incredibly dramatic as to cause Teddy Roosevelt to exclaim, "The scenery bankrupts the English language!"

After threading through Victor Pass at 10,202 feet, we headed for the town of that name, a dilapidated relic of the gold rush of 1892. Its boom-time population was 16,000; now, only 400 or so ever-optimistic souls languish there. Lowell Thomas graduated from Victor High School; Jack Dempsey trained in the city hall; Bernard Baruch was a Victor telegraph operator. Texas Guinan played church organ in nearby Anaconda. The popular old-time vaudeville team of Gallagher & Shean got a singing start as motorman and conductor of an electric streetcar—the Hobnail Special—that carried miners between Victor and Cripple Creek 24 hours a day back in the golden times. State Highway 67 follows that line's roadbed. We scooted along it past the area's main industry, Carlton Mill, world's largest gold reduction plant—four and a half acres under one roof, but then shut down—and onto what's left of Bull Hill Station: a rotting water tank, a day coach without wheels, and faint traces of two or three streets petering out across the flats.

We saw the site of Goldfield, which had 1,800 residents before the big fire of 1899. Up a gulch was Independence. Its gold mine sold in 1902 for $11 million—unheard of price for those days. In 1903/04, that town had the bloodiest labor war ever in the United States. Only one old lady lives up there now—all alone, the last independent.

Remains of the Economic Gold Mill resembled ancient cliff dwellings. We drove by the Anaconda Ore House, descended a long slope, and came upon Cripple Creek, at the base of softly rounded hills pocked with prospector holes—7,000 of them, for every inch of the slopes had been probed by avid gold seekers.

On the brick wall of a building facing us, a faded sign proclaimed: MT. PISGAH . . . *"Better than the Canadian Rockies,"* says Mrs. Crowley of Topeka, Kansas. On another wall banner across the street were painted two huge soles of feet—one with sad face, the other happy. In between them large letters advertised CHASE'S WALK-EZY FOOT BATH TABLETS.

This was the richest of the bonanza towns, producing half a billion in gold ore. Its mining district, only about six miles square, was one of the world's most fabulous. In 1901, a peak year, $24,986,990 in gold was mined in the district, an amount surpassed only by the much larger Witwatersrand field in South Africa. At that time Cripple Creek boasted 41 brokerage houses, 73 saloons, 15 newspapers (including *The Colored Tribune,* published for the large Negro segment of the population), one hospital, two undertakers, one coroner, 16 churches, nine photographers, four bookshops, 49 groceries, 20 meat markets, 14 bakeries, 11 laundries, five livery stables, 11 blacksmith shops, 11 dairies, streetcars, mercantile shops rivaling those of Denver, scores of gambling halls, three opium dens, several burlesque houses (including Crapper Jack's, The Red Light, The Bon Ton), two opera houses, a vaudeville theater, and 300 prostitutes in a score of fancy houses plus a quarter mile of unpainted pine shacks known as one-girl cribs. The city, with 25,000 population (today it is 614), was Colorado's fourth largest and the center of the gold mining district of 12 communities with population totaling 55,000, served by three different railroad lines and two electric interurban systems. As many as 58 passenger trains arrived and departed daily at Cripple Creek terminals.

The mountain grazing meadows were far richer in minerals than in pasture. The grass-roots gold here often could be mined with little more than a pitchfork. Mere tyros at gold hunting made fortunes in the area. A druggist named Jones, having no knowledge of prospecting, simply sailed his hat from a high point and staked a claim where it landed; the mine, named the Pharmacist, produced well over a million dollars. A mechanic named Bernard, equally inexperienced, staked his claim around a pile of rocks on which he'd found an elk horn. He called his mine the Elkton and traded a half interest in it to pay a grocery bill of $32.47; the diggings uncovered a $16-million vein. Two young Irishmen named Doyle and Burns had to borrow clothesline with which to measure off their claim, which turned out to be the richest of them all, producing over $65 million.

While Whiskers and the kids took our dirty duds to a Laundromat, I looked up a friend of another visit to Cripple Creek several years back, Bill Robinson, a one-time Kansas flatlander who then was editor and publisher of the Cripple Creek *Goldrush*—"A Weekly Newspaper Attempting Business in Teller County," according to its front window sign. Bill took me to a big bus parked alongside the two-story false-front building that in the old days housed Johnny Nolan's infamous gambling parlor and saloon. Bill, it turned out, was trying to make a go of an ambitious bus tour of all the notable old-time spots of the Cripple Creek gold district.

The tourists weren't going for it. Not enough flash for them, I judged, after Bill had outlined the route for me. Wonderful, if you know all the colorful and fascinating history of the place, but dull if you came onto it cold. You point to a spot and say that's where Bob Womack, the cowboy, discovered the first gold and the tourist from Omaha, Nebraska, says, "So what?" You take some peach-fuzz kids from Dayton, Ohio, to Arequa Gulch, where Jack Dempsey, then a miner, fought his first fight for pay ($50) and they say, "Who in heck was Jack Dempsey?" You take an embalmer from New Jersey to the mouldering mansion of Winfield Scott Stratton, who sold his mine for $11 million and died owning one-third of all the Cripple Creek area, and the guy can't wait to get out and back to a bar. I had the feeling the bus tour was doomed, but I could be wrong.

From Bill Robinson, I gathered that Cripple Creekers like to believe they can win out against all odds. They stick stubbornly to the belief that their town not only has a glorious past, but a great future—if the town fathers can just get hold of some respectable cash to back up their ideas. Other mining towns revel in their decrepitude, but not Cripple Creek. To suggest to a resident that this is a ghost town is the bitterest insult a visitor can offer. And yet everyone in town admits that Cripple Creek is in sad shape. Along Bennett Street, the once busy main thoroughfare, every other storefront is vacant. Many buildings are sorely in need of renovation. Gold production has declined drastically; only a few hundred working miners remain of thousands. Shaft houses of abandoned mines stand decaying. Cripple Creek might offer almost everything that makes Aspen, for instance, a tourist draw—or Central City. Cripple Creek's setting is superior to that of both those mountain neighbors.

We went to meet another enterprising Cripple Creeker, a young sculptor-craftsman named Nicoli Semyonitch.

"His name sometimes gets mispronounced," said Bill, "so you got to be careful. He owns a building up the street here that he's fixing up, and he runs the town's trash route and he's got a beard. You'll like him."

To find Nicoli we had to climb to the roof of the Elks Lodge—which used to be the Stock Exchange Building—where he was doing a tarring job.

We both puffed up two flights of wide creaking wooden stairs, slipped through the beer-smelly bar, and, en route to a tall, narrow, vertical ladder that led to the skylight, I was given a brief look into the lodge meeting room, which is where all the trading action took place in the wild old days. Now, sombre elk heads look down from the walls and against them are stately carved-oak throne chairs labeled BROTHERLY LOVE, CHARITY, and JUSTICE. We pulled ourselves up the ladder and out onto the roof, which was being slopped with hot tar.

I stuck a little to Nicoli when he and I shook hands. He appeared to be in his early twenties. Nicoli's chief problem, I judged, was that which bothers many young people today—a hangup with father. Nicoli said he likes to ride motorcycles, wear a beard, and live the easy-go life of an artist. His father disapproves.

"Get a shave and a haircut, meet his people, be nice and agreeable— I'd be alright," said this young independent, "but I won't."

Nicoli was making a meager living as town scavenger, by selling a piece of sculpture now and again, and by doing such odd jobs as laying handsome, old-fashioned brick sidewalks. I asked where he'd learned such a craft.

"Learned it right here, catch as catch can. I grout with sand, but the original way was with steam-cleaned coal ashes. With the dust all taken out, the ashes won't erode, wash out, and you got a job that's just like a Roman road."

Nicoli's opinion regarding the future of Cripple Creek: "What this town needs is vital people instead of old elephants going to the grave-yard."

We climbed back down the ladder, trying not to look like old elephants, then drove out to visit a venerable doctor, the only one in the Cripple Creek-Victor area for more than 40 years.

"He's one of the best duck hunters and skeet shooters around here," said Bill, "and an awfully good trout fisherman. Loads his own shells and ties his own fishing flies. As a young man he was a miner; his father was a mine superintendent."

As we drove along Bennett Street I noticed a storefront theater that showed old-time silent movies.

"It's run by a couple from Omaha," Bill informed me. "The sister-in-law runs the machine. They only just come here for summers. That, our museum, the bars, and the melodrama show at the hotel are just about our only what you'd call commercial amusements. In the old days there was a fancy opera house—smack in the middle of the red-light district, which is all gone now, too, but there's still one house standing that's been made into a sort of museum. I'll drive you down there later for a look."

We found Dr. Denman and his wife watching a large console color television. Guests were expected from Denver and the liquor cabinet was on the *qui vive*. The TV wasn't tuned in very well and all the people looked purple. The doctor himself got a little purple when he began lighting into Moscow, the Communists, Castro in Cuba, and foreign aid in general, but soon calmed down enough to tell what it's like being the only doctor for 2,000 people in summer, 1,000 in winter.

"Only bad feature," he said, "it's confining. I don't get to leave town much. But I'm used to it. I had a district clinic as early as nineteen thirty-nine, long before anyone ever thought of Blue Cross or Blue Shield. A family paid me four dollars a month, and that included obstetrics and surgery. There were five thousand people living here then. I'd see, in a day, from thirty-five to forty patients—about a thousand a month. Farthest I ever went on a house call was out here to Witherspoons, twenty-two mile, just this side of Gundy. I always maintained that, barring danger—that is, if I could have a police escort—I'd make a house call at Nineteenth and Larrimore in skid row in Denver. I was willing to go anywhere I was needed."

As we drove away from Dr. Denman's, Bill Robinson said, "Groucho Marx got stranded here once with the family act and for awhile he drove a grocery wagon between here and Anaconda. Bernard Baruch worked in a mine at Altman. Then he became a prize fighter. He could've been heavyweight champion of the world; he could've taken Dempsey. We'll go see a guy who saw Dempsey fight here when he licked George Copeland in nineteen-thirteen—six years before he knocked out Jess Willard to become world's champeen."

This fellow, named Franklin Ferguson, was manager of the Mollie Kathleen Mine, now being operated for tourists. He'd been a miner, a grocer, a brakeman on the Midland Terminal railroad and a prize-fight promoter, and had never been very far from Cripple Creek, his birthplace. When only thirteen he'd seen Dempsey's bloody battle with Copeland.

"Jack was rough and tough then," Mr. Ferguson told us. "He didn't have the polish he got later. He worked in the Portland mine and his fight manager then was Morgan Williams. It was more brawlin' than fighting. I'd say Jack was around twenty-one when he took on Copeland. Jack himself said about it, he knocked Copeland down seven times in the seventh round and he himself was becoming arm-weary and he turned to the ref and said, 'Do you want me to *kill* this bum?' and then the ref stopped the fight. Copeland had come to Jack's dressing room before the fight and said, 'Oh, I thought I was gonna fight your brother. I might kill *you.*' It made Dempsey so mad he said, 'You better look out,' and so he whipped him good. After Jack broke his hands fighting Jim Flynn, he left town overnight. Didn't say goodbye to nobody or nothing. Made Morgan awful mad. Jack took all his trappings, his paraphernalia, and just left. No sir, he never came back to stay. He'd come here from Manassa, Colorado, and that's why they called him the Manassa mauler. Eddie Egan, he once fought a wicked fight here too, against George Copeland. Egan even bit Copeland."

Mr. Ferguson invited Bill and me to go down into the mine, and I was sorry not to have the kids along. A hard-bitten old-time miner named Ray Prim went along as guide in the drop cage just big enough to accommodate nine.

We dropped to the ninth level and got out in the cold damp of the shored-up rock cavity to mingle with a Chinese family and a group of nuns. Ray told me he'd spent 45 years underground in the mines, always working alongside a partner. "Sometimes you'd want to kill him," he said, "but mostly you had to get along together." He'd been 28 when he started and now was 73—and ready to be a miner again if gold mining again became profitable. He'd come west to Colorado in 1921 in an attempt to cure a son's bronchial asthma. Wielding a miner's pick, Ray explained the technique of gold-getting, at a place that is broken up at the beginning of each summer so that tourists can take with them pieces of gold ore as a souvenir.

"They've tooken out twenty-five tons of it so far," said Ray. The gold veins in the Mollie Kathleen run from three feet to a hundred and twenty, and always north to south. "Don't ask me why," said Ray. "Silver does too."

Back on the surface, Ray showed us the shiv wheel that pulls up the cage. "During the strike in Independence," he recalled, "a fellow pulling up thirteen men cut the cable and let them drop. Another time the cable operator didn't stop the cage and it kept right on coming into the shiv and chewed the men all up into bits."

As we left this mine on Tenderfoot Hill I noticed that its advertising signs called it, "Educational, Realistic and Fasanating." I agreed.

From there Bill drove me to Myers Avenue and past the bordellos' last stand, the house that never was a home, known as The Old Homestead, an ugly, two-story, square brick building painted white, with clumsy portico and bay window at its front. I rejoined my neglected family and took them for lunch to Cripple Creek's showplace, the Imperial Hotel, built in 1896 shortly after the town's most disastrous fire. In 1946 it was restored and renovated, with innerspring mattresses and other twentieth-century amenities and no loss of Victorian charm, by a couple of brave adventurers named Wayne and Dorothy Mackin, who'd come from Kansas City, where Mrs. Mackin had been a food broker.

The Mackins are still on the job after 20 years, and even though it was one of his two busiest times of day, Wayne took us on a capsule tour of the place, which is loaded with a conglomeration of turn-of-the-century furniture, paintings, decorative objects, and prints. We were told that 700 rolls of antique wallpaper were used on the walls, some of which are fourteen feet high.

Room number 50 has a charmingly ornate brass-and-enamel priest's bed brought west by covered wagon. (How Mr. Mackin knew it was a priest's bed, I'll never know. Perhaps the mattress was dented only on one side).

The dining room was jammed with portly middle-aged ladies wearing badges. Maybe the Garden Club, lady Elks or the Loyal Confederates of Pisgah. I couldn't read what the badges said. The buffet line had come to a standstill due to one member taking forever poking over the roast chicken—trying to decide on just the right piece. During the pause I asked the lady ahead of me about the badge people. She said they were *aarps*. I said, what? She repeated, *aarps*—the American Association of Retired People. Out of Denver, they come once a month on a bus to have lunch and see the show; gives them something to do besides clipping coupons and studying wrinkles in the mirror.

After lunch, we went to the basement theater—the stairwell down to the cafe-auditorium is papered with worthless gold-mine stock certificates. We settled the kids in for the matinee—*Hazel Kirk, or Adrift From Her Father's Love*—one of the authentic scripts of the 1850-1900 period that young professionals (all paid scale) perform in as straight a style as they are able. In the beginning, in 1947, the players had been college-kid amateurs, and there were singing waiters who relied on risqué material learned from old Sophie Tucker records.

I couldn't help thinking that here were the Mackins, most successful entrepreneurs in town, and little they were doing concerned Cripple Creek history. Their establishment could have been set up anywhere in the High West and prospered. And there was Bill Robinson, studiously loyal to the town's historic past, conscientiously trying to show visitors what it really was like in this town that holds his heart, and nobody gives a good damn. Even the operators dressing up the bawdy house into something romantic were coining more money than Bill. I admired him for his integrity and his grit.

After promising the kids, cross our hearts, that we'd be back in time for the olio, I took Whiskers in the camper for a swing around town. We skipped the Elks Club roof (you see one, you've seen them all), but visited all the other places I'd been to with Robinson—though I wasn't drawn back to the doctor's place. This time I stopped at The Old Homestead. According to legend, it had been the fanciest brothel in town—$100 a night, including breakfast; three parlors downstairs, five bedrooms upstairs. The rooms now are furnished with period pieces; and mannequins, dressed in costumes of the day, are posed—in the words of this enterprise's advertising brochure—to "replace their flesh and blood sisters, to lend realism to the scene."

"I never heard of *anyone* going to bed with her hat on," commented Whiskers.

A modern advertisement for The Old Homestead says: "It is appealing to adults and children alike, for this house is one of the few existing examples of the late 1900 period in architecture and furnishings."

A doggerel poem by Rufus Porter, self-styled "hard rock poet," written about the bawdy side of Cripple Creek history, ends with this verse: "So you who write historic slush / Please try to keep it true— / The great camp needs no white-wash brush / For Meyers Avenue." With that in mind, I dug in old newspaper files for some unvarnished truth about the notorious sex traffic on that thoroughfare. Certainly, the place could not have been as frivolous and gay as its present exploiters claim. I found that prostitution in Cripple Creek was not illegal. Each madam was taxed $16 a month and each of her girls paid $6. Dance hall and crib doxies were taxed only $4 monthly. The girls had to pay for an enforced regular physical examination. Many of the inmates of those disreputable houses were teen-agers, and most were alcoholics or morphine addicts. Quite a few became suicides by taking overdoses of that drug, chloroform, or carbolic acid.

The greatest madam of them all, Pearl DeVere, mistress of The Old Homestead, died in 1897 from an overstrong sleeping potion. Her funeral was attended by a 20-piece Elks Club brass band, four mounted policemen, buggies loaded with professional associates, and carriages overflowing with floral offerings.

We went to Mount Pisgah cemetery, at the end of town, and found Pearl's grave, marked by a large stone shaped like a heart. This burial place is free to all comers—no charge for lots. Most of the sunken, neglected graves are enclosed by iron picket fences or primitive arrangements of posts and chains; one plot contains 50 perfectly blank headstones, marking graves of unknown soldiers of World War II.

From there we visited the town's latest restoration, the 1901 Teller County Hospital that has been adapted as a hotel. Guests get a kick out of staying in rooms that still have their original identity plaques over the doors: *Emergency, Maternity, Nursery, Consulting, Occupational Therapy,* and so forth. Through the open door of the room marked *Intensive Care* we could see two exhilarated couples having cocktails. The *Operating Room* has a tile floor and dado; marble washstands are in all the rooms. *Quarantine* and *Isolation* are the smallest and naturally have the lowest rates.

We got back to the kids just as the melodrama was reaching its compelling climax. Onstage, something (stomach cramps? elephantiasis? rape?) had happened to the young daughter of the kilted, aged Scots laird (aged about 23). He was down on his knobby knees, clenching fists, face contorted and turned heavenward, spotlightward, declaiming, "Oh, *Gawd!* This be Thy pun-ish-mend. I canny see! I canny *see!*" He brought down the house and the curtain. I've no idea what it all meant, and the kids, unable to enlighten us, asked if they could have another soda pop. We stayed for the lively olio and sing-along with piano and a good banjo—as good as Eddie Peabody, I thought.

"He's not," said Whiskers. "But I'd like to hear him do 'Under the Double Eagle,' like we used to when I played guitar for Harry Harrison's Banjo Band back in San Bernardino. On Thursday nights at the Sante Fe shops we played between wrestling matches."

I guess a man never really knows his wife.

The Greatest Rockies

We left town at dusk. The mountains around us were the lush, warm, purply kind that Joseph Urban painted as backdrops for Florenz Ziegfeld's extravaganza *Whoopee,* which I saw from the second balcony of the old Nixon when I was a schoolboy. Eddie Cantor was the star, and Ruby Keeler deserted the show in Pittsburgh to marry Al Jolson, but I remember best the show girls. When I half-closed my eyes I could see them again—the line of long-legged, half-naked Indian maidens in trailing feathered headdresses that reached the ground, riding sideways on snow-white bareback horses, slowly stepping down the mountain trail, their bosoms (the girls', not the horses') catching the last golden rays of the setting sun, to the beat of tom-toms and the swell of the 28-piece pit orchestra. (I kept the program for a long time.)

As soon as we came to a good spot with trees and a view, I pulled off to camp for the night. While Whiskers whacked together a steak dinner in the camper, the kids made a fire and we all sat around it and ate. We pulled mattresses and blankets outside and slept under the stars, and I understood what A. B. Guthrie, Jr., meant when he called them campfires of the sky. It was lovely, except that along about two A.M. I had to crawl out of my improvised cocoon and pull into another sweater to ward off the chill.

We'd forgotten to fill our water tank and had no water for washing the breakfast dishes. (Later I noted Lulu's journal entry: "Scrambled egg is hard to get off forks with only watermelon juice.")

Just after daybreak we hit the road. There was hardly any traffic, so for the first time I let Whiskers take the wheel to get the feel of the camper. We continued south, then west to Cañon City, and from there we wound around so that we'd cross the world's highest bridge, spanning the Royal Gorge, a chasm of solid granite more than a thousand feet deep.

A park ranger told the kids that the galvanized steel wire of the cables, if stretched out, would reach from Denver to New York City and beyond into the Atlantic halfway to London. They weren't impressed.

"I think it's silly," said Lulu. "Who's gonna string up all that wire again?" I agreed.

After about 60 miles of driving west, we saw the Sawatch Range looming ahead. Flanking the Arkansas River for 75 miles, these mountains have rightly been described as "the crowning glory, the ultimate pyramid of all the Rockies." More than a dozen of the peaks rise to above 14,000 feet in altitude. To our left, as we drove along, marched a parade of mountain giants.

Covering 104,247 square miles, Colorado has six times as many mountains as Switzerland. In this state the Great Divide bulges to a width of 300 miles and reaches its climax of height and complexity. Within Colorado there are two dozen distinct ranges—1,500 peaks higher than 10,000 feet and 54 more than 14,000 feet in altitude. All of them together are known as the Rockies.

It's hard not to write purple prose about Colorado's mountains. They have inspired many writers—especially Chamber of Commerce scriveners and those who compose travel brochures—to lose their cool.

"There's a mountaintop waiting for you. The mighty panorama, hewn of timeless granite, is right out of Creation. An endless color galaxy of peaks and pinnacles soars above color-belted canyons—deep rivers of silence. Massed spires of spruce climb the tall sky. In the vastness of the gallery of Ice Age architecture, little thoughts vanish and the mind reaches upward in winged flight, as a bird freed from its cage."

That's a pretty fair example, from a promotion book produced by the State of Colorado's Division of Commerce and Development, Advertising and Publicity Section.

Even big-time pros sometimes go overboard when it comes to writing about the Rockies, but never A. B. Guthrie, Jr., who has said: "The Rocky Mountains are a feeling. Let description rest there."

When we got to Leadville in midmorning, Whiskers complained of a toothache so bad that she stayed abed. While the kids tidied up the camper, I looked up an acquaintance, Jack East, to see if he could recommend a good dentist. My wife has a long-standing aversion to doctors and dentists, but I figured if Jack knew a first-class man, maybe between us we could shanghai Whiskers into his chair.

I found Jack at his radio station and he knew of a dandy dentist—had an office right upstairs in the motel where the station is located and luckily had a cancellation at two that afternoon. I passed that information along to Whiskers. She said flatly she wouldn't go. I called the dentist and confirmed the appointment.

The call letters of Jack East's radio station are KBRR in honor of Leadville's severe winter climate. Natives claim the town has ten months of winter and two of late fall. Highest temperatures—in July—are in the low seventies. The earliest recorded frost was one July 22nd; the latest spring frost, on a June 6th. Northerly winds blow nine months of the year. Average annual snowfall is 124.7 inches. In winter grave-diggers must resort to dynamite to get their work done.

Each February Leadville holds a winter carnival that features ski-joring (skiers pulled by horses), dogsled and snowshoe races, snow sculpturing, ski games, a parade, and a Grand Snow Ball. But nothing these days matches the great ice palace that was built during Leadville's heyday, a building made entirely of snow and ice. The whole affair was 325 feet in length, with a main rotunda 90 feet high and 40 in diameter; there were two enormous wings and supporting towers, turrets, and battlements. Inside was an ice rink, dance floor, dining room, gambling hall, merry-go-round, and an ice statue of Lady Leadville 19 feet high, standing on a 12-foot pedestal.

Leadville is magnificently situated at an elevation of 10,200 feet in the upper valley of the Arkansas. Its name is one of the most noteworthy in mining annals of the world—first as a fabulous gold camp, then as one of the richest of silver boom towns (in 1880, $11.5 million in silver was taken from its hills).

Leadville was prospering, Jack told me, and he looked for even greater strides ahead since the government's long-standing restriction on silver (since 1893) had been lifted. "The price now is up to one-sixty an ounce. My dad, who's kept close tabs on silver all his life, thinks it'll go as high as two-fifty."

Much of Leadville's present prosperity stems from molybdenum, a toughener of steel and cast iron, a silver-gray metallic element with an extremely high melting point. Molybdenum's major uses are in the automotive industry and in the manufacture of tool steels and weapons of war. The world's biggest producer, the most extensive underground mining operation on the North American continent, is located at Climax, 11 miles north, which has the highest post office in the United States.

Jack, a stocky pack of energy, has always thrown himself wholeheartedly, unselfishly, behind any project that promises to benefit Leadville. You can safely say he is this lofty town's loftiest booster. This time his enthusiasm was directed to a newly established community college.

"Here we are locked up in these mountains for most of the year, and we voted-in this college nine to one by passage of a three million dollar bond issue," Jack said proudly, "while over in Jefferson County, just out of Denver, the state capital, their junior college proposal was badly defeated. And they call *us* the backward mountain people!" The institution has been named Colorado Mountain College over objections of those who wanted to call it Ski College U.S.A.

"It's a whole new mature approach to learning," Jack said. "Non-regimentation. The students work out their own information in a multi-media learning resources center. Travel at their own pace. There'll be seminars, discussion groups, and a general assembly once a week. No instructors as lecturers, but with twenty-five tutors and specialists available on the two campuses—we're even different in *that* way from other colleges. We'll have an east campus here and a west one at Glenwood Springs, which is about ninety miles west by highway. Only one other school like it in the entire country—at Pontiac, Michigan."

He gave me a brochure listing an impressive number of liberal arts, preprofessional, occupational and career programs—everything, it seemed, but agriculture.

"The only agriculture we have around here," said Jack, "is mountain burros." They're mostly used in the annual World's Championship Pack Burro Race, a frenzied bash of midsummer madness that has been taking place here for the past 20 years. The race, of men trotting alongside burros, is run from Leadville to Fairplay, 23 miles to the east, over Mosquito Pass, highest on the continent (13,188 feet).

Back at the camper, Whiskers was feeling better, so before lunch I took her and the kids around to the Healy House, a 24-room mansion of the 1870–80 mining period, furnished with black-walnut antiques and decorated by priceless original wallpapers of the day. Miss Nellie Healy's sitting room has a "fainting couch" and framed bouquets of flowers fashioned of human hair. The kids were surprised that I knew that a crocheted cover to keep the chamber pot lid from rattling is called a "husher."

Next door stands the town's most unusual building, the two-room log cabin of James V. Dexter, millionaire mine owner, banker, art connoisseur and cutthroat poker devotee. In sharp contrast to its rough façade, the cabin's interior has fine woodwork, hardwood floors, and is furnished in exquisite Victorian style.

While Whiskers was having her tooth worked on, the kids and I went for a look at Leadville's noted opera house, financed in 1879 by Colorado's fantastic Cinderella man, H. A. W. Tabor, who built a $12-

million fortune from a $17 grubstake, given to a couple of diligent German shoemakers-turned-prospectors. By sheer dumb luck they struck an exceptional silver lode at the only point on a hill where the vein surfaced.

A company of dedicated young thespians had taken over the opera house, refurbished the florid old style, and were presenting alternately *Charlie's Aunt* and *The Chocolate Soldier*—a far cry from the roistering days when such notable scenery chewers as Chauncey Olcott, Maude Adams, and Edwin Booth trod these boards and hippy, wasp-waisted prima donnas in red silk tights gleefully gathered up gold coins tossed to the stage from the elegantly draped boxes. *Othello* was once presented here as *The Artful Dodger, A Riotous Farce,* and Oscar Wilde appeared in black velvet knee breeches, silk stockings, lace collar, and a shirtfront cluster of diamonds. The subject of Mr. Wilde's lecture to an audience of dirty-necked miners was: "The Practical Application of the Aesthetic Theory to Exterior and Interior Home Decoration, with Observations on Dress and Personal Ornament." The miners didn't dig it, but they admired Oscar's platform manner. He was what we'd call "stoned."

"That portrait of Maude Adams has been hanging in the box office ever since she played here," said the young fellow handling the tickets. He'd sold only nine for that matinee.

"Afternoons are never very good," a youthful usherette explained. "And during Burro Week we give up night shows to let the Catholic Youth Organization put on their annual melodrama. But we'll do good at our Saturday midnight show and the six o'clock Sunday. The hangings are a hangup for us, too."

"The what?"

"The nightly hangings. There's a bunch called the Leadville Raiders that stages a mock robbery of the Golden Burro Cafe every night, by Baza the Bounty Hunter and Hideous Henderson, and Hideous is gunned down in the street and then hanged from a gallows, put in a rough box and carted off to the cemetery. It always gets a big turnout." My kids exchanged nervous glances.

They wanted to see what an old-time mine looked like, so we drove out to what is left of the famous, immensely profitable Matchless Mine. Solely owned by H. A. W. Tabor, all through the '80s it brought him an average of $2,000 a day, with occasional monthly totals of $80,000 to $100,000. After the panic of 1893 had ruined Tabor, these were his deathbed instructions—in the spring of 1899—to his second wife, Baby

Doe: "Hang on to the Matchless. It will make millions again." It never did, but she hung on faithfully for 35 years, living until her death in 1935 beside the mine shaft in a rude shack, which today is much too clean and orderly to represent the environment of a daft old lady, who, when she died there at age 79, was wearing newspapers underneath her clothing to ward off the cold and had her feet wrapped in gunnysacks. It was a sad ending for a woman who'd been young, beautiful, and rich enough to have her wedding invitations engraved on solid silver and to be honored at that ceremony by the presence of President of the United States Chester A. Arthur.

Uppity Aspen, Georgetown, and Central City

Last time I'd been to Aspen, the upstart princess of the Rockies, I'd found the little town charming, though overbearing, and basking in a snobbish exclusivity that I couldn't warm up to. Aspen is beautifully situated, nestling beside the Roaring Fork River at 7,800 feet, sheltered by mountains that reach upwards of 14,000 feet.

Our route took us through Independence Pass, open only in summer. Between Leadville and Aspen are the state's highest peaks, Mount Massive and Mount Elbert, 14,418 and 14,431 feet in altitude respectively. The mountains of Aspen poke into a sky that in summer is always a marvelous blue, for the air is uncontaminated. The sun shines most of the time and average humidity is about 25 percent.

Aspen was founded in 1878 by silver prospectors who'd been shut out of Leadville. The mining field reached its peak in 1887. Aspen then was a boisterous camp of 15,000, and the take from the mines—$6 million annually—turned roughshod men into instant millionaires. Smelter figures indicate that almost $117 million worth of ore was taken from Aspen's mines during the boom years. After the silver panic brought on by the repeal of the Sherman Silver Purchase Act, Aspen's population began to dwindle. By 1930 it was down to 700 people, and houses were being sold for as little as $50; many attractive ones went on the chopping block as firewood.

During World War II Aspen's dreamy slopes were discovered by our nation's first ski troops, the Tenth Division Mountain Infantry, in training at Camp Hale, located at Pando, ten miles north of Leadville.

One of those skiers, an ex-world champion, Friedl Pfeiffer, sensed Aspen's skiing potential; there now are four superb ski areas with 22 lifts, including the world's longest, capable of putting 15,000 skiers per hour on more than half a hundred runs and slopes.

In 1945, Friedl got together with Walter P. Paepcke, then board chairman of Container Corporation of America, and worked out a master plan for Aspen's revival: ski center in winter, cultural festival in summer. Artists and craftsmen, wealthy sportsmen, movie stars and other glamour pushers, midwestern escapists, eastern couples yearning to be western ranchers, ski bums and opportunists of every stripe—all were attracted to Aspen.

Paepcke had hoped to make it a Williamsburg of the West by preserving the quaintness of the nineteenth-century mining-camp atmosphere in an authentic and dignified way. But the ski enthusiasts and hungry entrepreneurs couldn't have cared less about this sort of purity. Soon the town's buildings became a motley assemblage of imitation Swiss chalet, functional modern and late nineteenth century. It was an architectural mess, and it still is.

Through the Music Associates of Aspen, Inc., the world's finest musicians and concert artists are brought to town each summer for its renowned music festival, an American Salzburg that draws turnaway houses.

This annual event gave Paepcke aesthetic pleasure, but he was more stimulated by the seminars of the Aspen Executive Program, established in 1950 at the suggestion of *Time, Inc.,* tycoon Henry Luce, who'd said to Paepcke, "Walter, what about the forgotten man in cultural affairs of our society—the great, unwashed American businessman?"

The Executive Program is capsulated in an official statement: "bringing together the economic leaders of the nation into closer contact and understanding with the leaders of government, the community of intellectuals and pathfinders in the arts ... to prevent stress from becoming distress ... essentially a process of cross-fertilization between outstanding men of many fields who join in the enterprise of trying to understand basic concepts of the socioeconomic world we live in, of theology, of man, of science and politics."

It is a program for tired tycoons with a gnawing need for reenchantment. Bona fide Aspenites sometimes refer to the visiting executives as "Yankee clippers." Their brain-stretching is induced by exchanges of ideas with their peers and by required reading of such authors as Aristotle, Plato, Socrates, Karl Marx, and Alexis de Tocqueville. Mild athletics, calisthentics, steam baths, and massages are available to take out physical kinks.

Paul Engle once declared that the Executive Program "tries to build its own Independence Pass over the snows of prejudice into the ore-bearing minds of men."

For all the idealistic fanfare, the place remains glossy, highly sophisticated. Paying supplicants at the high-flown executive sessions—which cost each man about $900 for two weeks—have no need for lifeboat drills on these cruises into the upper latitudes. No one rocks the establishment boat, and despite Aspen's widely heralded independent thought and chimerical humanism, the atmosphere there remains archly academic and conservative, true to the town's past. Even in the most rambunctious mining days, Aspen was a staid community of prosperous, cautious, and orderly conformists. The chief scalawag then was a city nighttime marshal who had the decency to rob the bank of Leadville rather than the Aspen one which he'd been paid to guard.

A memorable vestige of the old days is the Jerome Hotel, an Aspen landmark since 1889. The antiquated waterpowered, mirror-lined elevator (controlled by passenger-pulled ropes), alas, is no more, but the lobby is still a period piece of note.

The town's shops mostly are elegant boutiques with elegant prices, although we came onto one harum-scarum bazaar that resembled a thrift shop on a bad day, while displaying such expensive and exclusive merchandise as hand-embroidered Peruvian jackets and Finnish blanket coats.

"I like it here," a moppet customer ventured to our Lulu. "It's just like my room at home."

We drove into higher country, 11 miles up Castle Valley to Toklat Lodge, in an Alpine meadow near one of the area's first mining camps, Ashcroft, now a ghost town (adult population: two). The fields were splashed with Colorado orchids, golden lady's slippers, spireas, and tiny calypsos. The aspen trees in full leaf had a soft yellow-green all their own. The lodge at Toklat is built of native redstone and marble from nearby Crystal River Valley, source of that used for the Lincoln Memorial and for the Tomb of the Unknowns in Arlington Cemetery. The lodge's gift shop was atumble with Eskimo crafts—custom-made mukluks, Cowichan hand-knit sweaters, and all sorts of mountain viands: dried wild mushrooms, smoked trout and sausage, cheeses, herbs, honey, Yukon syrups, and teas from the highlands of Ceylon, India, and China.

In sharp contrast to the touristry pace and self-conscious intellectuality of Aspen is quiet, unassuming Georgetown, off to the north and about 45 miles west of Denver. To get there we climbed over Vail Pass through forest land and onto the level floor of Blue River Valley, from which we ascended to cross the Continental Divide at Loveland Pass, the highest continually open major highway pass in the United States (11,988 feet).

Perilous switchbacks through massive salmon-colored rock eased us down into Georgetown, lounging Swiss-like in a green pocket of high barren mountains. In its golden days, the town was inhabited principally by white-collars and mine owners (nearby Silver Plume housed pick-and-shovel grubbers). It is the only major Colorado community that didn't experience holocaust. With buildings in good condition dating back to 1859, the town retains a genuine aura of the past. There is little of the usual tourist claptrap: no glowing madonnas, painted plaster kewpie dolls, plastic Indian bonnets, toy guns in holsters, ceramic horses from the plains of Japan, no fringed satin pillow covers inscribed to "Mother," "Sweetheart," or "My Hero." Nothing here but quiet, unobtrusive charm to be absorbed slowly. And that's what we did.

We visited the Hamill House, once Colorado's most luxurious home —camel's hair wallpaper, parquet flooring, gold-plated doorknobs, onyx fireplaces. We admired, from the sidewalk, the privately occupied Maxwell House, a sand-tan Victorian sweetheart—dormered, turreted, trimmed in pink, white, and black—and we spent some time inside the Hotel de Paris, Georgetown's proudest sight, now a museum administered by the Colonial Dames of America. Built by a deserter from the U.S. cavalry, a Frenchman who called himself Louis Dupuy, it opened for business in 1875, offering guests steam heat, hot and cold running water, woodwork carved by French and Italian craftsmen, marble lavatory bowls, diamond-dust mirrors, thick-pile carpets, gaslight, a library stocked with hand-tooled leather-bound volumes, a large dining room with Limoges and Haviland service, and a labyrinthine wine cellar, where stood dozens of casks of imported wines and bottles by the hundreds in bins.

Dupuy's was the showplace of the wild and wooly High West.

On the narrow, short, main street we admired a fine mounted specimen of a Rocky Mountain grizzly bear in the show window of a small taxidermy shop and were drawn in to meet the owners, a young bearded Parisian, Gilbert Lomont, and his American wife, Marsha Jo, down for the summer from Golden, home of the Colorado School of Mines, near Denver. They were concerned that Georgetown was going to be overlooked by tourists when the widening of U.S. Highway 6 was completed at the edge of town.

A few doors away, in a tiny theater neatly fitted into the second floor of the firehouse of the Star Hook & Ladder, the McClellan Players were about to raise the curtain on *Lady Audley's Secret, or Death in Lime Tree Lane,* "in the version first presented at the Royal Victorian in London, 1863." We were sorry not to be able to stick around for this classic folderol, but felt we had to be pushing on.

To Whiskers, the most memorable sight of Georgetown was that of Harrison's Yellow roses growing wild in the gardens of deserted houses. "It's the pioneer rose," she said, "the toughest one."

After leaving Georgetown, we drove up Mount Evans, at 14,264 feet the nation's highest motor road, and then went to Central City to see that town's biggest tourist draw, the Opera House, on Eureka Street, built in 1878 with walls of granite four feet thick, its interior lavishly decorated Empire-style. Since 1932, when Lillian Gish starred in *Camille,* professional productions of grand opera and musicals have been presented each summer. In recent years such footlight greats as Maurice Evans, Katharine Cornell, Shirley Booth, Helen Hayes, and Mae West have appeared here on the boards once familiar to Edwin Booth, Joseph Jefferson, John L. Sullivan, Cornish wrestlers, graduates of the local high school, bombastic politicians, and—for one time only—the embalmed corpse of Sheriff Dick Williams.

In the Teller House bar next door are buckeye frescoes of the 1880s —classical Greek gods and goddesses: Leda and her swan, Venus with her apple, Mars and his biceps, and so forth—the work of an itinerant romantic Britisher.

Along the town's main stem shabby bars alternate with shops offering all the sleazy wares absent from Georgetown—plus Karmel-Korn. One of the bars had five old-time mechanical music-makers jangling away at once.

"En avant," I said to Whiskers in my most elegant Hotel de Paris French, "to *plus les cowbeaus* and *les Indiens rouges."*

To climax our Colorado ramble, we made a sweep through Rocky Mountain National Park, which straddles the Continental Divide, here a 35-mile chain of tremendous peaks. This 405 square miles of the Rockies' Front Range is one of our nation's highest regions, the essence of American mountain grandeur. Valleys roll away at 8,000 feet; the peaks rise thousands of feet higher. Sixty-five of them top 10,000 feet, 16 more stretch up to the 12,000-foot mark. Long's Peak attains an elevation of 14,256 feet. Perpetually snow-topped, it is a stark mass of reddish-gray granite with a sheer 2,000-foot face to the northeast.

The park is more than a glut of mountains; its appeal lies in the variety of its countryside. There are lovely upland meadows and glades with forget-me-nots no larger than pinheads. Enchanting dense forests of spruce, fir, and pine rise everywhere. Groves of aspen shimmer like fans made of emeralds. Lakes of brilliant blue stretch along overhanging ledges; others are formed from glacial ice. Below in the valleys rivers twist like silver ropes; swift streams tumble at roadside. There are beaver ponds and an abundance of walking and riding trails. Albert Bierstadt, German landscape artist, long acclaimed as the most romantic depicter of our Wild West, described this park as America's finest composition for the painter.

At Grand Lake is the highest yacht anchorage in the world (8,437 feet), site of an annual sailboat regatta. Beyond, to the north, are handsome mountain lodges and guest ranches. Upon leaving the roar of the Colorado River, we climbed over Milner Pass and drove on to where we could look over a 350-foot cliff to Iceberg Lake, a rockbound crystal pool with floating blocks of ice. A short distance farther on is the highest point of this road that rides the range's crest—12,183 feet above sea level. Our faithful camper didn't even wheeze. I did.

We poked along, stopping many times at viewpoints that took away what breath we had to spare. There were wild flowers in profusion, even a few bog orchids in the marshy regions. It was the wrong time of day to see wildlife, although deer, elk, and Rocky Mountain sheep are plentiful. All we saw were a few chipmunks, but the kids said they didn't count. Within the park 283 species of birds have been noted—

not by us. A hummingbird mistook our truck's left mirror for a fellow hummingbird, and we glimpsed what I took to be ptarmigans (the kids said pigeons), but that was all.

"Wouldn't it be nice," asked Tia, "if bird watchers could fly like the birds? Then you could see a lot more of them."

We pulled out of this high wonderland at Estes Park. In this part of the West a mountain valley is called a park, and this one was the domain of Joel Estes in 1860. He cleared out when two other families moved in to share the huge rugged hollow—couldn't stand the crush of humanity. Now Estes Park Village in summer is overrun with noisy nature seekers. After our day in the open we felt exactly like old Estes and lingered in town only long enough to gas up and fill our water tank.

"I bet we've been on all the highest Rockies," said Tim, "and over all the highest passes."

"Not quite," I told him. He was forgetting that the Rockies are more than 2,000 miles long.

Lofty Heroes

A Cave &
Custer-cum-Hollywood

From Estes Park we headed north toward South Dakota, passing through Laramie, home of Wyoming's highest institution of higher learning, the University of Wyoming, at 7,200 feet above sea level the coolest summer school in America, although many of the hotheads at Frontier Days had come from there.

I was sorry that our route led east of Rawlins. On display in a bank there is something I'd wanted the kids to see as evidence of sadistic pioneer behavior: a pair of shoes made from the tanned hide of an old-time bandit named Big Nose George. I've been told there's also a tobacco pouch extant—in the possession of a local doctor—that was fashioned from an especially vital part of Big Nose (and I don't mean his nose), but I cannot vouch for that.

We drove north from Laramie through Wheatland and east to Fort Laramie, a rallying point for emigrants of the mid-1800s that developed from a trading post established in 1834. In the single year 1850, army officials reckoned that people passing this fort—afoot, on mule and horseback, or riding in wagon trains—on their way to gold rush country in California numbered, incredibly, more than 50,000. But military figures then likely were as unreliable as they are today.

At Lingle (pop. 437) we turned north again, and east of Mule Creek Junction crossed into South Dakota, a state with a lot of room—16th in size, 43rd in population.

In the morning we headed for Hot Springs, once the state's most fashionable health resort. At the turn of the century, 16 excursion trains daily brought folks to the mineral springs, and glamorous worldly types signed in at the majestic Evans Hotel, which is still doing business at the same old stand.

Stopping there for breakfast, we were reminded that South Dakota's Black Hills are a favorite honeymooning spot of neighboring states to the east. A parked car with Minnesota license plates bore sardonic sendoff messages—*A LOST PLAYBOY!*, *TOO LATE!* and *SUCKER*—lettered on the back deck and windows with jet-sprayed shaving lather.

We were astonished to hear a waitress inquiring solicitously of some guests from Iowa about their young daughter's rattlesnake bite, inflicted the day before when she'd foolishly ventured off the macadam and into the brush. Our kids tried to be blasé about it; nevertheless they blanched a little.

The main street of this town, lined with quaint pink sandstone buildings, stretches for a mile and a quarter along the Fall River, a warm stream that never varies in temperature. There is trout fishing all winter; watercress grows on the banks, and bullfrogs croak though rime-frost forms for half a mile around.

Tim has a thing about caves. Ever since we'd left home he'd been bugging me to find one for him, and ten miles north of Hot Springs he got his wish—Wind Cave, a limestone cavern with ten miles of subterranean passages, formed about 60 million years ago. It is located in a 44-square-mile national park that is a wildlife preserve of antelope, elk, bison, deer, and the official state animal, the prairie dog. In this part of South Dakota there are six other notable caves, boasting a variety of features, including stalactites, stalagmites, helicites, dogtooth spar crystals, a fissure 160 feet high, an underground crystal-lined Benedictine shrine.

Whiskers decided caves are not for six-footers and stayed behind while I accompanied the kids into the earth. We were led down narrow, carved-stone steps by a long-suffering ranger who sternly cautioned us that every bit of rock in the cave belongs to the United States government and must not be handled in *any* way. I think he needed to get out in the sun a little more. These ranger guides each make four trips per working day in summer, sometimes with as many as 75 people per group.

"This would be a good place to empty the camper's sewage tank," said Lulu, as we began the long cool descent. (We'd been having difficulty finding a disposal station.)

A mile and a quarter of underground calcite-lined passageways are lighted along trails descending 326 feet beneath the surface. The temperature is a chill 47 degrees.

Peculiar to Wind Cave are boxlike, subtly tinted crystal fins—sometimes called frostwork—which are in honeycomb patterns on rock walls and ceilings.

In the confines of a cave trail, one balky child or one timid fat lady can hold up the entire procession. The silliest question asked of the ranger in Wind Cave: "Is it fireproof?" "Yes," he replied. He took himself very seriously.

We returned to Hot Springs in time to go swimming and trapeze-swinging in Evans Plunge, noted as one of the very few spring-fed indoor pools and for years the world's largest (50 by 200 feet; built 1890). The water just bubbles up through the pebbled bottom, always at a comfortable 87 degrees.

That evening, five miles east of town, before an enormous natural stage more than a thousand feet wide and about as deep, we endured the Crazy Horse Pageant, which tells of events leading up to Custer's Last Stand and its aftermath—from the Indian's viewpoint. A raw wind chilled us and turned blue with cold the half-naked Indians—both real ones and painted local stagestrucks. But most summer evenings, we were told, are pleasant at this historical spectacular, which features stereophonic sound effects, narration, and Indian dialogue of questionable authenticity—all recorded in Hollywood. The slaughter of Custer's troops, which is what everybody comes hoping to see, was presented so far away, on a distant hilltop, that much of the drama of the grim event was lost to the audience.

We slept that night snugged into a high piney canyon, our camper air-conditioned by gentle breezes. In the morning we pushed east through wheatlands—endless undulating golden sweeps broken only by the low upthrust of an occasional hamlet, a stand of weathered grain elevators, and distant clusters of storage sheds huddling together like bashful bathhouses at a beach. Then we came into reaches of pastureland where often all in sight belongs to a single man—a lonely, lazy land joined to the outside world only by the sky and a double strand of telephone wire skimming the roadside on skinny crooked poles.

Soon we entered true Indian country, the land of Red Cloud— *Makjpia-sha,* whose father died of white man's drink, and who was named for the ball of fire meteor that passed over Sioux country in 1822. Here also lived Crazy Horse, *Tasunkie Witko,* the fair-skinned, light-haired, gray-eyed one who never was photographed, who never signed a peace treaty with white men. They called him "Curly." This territory was home to Spotted Tail, Swift Bear, Touch The Clouds, Little Big Man. Here moldering in the earth is the Indian known to white men as "Man Afraid of His Horses," but to his peers by his correct name, "Man Whose Horses Inspired Terror." Lakota Indians of the Dakota Nation—bellicose, driven west by the Chippewa (Ojibwa) of northern Minnesota—were first called Sioux by the French, from an Algonquian term, "Na-do-we Siw-eg," an allusion to snakes.

The low hills here looked as though they'd been made by swoops of a giant eagle. General Harney made his historic march "to overawe the Indians" over this route. Great clumps of oak, box elder, and cottonwood, fringed by plum and chokecherry bushes, swept by as blurs of green. There was mile upon mile of eerie solitude. I could be happy in such a place if only it didn't get so blasted cold in winter.

"Out there in the winter," a gas station man in Hot Springs had told us, "the wind whistles Dixie, an' it can git to be forty below with no trouble at all." But now the wind wasn't even sighing, and it was oppressively hot. The sun is so uninhibited here that often the temperature hits 120.

I was a modern motorist no longer, but a naked brave, my thighs locked to the bare back of a wild-maned mustang, whipping across the plains on the tail of a thundering buffalo. I'd almost got him speared when I felt a poke in my ribs. "Wake up," said Whiskers. "You're over the white line."

God's Paleface Braves

Fifteen miles beyond the White River we came to the Holy Rosary Mission, established in 1888 at the behest of Chief Red Cloud for the education of Sioux children by Jesuit missionaries, whose own hands built the rambling European-monastic affair of brick kilned on the spot. I'd been here once before, several years ago, and met the dedicated Father Robert W. Lambeck, then headmaster of this remote boarding school (kindergarten through high school—487 pupils). In Father Lambeck's small office we'd discussed the changing intellectual, moral, and family problems of reservation Indians.

"The Indians," Father Lambeck had told me, "are struggling between pre-reservation values and those of the white man's twentieth century—not lost in limbo so much as robbed of their identity—victims of a deliberate attempt of the United States government to destroy them as a people by knocking off the top dogs to ruin morale."

On the wall behind the cluttered desk there had been crossed tomahawks, and Red Cloud's portrait draped with a king-size primitive wooden rosary. "It's hard to get the children used to our ways," Father Lambeck had claimed, " 'Grandpa never did it,' they say, 'Daddy never did, why should I?' "

When I'd asked what it's like working with people who are overburdened with feelings of inferiority, the priest had said, "They're childlike in their cunning and also very astute. And they remember the past very well. The battle of Wounded Knee remains real to them. Sometimes when we displease them, they'll say, 'We gave it to Custer; *you* better watch out.' "

Pine Ridge, one of South Dakota's eight Indian reservations, is seventh largest of our nation's approximately 300. It measures about 90 by 50 miles, lying just east of the Black Hills between the Nebraska line and the Badlands to the north. Nearly 10,000 Teton Sioux of the Oglala tribe live here. Almost all the best farmland—42 percent of the reservation's total acreage—has been bought up by white men, sold to them when government regulations were less strict. What land is left is held in trust for the Indians by the Department of the Interior, which handles all leasing arrangements and issues monthly checks to owners from a computer in Aberdeen.

The Oglala Sioux are not the poorest nor the richest of our Indians. The Hopis, Apaches, and Papagos are worse off; the Navajos and the Indians of Palm Springs, California, are more affluent, as are the Oklahoma tribes who own oil lands. Of employable Indians on the Pine Ridge Reservation only 43 percent have jobs. The Oglala Sioux live principally off the land, which they work themselves or lease to white ranchers, or they work for the federal government or white men who own most of the area's small businesses—principally filling stations and grocery stores. Average annual income per family is less than $900, aside from that of a few prosperous ranchers, Interior Department employees, and members of the Tribal Council. The tribal officials each receive a yearly salary of $7,500, voted to themselves and paid out of proceeds from tribal lands under grazing leases.

At the mission not much had changed except personnel. A new superior, Father Earl J. Kurth, had replaced my friend. Father Kurth wore boots—one black trouser leg tucked in, cowboy style. There was a new prefect, a young enthusiast from Minneapolis named John Staudenmaier, and a new public relations priest, an affable young Irishman named James Fitzgerald.

"I really work in the Development Office," he explained, "otherwise known as begging. At Christmastime we do a one-million-copy mailing to raise funds."

The mission's perennial and most discouraging problem is that of finance. The annual cost of education per pupil in 1968 was $500; the federal government grants a maximum of $50,000 yearly, the amount based upon attendance. Dropout rate has been as high as 47 percent, but averages 25 percent. The school's annual fees—$25 for one, two for $35, three or more $50—seldom are fully paid; one family enrolled nine of its 25 offspring and were able to pay for only two.

We arrived just at lunchtime and so were graciously invited to share the simple meal being served at a long bare wooden table in the students' dining room (school was not in session).

After lunch Whiskers and the kids were taken on a brief tour: the church (its walls beautifully stencilled with Indian motifs by a gifted Sioux named Felix Walking), the dormitories (forests of war-surplus double-decker bunks), the aromatic kitchens (where some of the mission's 14 nuns were at work), and the communal bathroom (a score of old chipped enamel tubs and the roof falling in).

The students' family names are colorful: Big Crow, Red Bear, Fast Horse, Afraid of Hawk, Brings Plenty, Crazy Thunder, Pawnee Leggings, Pumpkin Seed, and the like, but first names are as ordinary as any other Americans'.

We paused briefly for a look at the Head Start program, a supervised group of little Indians riding tricycles, hammering, playing with blond dolls, finger-painting, working with clay. One tyke, aged about five, brandished a toy tomahawk.

We were shown the gymnasium, a low-ceilinged room that had ten pillars—basketball there must be somewhat like playing the game in a forest.

"The federal boarding school at Pine Ridge has the best gym," said Father Fitzgerald, "and gets the best athletes."

The mission's library is in the charge of chubby, elderly Father Wilfred Mallon, a Ph.D. who in three years built the book collection from 250 volumes to 10,700—only 28 of which had to be purchased. The average annual withdrawal is 23 books per student in contrast to the average in the South Dakota public school system of 12 per student. The young Indians have no interest in sea or detective tales, but love ghost stories. Ancient Rome and Greece fascinate these readers; *Macbeth* is the most popular of Shakespeare's works. Though their parents are anti-Negro, the mission's Indian students are intrigued by literature about that other minority. *Native Son, The Outsider,* and *Black Like Me* have proven extremely popular.

Of the first 50 books loaned during the library's initial week of operation, 38 became badly overdue; in 1967, only 13 books were overdue during the entire year. Just three books have been lost—one was Karl Stern's *The Pillar of Fire* and the other two are known to have been stolen during a dance to which the public was admitted.

Father Mallon maintains rigid discipline with book borrowers. "You don't know how good it feels," one told him, "to have something you have to do and know you're going to do it." One little girl, bringing back an encyclopedia, reported, "The other kids told me if I lost it you'd pull out my leg and beat me with the bloody end."

Father Mallon is justifiably proud of his work. "Reading changes them," he said. "Talking to them doesn't. They respect books. In six periods a day of library classes I've not had to pick up one piece of paper off the floor nor had to put in thirty minutes a year in upkeep on the shelves. People who say Indians are naturally careless and messy just don't know very many young Indians."

I asked Father Mallon what had been his singular greatest satisfaction as librarian. He thought a moment, then said, "It was when the son of a habitual drunk, a local musician, after reading many history books, asked me, 'Could *I* be a history teacher?' "

The prefect, John Staudenmaier, took us to what he called "the

Dogpatch of the reservation," nearby Calico. "It's actually more a camp than community," he said, "what the Sioux call *tiospaie,* a group of kinsmen living communally."

We traveled in a green Chevy of uncertain vintage. "They call my car 'the water buffalo,' " said the prefect. "It's high-centered—'hunggop,' as the kids say—and can make it through all but the deepest mud. One thing here on the reservation, all Indians drive slowly—the tires are so bald, they don't dare go over thirty-five. And every car will always be *full*—trips are pooled; gas is never wasted on individual jaunts."

John's trip was to inform members of his softball team that a practice had been cancelled. "They don't go much for hard baseball," he said. "Pony racing is the most popular sport of the young men—that and rodeo—but as a rule, Indians are not competition orientated."

We went first to a two-room log cabin, the home of Harold Tobacco. A dilapidated trailer, the sleeping quarters of seven people, stood alongside. "This is luxury living," said John, "compared to what you're going to see."

He was right. Some subsequent homes were unpainted sliced-log houses, but most were nothing more than tar-papered wooden shacks, makeshift and falling to pieces. Outhouses. No electricity or running water; heat and cooking was by wood fire or propane gas, and light by kerosene lamps. The government supplies such Indians with a monthly ration of rice, flour, powdered milk, peanut butter, margarine, lard, raisins, oatmeal, cornmeal, canned meat, dried beans, rolled wheat; $50 in cash comes from local welfare.

Scattered in every yard were broken-down, partially demolished automobiles—usually without wheels, for they are the parts most cherished. Sometimes there was a pole-and-pine-bough shelter, the traditional outdoor, breeze-cooled summer kitchen—known to whites as a "squaw cooler" (the Sioux dislike the terms squaw, buck, and papoose). Grimy blankets sagged on clotheslines. These people were pitiably poor; dreariness was chronic. Yet every home hosted a few dogs, and though little respect for bourgeois values was indicated, the cattle and horses were sleek and beautiful; one Indian woman, working in a cornfield, had a pet fawn alongside her.

On our way back to the mission, John stopped at a tiny wooden church, Our Lady of the Sioux. The antependium (altar covering) was made of six buckskin hides, hand-tanned as soft as velvet. The candle holder was of buffalo horn, and a peace pipe, hanging on the wall, was adorned with eagle feathers. "The eagle symbolizes unseen reality—freedom, wisdom, and eternity," we were informed, "and the bison has to do with economic life—the earth, warmth, and fertility."

Back on the highway we picked up a hitchhiker, a thin old Indian. "Goin' to Rapid for my pills. Got no good doctors down here." He'd been a professional baseball player, he said; as we drove along he freely spouted his knowledge of that sport. He was a little drunk.

John told us later that drinking is a major problem. The tribe has voted the reservation dry, but towns outside the territory sell beer and booze, and that's where the Indians shop, cash their welfare and mother's aid checks, go to bars and dance.

"We call them parasite towns," said John. "Those of us at the mission wish that alcoholic beverages could be legalized on the reservation. Then the money could be spent here at home; small businesses would increase and create about four hundred jobs. Too, there'd be less chance of highway accidents due to drunken driving—we get some awful ones now on Saturday nights."

The drinking problem reaches down from adults to the children. "They start drinking at the fifth grade," John said, "and by the seventh it's real difficult. By twelfth grade there's hardly any student who hasn't been drunk. There are incipient alcoholics in high school—kids that show up in the morning with the shakes, kids who have to have a drink before breakfast. Smoking, too, takes hold early. It starts at third grade level, and by the time the kids are in high school ninety-eight percent are smokers."

Before leaving the mission we walked up to the adjoining small hilltop cemetery via a dirt road that had ruts deep enough to take my leg to mid-thigh. Red Cloud, whose dream of learning is being fulfilled, rests beneath a small stone monument. Enhanced by paper poppies and plastic lilies, it is the burial ground's most impressive marker, though the stone image has a badly chipped nose. The inscription says: "Brethren be of one mind, have peace, and the God of peace and of love shall be with you." Sounds too mealymouthed to be anything that Red Cloud said. Very likely the words were urged on him by well-intentioned priests. I prefer Red Cloud's scornfully ironic advice to his people after abandoning his vow to fight for their lands forever: "You must begin anew and put away the wisdom of your fathers. You must lay up food and forget the hungry. When your house is built, your storeroom filled, then look around for a neighbor whom you can take advantage of and seize all he has." That was the way, he implied, to become rich and virtuous like a white man.

The Defenders

Continuing southward, we competed in a short drag race with a lad, barefoot and bronzed, aboard a pinto pony (the camper conceded). A yipping, yelping gang of mongrel dogs escorted us into Pine Ridge, the Indian agency town of 1,256 people: American Legion post, Lions Club, Ladies Aid, PTA, Boy Scout troop, Reservation Police, health service and hospital, Bureau of Indian Affairs offices—center of this Indian universe.

In Pine Ridge we visited a small Indian-run industry where plastic leaders are knotted onto fish hooks for a Denver-based company. By doing piecework, an Indian here can earn as much as $37.50 a day; some workers tie as many as 300 dozen leaders daily, but most do from 120 to 180 dozen. Acceptable minimum production per employee is 83 dozen a day. There are not nearly enough employees.

"We're always behind in our orders about sixty thousand gross," the boss, Emil Red Fish, told me.

A certain amount of apathy exists among Indians toward accepting jobs that take them away from the security of home life. One of the commonest reasons for Indians shunning government training programs is that once a white man's trade is learned, the reservation offers little opportunity for working at it.

We dropped in on the town's moccasin factory, where 33 workers turn out about 750 pairs a day. Lacers and beaders ply their crafts at home. Manager Charles Quiver was the only employee left of the work force of six months before. "The Indian is funny," said this Indian. "He'll take off for a doin's anytime. He wants to go to a dance or such, or hunting, he just quits and goes. It's hard, too, for him to adapt to assembly-line production. He likes to work more individual."

Tacked to a pole outside was a poster announcing the annual four-day Sun Dance, a kind of country fair and tribal jamboree combined with an ancient religious ritual. The placard indicated that the once bellicose

Sioux now entertained thoughts of peace. "Richard 'Buddy' Red Bow," it read, "17 years old, member of the Oglala Sioux tribe, will pray for worldwide peace by performing the traditional Sun Dance worship. Red Bow will pierce his flesh and offer his blood, praying for the safety of American Servicemen and a peaceful speedy end to war in Vietnam."

Across the Nebraska border only a few miles south is the parasite town of White Clay, a huddle of listless establishments strung along the highway. The first store sports a large sign, "THE OUTLAW—We Buy and Sell Anything." Underneath is painted "*Lakota . . . Masopiye Sima-Tiyoblega Canmakin,*" followed by "King Korn Stamps, USED CARS, Ponies FOR SALE." A wall sign on another store announces, "*Masopiye Woute Talo Hayapi-owote*—GROCERIES MEATS CLOTHES GIFTS." The first cafe we went to offered *sunka kata* (hot dogs) and *taspan opemnipi cagasni akan* (pie a la mode), but didn't sell beer—the proprietor dispensed wine out a back window. A dingy place across the highway looked more promising. Its wide earthen sidewalk was a veritable mosaic of beer-bottle caps, flipped off and ground naturally into the dirt by men's boots. The space behind the bar allowed for a lot of action; a man there could swing a pickax handle very nicely.

The big-shouldered, smiling bartender—half Indian, half Mexican—said he'd been on the job since 1953, three days after sale of intoxicating liquor to Indians was legalized. A knife-scar across one cheek marred his dashing good looks. While he talked to us, someone touched him from behind; his reaction was catlike. Instinctively, he whirled, ready for any comer. He said the bar expected to take in from $1,600 to $2,000 a day during the upcoming Sun Dance Celebration.

"It'll be so crowded in here," he boasted, "you'll have to bring your own breath. We outsell Alliance, Nebraska, which has over seven thousand people, and we ain't even big enough to get into any atlas. The Budweiser Company sent men all the way out from Saint Louis to see how come we, being so small, was doing so good."

For the Indian bent on merrymaking there are other such gardens of pleasure around this Indian reservation and its sister, Rosebud, to the east—notably in the South Dakota towns of White River, Winner, and Martin; and Rushville, Gordon, and Hay Springs over the line in Nebraska. The police of these towns are not noted for their fair treatment or gentleness with Indians. Subjugation by brutality or the use of tear gas is commonplace. Indians sometimes are chained to their cell bunks, often are held incommunicado, and always are given harsh sentences. In an outstanding case in the town of Martin, a young Indian named Le Roy Janis —while being arrested for remonstrating with a barmaid for refusing to serve a drink to his wife—was sprayed by a tear-gas gun allegedly held two inches from his face. According to newspaper accounts some of the chemical struck a three-year-old daughter of another Indian, Andrew Imitates Dog, who promptly joined the fray, backed up by sympathetic fellow Indians. The jail, with accommodations for eight, eventually was occupied by more than 30 persons, including the child and her mother. Mr. Janis, his face blistered, eyes swollen shut, was refused medical aid, and throughout the night the child cried for milk. Janis was held incommunicado for four days before legal help arrived from Rapid City, 200 miles distant. The Association of American Indian Affairs had to search that long and go that far before finding a lawyer willing to represent an Indian. Janis was fined $70 and given a 30-day sentence. The imprisoned child was released, but both her parents were sentenced to two months in jail.

Frequently, living conditions in the jails of these small towns are unspeakable. Indians with whom I talked said that mattresses are so dirty that grease can be scraped off them with fingernails, and that bathing or washing of clothing and dishes usually must be done with cold water in either the mop bucket or toilet bowl.

Some notion of the attitude of lawmen toward Indians in these parts is gained from a statement made by a police chief to the *New York Times* regarding an Indian-police melee in one of the parasite communities: "We should have been using live ammunition instead of tear gas in a mob like that. The Indian is not a law-abiding person. As near as I can figure out, it's about like the Negroes down South—you can't let them get the upper hand."

Sioux Slaughter

East and north of Pine Ridge is Wounded Knee, where on December 29, 1890, the Sioux—most fearsome, militant, relentless, and lordly of all Western Indians—put up their final resistance to white supremacy. The event, referred to by white historians as the Battle of Wounded Knee, is designated by the Sioux as the Chief Big Foot Massacre.

Some place blame for the disaster on trigger-happy troops led by inexperienced, panicky officers. Others, less charitable, claim that this action by soldiers of the famed Seventh Cavalry was a deliberate wreaking of vengeance on the Indians for the defeat of that outfit under Custer at the Little Big Horn in 1876, 14 years previously. Journalists of the time labeled the Custer encounter a massacre by the Indians; the Sioux prefer to call it the Battle of Greasy Grass. They are sorry it happened, because after that victory the army really went for the Sioux, grinding them down until they were unable ever again to muster their forces effectively.

The infamous slaughter at Wounded Knee was the climax of the Messiah War, caused by the arousing of certain Indians by a fanatic Nevada Paiute named Wovoka, who claimed—following an eclipse of the sun in 1889—to have had a vision that made him the Indian messiah, destined to lead a campaign that would resurrect the dead, bring back buffalo to the Indians, restore their stolen lands, and drive out whites. His principal propagandism was a ghost dance, during which participants wore a magic shirt supposed to be rendered by the dance immune to bullets—a sort of early-day bulletproof vest, except that it turned out to be worthless.

Big trouble had started when Sitting Bull was killed on the eve of setting out with his followers to join the ghost dancers. Orders had been given then for the arrest of Chief Big Foot's band, thought also to be planning to follow the messiah. This group of Indians, 319 in number, including women and children, was overtaken at Wounded Knee by a contingent of about 700 soldiers and Indian scouts.

Big Foot's warriors were disarmed by the soldiers—relieved of a miserable few rifles of little value. Then from the tepees, wagons, and bedrolls was taken everything that could possibly be construed as a weapon: axes, crowbars, knives, cooking utensils. The Indians, already almost destitute, were stripped of their hunting, skinning and tepee-repairing tools—an unreasonable action deeply resented and believed by many to have been a deliberate attempt to provoke a quarrel. The Indians now were completely defenseless. No one today is sure just how the cowardly attack began. Some say that one of Big Foot's bodyguards, named Yellow Bird, had concealed a gun beneath his blanket and during a scuffle it was discharged, thus setting off the tragic skirmish. Others claim that the opening shot was a prearranged signal instituted by one of the soldiers.

The messiah followers suddenly found themselves in the midst of hell. Following is an account of the brutish action by James Mooney, a conscientious newspaper reporter of the day:

"At the first volley the Hotchkiss guns trained on the camp opened fire and sent a storm of shells and bullets among the women and children, who had gathered in front of the tepees to watch the unusual spectacle of military display. The guns poured in two-pound explosive shells at the rate of nearly fifty per minute, mowing down everything alive ... in a few minutes ... the surviving handful of Indians were flying in wild panic to the shelter of the ravine, pursued by hundreds of maddened soldiers and followed up by a raking fire from the Hotchkiss guns, which had been moved into position to sweep the ravine. ... Fleeing women, with infants in their arms, were shot down after resistance had ceased and when almost every warrior was stretched out dead or dying on the ground."

Dead bodies were found as far as two miles away from the center of the tumult. Negro troops were sent in to finish off the wounded. (This may account somewhat for the hatred of present-day Sioux for Negroes.) After the massacre, a blizzard raged for three days; the bodies finally rounded up were frozen into grotesque shapes, which made problems for the grave-diggers. Twenty-two congressional medals of honor were awarded soldiers who took part in the affray.

The official death toll is subject to dispute. On the state historical highway marker, it is given as 40 braves, 200 Indian women and children, and 20 U.S. soldiers. The federal government's companion marker states: 146 Indians and 31 soldiers killed. The Indian agent in charge of Pine Ridge at that time gave 300 as the number of dead Indians. The official military quotation was 90 warriors killed and approximately 200 women and children.

Alongside a neat clapboard church on a grassy knoll, the Indian dead are buried in a mass grave measuring 95 by 6 feet and are commemorated by a stubby granite shaft bearing the names of 44 of the most prominent braves who perished that day not so long ago. The monument was erected by surviving relatives and friends of Joseph Horn Cloud, whose father was killed here.

As we pulled onto the high spot, a couple of tourists from Indiana were standing by the monument with their three kids. "What are we supposed to be looking at, Daddy?" asked the oldest and least tired.

"History," he said.

From this hallowed ground we traveled north through grasslands, where the name of each nutritious blade is known to every catttleman:

blue grama, buffalo, threadsleeve sedge, bluestem, wheatgrass, needle and thread, turkey-leg. We breezed through unpretentious wayside settlements —Potato Creek, Porcupine, Sharps Corner.

At one crossroads we encountered a newlywed couple taking their honeymoon on horseback. The husband was no skylarking youngster, but a middle-aged farmer, grizzled and sun-leathered. His bride—much younger—was sedate and plump. They were 335 miles away from his mother's 160-acre farm to the east ("I farm forty acres of it"), had been out two weeks and expected to make it to Cody, Wyoming, in another three.

"Don't you care to know somethin' about our marriage?" the mounted benedict asked hungrily, wanting us to share and savor his life's great adventure. "Somethin' ever'body don't do, that's fer sure."

I agreed.

"We was married at five A.M. in the Presbyterian church—had to get my best man outa bed—and had a six A.M. wedding breakfast to get an early start." They'd been on the road that day since eight o'clock and had stepped off 19 miles.

"We average twenty-five a day," said the happy horseman. "One day we made thirty-five, another it was thirty-one. I shoe my own horses. Their names is Sweetheart, Pepsi, and Flake."

As we drove off, the bride looked longingly after our camper.

"They should have painted 'Just Married' on the horses' behinds," suggested Lulu.

Just outside Rapid City we stopped for coffee. On the TV behind the counter a commentator was discussing recent Negro rioting back east.

The stocky olive-skinned waitress said, "If one of them was to sit down here, I wouldn't serve him. An' you can't say I'm racial prej'ice because I'm Indian an' I won't wait on no damn fullblood neither. I wouldn't want my daughter to marry one of them anymore'n I'd want her to marry a nigger."

The Democratic Quartet

When Mount Rushmore was known as Slaughterhouse Rock in the 1870s, nobody paid it any mind. Now, renamed and immortalized as "The Shrine of Democracy," it is visited annually by about a million people. It's *the* thing to do if you're anywhere near South Dakota. We did it—but could have done without it.

The best approach to Mount Rushmore is from the southeast via Iron Mountain Road, which scales that mountain, passing through two tunnels hacked from solid rock and neatly framing the famous sculptured heads. Some of this route is narrow and one-way; there are four unique "pigtail" bridges built of logs—corkscrew-like affairs that turn back on themselves to allow for easier climbing. Every one of the remarkable views afforded by this road was selected—despite protesting engineers—by the late South Dakota senator Peter Norbeck, tramping on foot over the rough country.

Coming from the north, as we did, the turnoff is at Keystone, where a motorist must run a gauntlet of a clutter of garish tourist traps sporting ugly, screaming signboards. We were dismayed to find such honky-tonk on the doorstep of dignified Mount Rushmore. It's a free country and all that, but these particular grabbers for the visitors' bucks seem to carry democracy too far.

Despite their corniness, there is a certain majesty in these heads of the presidents carved in the stone face of the 6,000-foot mountain by Gutzon Borglum, one of nine sons of a Danish immigrant. Jefferson, however, frequently is mistaken for Martha Washington. Each face is 60 feet high. Washington's nose is two feet longer than the face of the Egyptian Sphinx from chin to top of head. A favorite tourist quip: "The faces are familiar, but I can't place the names."

The carving took six and a half years of actual work over a period of 14 years, ending in 1941, seven months after Borglum's death at 74. His son, Lincoln, supervised the finishing touches: Roosevelt's cheeks; the lapels and collar of Washington's coat; and some trimming of Honest Abe's beard. The total cost was $989,992.32. (Why do these preposterous projects always have such persnickety accountants?)

At Mount Rushmore's parking lot there were license plates from every state but Alaska, Hawaii, and Mississippi. In the dining room and gift shop the first question of college-student employees is, "Where you from?"

Mount Rushmore's Buffalo Dining Room offers buffalo steaks. We found the meat gamey, somewhat like venison, but sweeter. It is processed at the modern packing plant of the State Game, Fish, and Parks Department. To maintain ecological balance, the department annually thins Custer State Park's herd of buffalo (the world's largest, 1,800 head). Whiskers had a sensible suggestion: "Why not give each Sioux Indian a buffalo? Then they could build up a tribal herd, eat and sell the meat, tan the hides, use up the bones, horns, and stuff."

The table service, in the hands of youngsters from seven foreign countries and 23 states, was the swiftest I'd ever experienced, for their tips depend on hustling customers for a fast turnover. (There is a long waiting list for these lucrative jobs.)

An enormous gift shop adjoining the dining room peddles expensive foreign imports as well as every sort of item on which it is possible to imprint or press into bas-relief the heads of the four Mount Rushmore presidents. On our way out of this bizarre bazaar, we saw in the coffee shop a lady spooning ice cream to her carefully clipped silver-gray poodle. The dog was wearing a baby bib bearing the likenesses of George, Tom, Teddy, and Abe.

The Ranger's nightly lecture in the amphitheater was boring. He read from a prepared text, while recorded music worried along behind slides—mediocre and poorly illuminated. I'd expected better. My interest in the talk rallied at one point, when, while describing the winches used for lowering workmen down the mountain face, I thought the ranger said wenches and conjured up a delightful picture of dangerous dalliance in Jefferson's ear, Washington's nostril, or some other such cozy love nook.

There is no lack of material to draw upon for a livelier lecture, giving more of an insight to the romance and prodigious labor of the gigantic undertaking. Funny, human things *did* happen. For instance, there was the shock when, during the monument's dedication over the NBC radio network, the commentator out from New York City majestically identified the Theodore Roosevelt head as that of the incumbent President, Franklin Delano Roosevelt. The lecture audience might have been amused to know that the most-asked question at Mount Rushmore is, "How much cement did it take to make them?" (Another popular question: "Where do you store them in winter?") Robert Dean's book, *Living Granite,* tells of four tobacco-chewing cowboys who came visiting while the work was in progress and were able to identify only George Washington, prompting the exasperated Borglum to say, "Good God! This country is still in the cow-milking stage."

It seems to be the policy at Mount Rushmore to de-emphasize Borglum's role. The directors of this theatrical presentation of the principles of democracy appear to be so enamored of the austere nobility of the monument itself that the humanness of its creator is slighted. The visitor learns nothing of this unusual man's loves, hates, or battles; his appetites, morals, or family relationships.

Dutifully we viewed the nightly illumination of the four eminents. I half expected the lighting, from a battery of 72 searchlights, would be red, white, and blue—and possibly gold—but it was just plain dazzling white, and everyone stood reverently at attention while a recording of the "Star-Spangled Banner," sung by the Mormon Tabernacle Choir, came wavering over the loudspeakers of the worn-out P.A. system.

As the crowd began to disperse, a flurry of excitement was caused by the appearance of a mountain goat on Teddy Roosevelt's moustache. Wishing to avoid the bumper-to-bumper crush of departing instant patriots, we turned right at the exit fork, drove up the grade toward the mountain's back side and were rewarded by the magnificent sight of George Washington alone in brilliant cameo against the starry sky.

We stayed that night in a motel just beyond Calamity Peak, a cozy, old-fashioned, family-owned affair, handed down from father to daughter —one of a sort seldom seen in these days of production-line commercial bedrooms. Our bedspreads were chenille; the sheets had been sun-dried. The rooms were pine-paneled and had genuine Navajo rugs on the floors. We were lulled to sleep by the gurgling of a neighboring stream. Delightful. In the morning we were awakened by a considerate father in the next unit yelling at his kids, "BE QUIET! People are *sleeping* next door!"

After breakfast—fixed in the camper and served on a picnic table alongside the stream—a friend who knows Lincoln Borglum took us to call on him at his father's roadside studio, not far from Gutzon's masterwork. The old building, with a 25-foot ceiling and a walk-in fireplace, harbors bats.

"I fight them with mothballs," said the younger Borglum, a tall affable fellow I judged to be in his early fifties.

The studio was cluttered with mementos of Gutzon Borglum's sculptural life: a life mask of William Jennings Bryan; a bust of Nathan Hale, made in Paris; the death mask of Pancho Villa, with bullet hole over left brow; working models for Mount Rushmore; a bust from life of Teddy Roosevelt. A billiard table that apparently hadn't had its balls racked up for some time held dusty cartons and stacks of old books, a nondescript collection of rusting tools.

The focus of attention in the cavernous room was a 17-foot-high scale model of a Christus with upraised right arm—a sort of bearded Statue of

Liberty minus torch, book, and spiked crown. The statue, to be 200 feet high, will be cast in concrete atop Spearfish Mountain and called "Christ on the Mountain." The idea originated with a South Dakota senator, the late Francis Case; a commission has set out to raise $300,000 for completion of the work. A hard-working member of that commission is Josef Meier, who since 1939 has been portraying Christ in the Black Hills Passion Play at Spearfish, one of the area's most popular tourist attractions.

Crazy Horse's Champion

The big man of the mountains in the Black Hills these days is Korczak Ziolkowski (KOR-chok Zill-CUFF-skee), a full-bearded bear of a fellow of Polish descent from Connecticut. He has dedicated his life to the creation of an enormous mountain monument to that Indian's Indian, Chief Crazy Horse. Near Custer, the Black Hills' oldest town (1875), the colossus is slowly emerging from an 18-million-ton chunk of granite that rises abruptly from a rangeland plateau to an altitude of 6,200 feet.

The statue is destined to be the world's largest, a carving 641 feet long by 563 high—taller than the Statue of Liberty by 258 feet and Mount Rushmore by 287. Naked except for a 44-foot-high feather to be constructed of cement upright from his mane of flowing stone hair, Chief Crazy Horse will be mounted on a galloping horse, emerging from the rough rock with only the back, head, and forelegs chiseled. The rider's outstretched arm, 263 feet long, will rest on the animal's plunging head—219 feet from ears to muzzle. The horse's nostril will be spacious enough to contain an eight-room house. The opening between rider's arm and horse's back will be the height of a ten-story building. Furthermore, the statue will be in the round, not a bas-relief like Mount Rushmore. Fantastic? Yes, but not a gigantic hoax as some South Dakotans have long accused Ziolkowski of perpetrating. Not much of the chief and his horse can yet be seen, but Ziolkowski claims that his masterwork will be finished—God willing—in another 12 to 15 years.

I've known this visionary, heroic man for several years, but Whiskers hadn't met him, and since our oldest son, Toby, was working with Korczak for the summer, we were anxious to get to Crazy Horse Mountain.

We drove to Custer by way of the Needles Highway, named for a section of flinty monolithic rock, the original granite core of the Hills, formed by the wear of the elements into grotesque yet graceful pinnacles and spires. The initial idea which grew into the Mount Rushmore memorial had been to carve Washington and Lincoln on two of these granite upthrusts, but when Borglum was called in, he declared the plan inadequate and proposed much larger figures on the entire side of a mountain. Towering over this road is Mount Harney, highest point in the United States east of the Rockies, 7,242 feet.

We got to Crazy Horse before noon. Korczak was still up on the mountain with one of his sons, Adam. The oldest boy, John, 17, had rejected the trade of mountain carver and left home to go on his own in Denver, much to Korczak's bafflement. All the others of his stair-step brood of ten, except the toddlers, were working about the place—escorting and spieling tourist visitors, minding souvenir and soft drink counters, performing various household chores.

We found Toby with 12-year-old Mark, who was diligently pouring plaster models of the monument to sell to tourists. Korczak soon appeared, comically hunched over the steering wheel of a battered jeep, his huge hulk seeming to fill the front seat (he weighs a muscular 220).

He cleaned up a bit and made a shaker full of sweet Manhattans, his favorite relaxer. After wrapping ourselves around them, we all sat down to a formal luncheon—the best china, linen napkins, lace place mats, silver service, and wine—in a spacious octagonal pine-paneled dining room with gallery above. It is the newest addition to the 37-room Ziolkowski home-studio complex, built of enormous logs, largely cut by hand-ax and finished in Korczak's own sawmill. The round, polished mahogany dining table, at least eight feet across, had been lowered into the room before the roof was put on. Of the candle sconces and crystal chandelier, Korczak said, "They're not from Tiffany's, just Sears Roebuck mail-order." We were dressed for traveling; Korczak was in his faded denim work clothes. It must have been like this, I thought, in the pioneer gold camps—rough-hewn with the elegant. Korczak was excited that noonday because he was about to break through the tunnel being blasted for the Indian chief's underarm space.

"I think we'll see light through by tomorrow," he said. "From the other side I can hear old Chris working the drill. If my calculations are right—and I *think* they are—one more little blast should do it."

After lunch we loaded into two jeeps—16-year-old Adam handling the one holding all the kids—and drove over a rude road clawed from the back of the mountain to the working area on top. Several times I thought we'd make a circusy double-backward somersault or a wicked sideroll and twister. At the top I learned that the kids' jeep had carried several cases of dynamite.

For years the only way to the mountaintop was a 741-step staircase built by Korczak and his carpenter in residence, Emil Uherka, who has supervised the driving of every nail around Crazy Horse. Up these steps, Korczak carried tools and equipment on his back, including a total of 29 tons of lumber and, piecemeal, 2,200 feet of pipe for supplying compressed air to his jackhammers. On some days he went up and down the steps a half dozen times—often just to answer the phone and occasionally with 50 pounds of dynamite cradled in his arms. Now, a phone line connects the top and home headquarters, and there is this road, built primarily so that a 16-ton bulldozer could be taken up.

"Before the dozer came," said Korczak, "it took us over two months just to move three hundred sixty tons of rock." To date, of the more than three million tons of rock that have been blasted from Crazy Horse Mountain, Korczak has pushed over the side almost two and a quarter million tons, more than five times the total amount removed from Rushmore.

The view from the mountain is superb. We sat around on the rocks storing it away while our traveling kids ganged up with Toby, Adam, and Casimir to push large boulders over the edge by concerted leg power. It gave Whiskers and me a turn to see the kids kicking out into space—it was such a long way down.

Korczak's most recent major project on the mountain was the construction of a gigantic platform scaffold, movable on narrow-gauge railroad tracks removed from a defunct gold mine. One of his convictions is that workmen finishing the sculpture must work from platforms, not while suspended in bosun chairs as at Mount Rushmore. A sign attached to the rig's side says in letters about six feet tall, "SLOW MAN AT WORK."

"It costs tourists ten cents," chuckled Korczak, "to look through my telescopes and find out what it says."

(Once, so visitors would have something tangible to gawk at, Korczak spent six weeks painting a full-size outline of the projected statue on the mountainside, swinging at the end of a one-inch rope with a can of white paint tied to his belt and a field telephone strapped to his back. He used 134 gallons of paint; to be visible from the home-studio the marking had to be six feet in width.)

"You notice there's no comma between SLOW and MAN," Korczak pointed out.

Ziolkowski works slowly because he works mostly alone. He has not the means to hire 25 or 30 men as Borglum did. Usually only one or two helpers are on the job—drilling and dynamiting or doing common labor. His present helping hands, besides Toby's and those ever-willing ones of young Adam, belonged to an aging miner named Chris Knudsen—half deaf, with several fingers missing and only one eye. At the dead end of the 70-foot tunnel we found Chris, white with rock dust (he scorns a mask) doggedly working a jackleg drill, a fiendish device that makes an ear-rattling clatter.

"You think it's bad now," said Korczak, "you should be here when we set off the dynamite. The dust gives you a headache so terrible you think your head is in a vise."

Korczak's insistence on perfection, his fierce application, and his Polish temper often upset what help he is able to attract to this lonely high point. The only associates, other than his exceptionally level-headed wife, who've been able to adjust to the sculptor's outbursts are the carpenter, Emil, and a sunny-minded housekeeper named Mary Blythe.

Ziolkowski's sculptural operation is incorporated as a nonprofit tax-free foundation. Its board of directors is headed by Joe Foss, World War II Marine ace and former governor of South Dakota. There have been few large cash donations from the public, but individuals and industrial firms sometimes contribute such things as tools, steel cable, and dynamite.

The cost of operations at Crazy Horse each year exceeds revenue from admission charges, and Ziolkowski, who works for the foundation without remuneration, annually makes up the deficit with a contribution taken from funds earned by his postcard, souvenir, food, soft drink, and binocular concessions, from a dairy which he operates, and from sculpture which he sells. It's a neat arrangement but doesn't allow for fast progress. Korczak has refused federal subsidy or state aid that would speed things up, for he is determined to keep the project a private enterprise that one day will attract enough cash customers to enable the establishment, at the statue's base, of a cultural, health, and educational center to benefit Indians exclusively—his real reason for undertaking the creation of the gargantuan statue.

Korczak told us what Harold Ickes had said when he'd been approached as Secretary of the Interior for permission to make a monument on Crazy Horse Mountain (then known as Thunderhead and owned by the National Park Service): "I don't care what the Indians want. I wouldn't cross the street to see Mount Rushmore, and no one is going to deface any more of *my* mountains."

Korczak chuckled. "I guess he forgot who America belongs to, but that's not unusual. Not too long ago Secretary Udall announced that *he's* the biggest real-estate owner in the United States. He, personally. How do you like them apples?"

Ziolkowski and his project have antagonized the more conservative elements of the Black Hills ever since the first blast on the mountain back in 1948. (The idea for the monument came nine years earlier from an old Indian, Chief Standing Bear.)

Korczak's notions of what constitutes proper civic behavior don't always coincide with those of the Establishment. He has been widely criticized for playing a major role in transplanting the bones of Sitting Bull (Tatanka Iyotake) from their burial place at Fort Yates, North Dakota, to what he thought to be a more appropriate spot in South Dakota. Public officials considered the act grave robbing and were scandalized, but nothing came of the uproar. By the time the escapade was discovered the remains were resting under 20 tons of cement and a high pedestal weighing an additional 6 tons supporting an 11-ton granite bust of the great Indian leader (whacked out gratis by Ziolkowski). There was the further barrier of a high wire-mesh fence topped with barbed wire. This time Sitting Bull was in to stay.

"Someone had to do something," Korczak says of that experience. "The next of kin had the right to the remains according to law, but the North Dakota authorities, all the way to the governor, refused to give them up, with the state passing the buck to the federal government. Five towns began agitating to have the bones buried in their own backyards— all for commercial reasons: Bismarck and Fort Yates in North Dakota, and Sturgis, McLaughlin, and Bullhead in South Dakota.

"We had a meeting about it in our house with all the heirs present— twenty-nine people in all, mostly Indians, and two interpreters. Sitting Bull's illegitimate son was among them; he peed all over my furniture. Didn't mean to—he was ninety-odd years old and couldn't help himself. We excused him. There was Clarence Gray Eagle, a nephew of Sitting Bull, who was with him when he was shot; the undertaker Ray Miles; Walt Tuntland, of the Chamber of Commerce in Mowbridge where the bones were to go—he runs the Ben Franklin store there; George Walter, the banker, who bought the land the bones were to go in, a very important guy; Nancy Kicking Bear, Sitting Bull's oldest granddaughter; two of her cousins, Evangeline Spotted Horse and Sarah Spotted Horse, and a reporter from the Sturgis *Tribune* whose name I can't recall.

"Nancy Kicking Bear is a big woman—six-footer like Whiskers, only very broad-shouldered. Looks just like her granddaddy—very impressive. They all sat quiet for a good fifteen minutes. Then Nancy spoke. Her piece was followed by Sarah, who talked fifteen minutes and said she had an offer from Rapid City of $20,000 for the bones. Evangeline got up and said she agreed with her sister. Then there was seventeen minutes of silence—I clocked it.

"Finally, I decided someone had to speak up. 'Sarah,' I asked, 'who killed your grandfather?' She acted as if she didn't understand me. 'Sarah,' I said, ' you speak English as well as I do. Who killed your grandfather? Red Tomahawk—one of you— did it, and now you want to sell your granddaddy's bones for $20,000. Sarah, did you ever hear of Judas?'

"Well, they took a recess after that and I've never seen those two since, or thirteen others who disappeared with them. After the recess, Nancy Kicking Bear talked to Clarence Gray Eagle a mile a minute. I didn't know what she was saying, but she was angry as all get out. Then she said in English that she was sick and tired of white man's red tape. 'Let's go to Fort Yates and take the bones of my grandfather. It's all legal, not military land anymore; even the Pentagon can't stop us.' A date was set for a meeting at two A.M. outside Fort Yates—April twentieth it was. I remember saying, 'You can't do that; it's Easter Sunday—there's only one can come out of the grave on that day.' So they changed it to Good Friday instead. Then those who were left sat down and we had a good meal. The Indian women gave their wine to the men."

(Arrested on the Standing Rock Reservation by Indian police, Sitting Bull was shot to death simultaneously by police Lieutenant Bullhead and Sergeant Red Tomahawk. There ensued a terrible battle between 150 of Sitting Bull's Hunkpapa warriors and 43 Indian policemen—Blackfeet, Yanktonais, and Hunkpapas. Oddly, Sitting Bull's gray horse, a gift from Buffalo Bill, upon hearing the tumult, went through its repertoire of tricks. The Indians were terror-stricken, believing that Sitting Bull's spirit had entered the animal.)

Korczak strongly believes in the supernatural. Recently he'd been visited by some notable Indian friends who'd brought along a special kind of medicine man called a *shaman,* to consult the *yuwipi* (yoo-wee-pee—Lakota spirits) to learn whether Crazy Horse Memorial was destined for successful completion.

"They tied this *shaman's* thumbs and fingers together, then roped him, and he lay on the floor in the dark to invoke the *yuwipi* while some of the others chanted and beat on drums. Now, I don't know how it was done—it was weird—but little lights like fireflies appeared, moving all about in the room for quite a while, and when the room lights went on again the medicine man was free of his bindings and he passed on to me what the spirits had told him—everything was favorable at Crazy Horse."

There were times in Korczak's life when he needed the *yuwipi* more than he does now. Orphaned at age one, he was adopted at four by an Irish prizefighter and suffered a grueling, deprived life remindful of Charles Dickens' stories. Korczak's bed then, for instance, was a packing crate. Before reaching 17 he ran away from his keeper three times. A judge who helped wards of the juvenile court discovered Korczak to be a grandson of a Polish count, recognized his latent talent, and set him on the road to becoming a sculptor.

Korczak's early days at Crazy Horse were no picnic either. Process servers and sheriff's deputies were regular callers. He's been broke, badly bent, but never aimless.

"I always knew what I wanted to do," he said. "I'm a lucky man. Here I am living out the dream of my life—not getting rich, but making a living at it—and now the spirits tell me everything is going to come out all right, and I believe them."

And I believe in this latter-day mountain man. Ten, 12, 15 years from now I intend to go back to Crazy Horse and we'll have a picnic with both our families in the big stone Indian's belly button.

Sin City and Gold Town

Deadwood once was South Dakota's most wicked city. Deadwood Dick, Preacher Smith, and Poker Alice warily walked Deadwood's single street, Deadwood Gulch. In its old No. 10 Saloon, that stalwart superman marshal of lawless towns, Wild Bill Hickok, was shot through the head from behind during a poker game by a drunken hired assassin named "Crooked Nose" Jack McCall. Wild Bill (James Butler Hickok) is honored by a two-and-a-half-ton granite sculptured head by Korczak Ziolkowski. It stands on a brick pedestal near the freight station, but the exact spot where Hickok was killed on August 2, 1876, seems to be in doubt. Both No. 10 and the Wild Bill Bar claim the site. Both have the "original" gravestone, and No. 10 exhibits as well "the original Murder Chair," splashed with red-enamel blood.

Deadwood was the adopted hometown of Missouri-born Calamity Jane (Martha Jane "Canary" Burke), who'd arrived in the Hills as a mule driver armed with the two most necessary attributes of a good skinner: the ability to take a man's ear off with a bullwhip and a command of the kind of language that curls men's toes. She died in Deadwood and was laid out in a white dress with a pistol in each hand.

Wild Bill and Calamity are buried in Mount Moriah Cemetery, 300 feet above town on a rocky ledge. The burial ground is a favorite tourist spot, so naturally a ticket booth for the nightly summertime melodrama, "The Trial of Jack McCall," is set up as close as possible to the monuments. From up here the rooftops of the city make a patchwork quilt along the narrow gulch bottom. On both its steep sides, homes are terraced amongst the closely set pine trees. It is a rather charming scene from on high, much less so at close range.

Until fairly recently, this town was so unashamedly sinful that brothels bore neon signs; the doxies were evacuated by limousine during the great forest fire of 1961 and they never returned to rake the ashes.

Three miles from Deadwood, over curvaceous Strawberry Hill Road, is Lead (pronounced "leed," meaning mining lode or vein), at the head of Gold Run Gulch and spread a mile high over the surrounding hilltops. The only truly level place in town is Grier Park, made by blasting off two sharp mountain peaks. Phil Stong, the novelist, once described Lead as a town where "one can roll anywhere by lying down and aiming."

Lead boasts that it is "a mile long, a mile wide and a mile deep." The town stands over the richest, largest gold mine in the western hemisphere, The Homestake, which has yielded more than $500 million worth of gold and provided the fortune of William Randolph Hearst. A syndicate headed by his father bought the mine in 1877 for $77,000.

The extent of the mine below ground is fantastic—there are more than 100 miles of underground tunnels extending more than 5,000 feet below the city. The local sawmill provides 55 million board feet of lumber annually for beams and shoring. The mine's surface workings are on an incredible scale. Cages drop in their shafts almost a mile vertically and are hoisted back to the surface by cable turning around a drum 25 feet in diameter. Giant hoists operating at three times the speed of modern skyscraper passenger elevators bring up nine tons of ore in one load.

This is one of the world's strongest company-dominated towns. Practically all the land is company-owned, but any employee may build on a site and occupy it rent-free as long as it is not needed for mining purposes. The Homestake operates its own hospital and medical facilities (free to employees and families) and clubhouse (ditto, plus the general public) and runs a comprehensive civic athletic program. The company is so paternalistic that every attempt at unionization of the approximately 1,900 workers has been roundly defeated. John Gunther once said of Lead, "Compared to Homestake, Anaconda is the CIO."

For those who do not find enough of Christian brotherhood in Lead, there is Spearfish, 23 miles northwest as the carburetor flies. Since 1939, Spearfish has been the site of the Black Hills Passion Play, the Westphalian Luenen version dating from 1242. I'd attended during a previous visit to South Dakota and, while I prefer spiritualism to be less flamboyant, I'd enjoyed the pageant immensely. It depicts, in 22 scenes, main events in the last seven days of Christ's life, with a cast of hundreds—professional actors in speaking roles and local church folk as supernumeraries, listed in the official program as: "Roman Soldiers, Legionnaires, Disciples, Priests, Buyers, Merchants, Citizens, Temple Girls, Angels, Water Girls, Magdalene Girls, Mary Women, Dancers, Pilate's Court, and Mob." The humans are augmented by camels, sheep, horses, pigeons, and one jackass. There are chorals and organ music. The outdoor amphitheater seats 6,500 ($2 to $4 a head) and the shallow stage is 650 feet across— almost twice the length of the Ringling Bros. big top in its most glorious period. Natural acoustics and voice amplification equipment are superb— you can almost hear the winking of an eye.

I wanted Whiskers and the kids to see the presentation, but my suggestion met with little enthusiasm.

"Sounds too much like 'spec' at the circus," said my wife. (She referred to the traditional big walk-around pageant called the Spectacle.)

"Are there any elephants?" asked Lulu.

"No, but there are angels," I countered.

"Do they fly?" asked Whiskers.

I had to say no, so we passed up Oberammergau-west.

In the Big Horns

All-American Indian Days

Under a lowering big sky we left South Dakota and crossed back west into Wyoming, which probably was named by an eastern settler, for the word is a Delaware Indian one, *m'cheuwo'mink,* meaning "upon the great plain." Wyoming lies midway between the Mississippi and the Pacific, ninth in size among the 50 states and one of our country's most sparsely populated areas—only 3.2 persons per square mile.

The state is twice the size of New York State, yet only three cities—Cheyenne, Laramie, and Casper—can boast a population over 15,000. There are two others of more than 10,000, and 28 with between 10,000 and 1,000 people; the rest all rank below that level. Ten of Wyoming's 239 settlements each have fewer than a dozen residents. Nearly all the towns and cities are from 30 to 40 miles apart.

Wyoming is a vast high mesa with an average altitude of 6,000 feet. There are places where you can look farther and see less than anywhere else in the world. It is a ranching paradise, the last stronghold of the true American cowboy. Some sections have 150 kinds of grass; among them, the bluegrasses, wheatgrasses, fescues, and redtops are as nutritious as any steer can hope for.

More boots than shoes are worn in Wyoming, where no man is complete without his broad-rimmed range hat. There are 20 times more domestic animals than people. The grimmest historic battles fought here were between cattlemen, sheepherders, and nesters (territorial squatters).

Wyoming largely is a land of awesome silences, unbroken emptiness, endless reaches of sky. "You can still hear the land almost as it was," the Indians say.

But all is not rolling open land and fertile valleys, for this state is very much a part of the craggy High West. There are 11 formidable mountain ranges. The Wind River Range contains Gannett Peak, 13,785 feet above sea level, the highest point in the state and the Continental Divide's loftiest as it crosses Wyoming. The best-known Wyoming mountains are the snowcapped Grand Tetons in the northwest.

At Sundance, between the mountain of that name and Bear Lodge Range, we detoured to see the Devils Tower, the first national monument, a massive column of gray rock, with sharply fluted sides and almost flat, elliptical crest— formed by a rapidly cooled lava blister made 20 million years ago during the Black Hills uplift. The Sioux called the tower *Mato Tipi* (Bear Lodge), and they have legends concerning it. The most charming is that conceived by I-seo-o, a Kiowa scout, in which seven little girls are chased by bears onto a low rock, which then, in response to their frantic supplications, shot upward, thus thwarting the attacking beasts. The rock rose higher and higher, and as the bears leaped at it their claws caused the fluting. The children finally were pushed up into the sky where they remained, known now to white men as the Pleiades, or the Seven Sisters.

By way of Moorcroft, Gillette, and Buffalo we reached Sheridan, in the northeastern foot of the Big Horns. The next morning we were awakened by the sound of girlish giggling, the rattle, clank, and tinkle of Indian jewelry, the shuffle of deerskin moccasins, as candidates for the Miss (Indian) America Pageant went by our motel room door on their way to assemble for the grand Saturday morning street parade.

We'd come to town especially for All-American Indian Days, during which Indians from many states gather for sports, contests of skill, displays of arts and crafts—but most of all for competition dancing, the beauty contest, visits among themselves, and informal gambling (generally on an intricate hiding-guessing business called "the stick game"). The more serious purpose behind the three-day celebration is that of acquainting the public with the Indian's special problems and needs and of giving back to the Indian people self-respect denied them over the years.

Twice Sheridan has been awarded the George Washington Honor Medal from the Freedoms Foundation for its efforts in those directions. Only 13 years ago Sheridan stores and bars displayed signs reading, "No Indian Trade Wanted," and "Indians and Dogs Not Allowed." The big change in the town's attitude toward its bronze associates came about when Miss Lucy Yellowmule one year submitted her name to the annual Rodeo Queen Contest. She was the first Indian ever to do so and she won hands down. That busted the town's Indian bigotry wide open. The civic influentials decided to devote one night of the annual rodeo to an Indian pageant. After four years an All-American Indian Days board of trustees was formed, and through its efforts the pageant gradually expanded to its present form. It is a noncommercial venture—no paid employees and the show is run by Indians through an executive committee. The budget allotting prize money for contests and dances is small—only $1,200, paid out in units of from 50 cents to $75. Financing comes entirely from the North American Indian Foundation, a national organization.

We attended the afternoon program at the dilapidated fairgrounds. Awfully slow starting. An absolute shunning of showmanship as we understand it. It reminded me of a circus I'd seen in Mysore, India. Without fanfare it just began. No ringmaster. The performers took their good old time revealing their acrobatic skills; no one bothered to take bows. The acts went on, one after the other, with no announcements and complete diffidence. This American Indian show, however, did have a majordomo, a stout, middle-aged, bespectacled Indian, Joe Medicine Crow, who wore ordinary ranch clothes plus a full-feathered headdress and carried a briefcase. Slouched over the podium, he was charmingly gentle and casual about the whole affair.

"Do you think he's got water or gin in that glass?" Whiskers asked.

"Firewater," I said. "Booth's Old Tom-tom."

After we caught onto the pace and learned to appreciate the subtle barbs hidden in the quiet humor, we began to enjoy the program immensely: lance throwing, a tepee-building race by a few awkward women not highly skilled in that craft, delightful children's dancing, fry-bread contest (with samples). Then rain moved participants into the shelter of the grandstand to sit out the downpour with the fewer-than-100 relaxed spectators.

The night show, more organized, better patronized, opened with a concert by a drum-and-bugle corps—a dozen white men costumed in the blue and gold uniforms of Custer's Seventh Cavalry (of all things to flash in front of a bunch of Indians!). But the musicians' performance was so studded with brass clinkers that the Indians likely considered the masquerade appropriate and relished it.

Soon their own musicians took over, beating out dance rhythms on skin drums while hunched over them singing weirdly and looking a little like men at a crap game. After a special welcome dance, with all Indians taking part ("Shake the chewing gum off your moccasins," said the announcer drolly, "there's a lot of it down here"), the 36 Miss Indian America aspirants were introduced one by one, escorted to a downstage platform by two tall, muscular men in full battle regalia. As each girl was presented, Miss Indian America of 1966, Wahleah Lujan, from Taos Pueblo, New Mexico, read off the girl's credits: ". . . sings folk songs and plays the guitar at the same time . . . rock and roll singer, her nickname is Dawn because her Indian name is Dawn of the Morning . . . ceremonial princess of the drums . . . a delegate to the National Cheerleaders Convention of 1965 . . . a descendant of Chief Crazy Horse and Chief Rain in the Face and is very active in 4-H work . . . Miss Auto Oil Celebration Princess . . ."

Our kids each picked a favorite and placed small bets. Lulu's was Bernita Puhueyestewa, a Hopi from Second Mesa, Arizona. Tim chose Faith Anne Smith, a Chippewa from Illinois, the farthest-east Indian he could find. Tia, sentimentalist, put her two bits on Mary Magdalene Shoulderblade, a northern Cheyenne from Lame Deer, Montana.

I remained publicly neutral but secretly was rooting for a ravishing Navajo from Window Rock, Arizona, Sarah Ann Johnson.

The contest qualifications state that a girl must be between the ages of 17 and 26 inclusive and must be of at least one-half Indian blood and unmarried. She must "possess high moral character and have attained an intellectual position among her people." The winner must have "the quality, ability, and personality to breach the chasm between Indian and non-Indian during her travels, lectures, and public appearances."

None of the girls was a raw reservation Indian. All were educated young ladies with the advantages of government Indian school and/or college educations.

The program closed with men's and women's dance eliminations.

The homemade costumes were the equal of anything the circus has ever done—and that's saying quite a lot. The dancing was the liveliest I've ever seen. After the formal program came free-for-all social dancing, and the stick game, played far into the night.

Sunday morning there was an interracial, interdenominational church service at the fairgrounds. The invocation was by John White Man Runs Him, a Baptist deacon from Lodge Grass, Montana, and a descendant of one of General Custer's Crow scouts. The Lord's Prayer was presented in sign language by a group of Indian women. The sermon, by a Presbyterian Indian, got so loud at one point that it started some Indian babies crying—hurt their little ears. A Crow Baptist choir, in full fuss-and-feathers, beaded buckskins, and Spanish shawls, sang hymns in their native tongue, throwing in an occasional "Gloria." The most quaint turn of all was that of a trio of young buckskin-draped Klamath Indian maidens warbling "Inside Those Pearly Gates."

After the service, we were invited to a buffet luncheon at a nearby home attended by all the Miss Indian America girls in their ordinary garb and without tribal wigs. Yes, wigs. Some of the beautiful black hairdos seen at the pageant were wigs.

Miss Virginia Frank, a Navajo candidate from Shiprock, New Mexico, had performed a song at the Saturday night performance which she'd called "The Long Walk," or the "Happiness Song." I'd always thought of the Navajo's "Long Walk" as their most calamitous experience. Kit Carson, in order to put an end to the Navajos' raiding of Pueblo, Ute, and Mexicans, had destroyed their hogans, crops, and livestock. When the starving Navajos surrendered, they were herded off on foot to a reservation at Fort Sumner, in the Bosque Redondo of New Mexico, 300 miles east of Navajo country, where they were held in stunned captivity for four years.

I told Miss Frank that I detected ironic overtones in her version of the song. "No," she said, "this is only about being happy to go home. There is a sad song, but I don't know it. We wouldn't want to remember the sad part." I wondered if she weren't being hypocritically polite.

Miss Lujan told of her government-sponsored tour of West Germany, Belgium, and Holland to promote Indian jewelry. The junket didn't work out well because Europeans didn't understand the elaborate silver arm- and headbands and gaudy costume jewelry that had been sent over. "Simple things would have been better," she said. She was pleased that

Germans know so much about American Indians and dismayed that New Yorkers didn't know the location of her home village of Taos and even associated her with Mexico City instead of New Mexico.

I asked Miss Lujan what she, as a member of a minority, thought about the Negro rioting back east. After earnestly pleading with me to quote her accurately, she said, "We have more right than anybody to be demanding things, but that isn't the way our people are. My grandfather, who is Pete Bernal, tribal secretary and interpreter for the Taos people, would never allow us to do anything like that. We have a simple, down-to-earth philosophy. The Navajos, also, have such quiet dignity to them. That's the way they're raised. It's better if we don't march in the streets. Everyone knows what's been taken away from us. If they don't know they must be awfully ignorant."

She believed that the Indian has something to lean on in troubled times—not the past, but his culture. "It has survived the past, even though our land has been taken away and we've been pushed around. Yet we've still hung onto our culture. To me, it seems that the young American Indian is so much better off. He gets to see his own people's way of life and the white man's and can choose. There are good parts on both sides. It's an advantage to be an Indian, but you can argue with me on this, for many are torn between two cultures. But for me I think it is something grand. My parents are an excellent example. They were raised on a pueblo. Everything about them is Indian, but there is not enough work on the pueblo so they left it, but you can't take the Indian out of them. Their home isn't like any white man's home."

In midafternoon, on the fairgrounds at the Sale Pavilion, there was a seminar on Indian affairs. A half-dozen dour, middle-aged men sat at a long wooden sawhorse table down in the pavilion's earthen pit with bull droppings still underfoot (a subtle Indian comment?); a sparse audience occupied the terraced bleachers. Though interesting, the seminar never once touched on its promise to examine the social problems of the young Indian nor those of off-reservation Indians. The discussion was concerned mainly with changes in economy and property values that would be brought about by passage of the government's Indian Resources Development Act of 1967. Stiffest resistance to the bill was against the greater freedom allowed by it in selling, mortgaging, and developing tribal lands. Hard to understand were provisions that dealt with credit to guarantee loans, an insurance program, revolving loans, and the authority of a tribe to issue municipal-type bonds for industrial development on the reservations.

One man reported what Johnson Holy Rock, chairman of the Tribal Council of the Oglala Sioux at Pine Ridge Reservation, had said of this legislation:

"Their intentions in putting forth this bill are undoubtedly of the best, but they don't understand the Indian mind, and we here at Pine Ridge have simply said we won't accept it; we want to be left out; we're not ready for it; we know we'd lose more than we'd gain, and we've lost too much already."

One articulate woman addressed the seminar regarding official comprehension of Indian mentality.

"We don't *want* to join the mainstream," she said. "It's so polluted, we'd rather jump into the Rio Grande, muddy as it is. The Indian's laws and moral standards are superior to anything the white man has. Let the other fellow live the way he wants to, but don't pressure us to live your way."

The true fear among those at the seminar that day seemed to be that, through this new freedom, they would lose paternalistic benefits they enjoy, and that federal aid to Indians from such sources as the Office of Economic Opportunity, the public housing and poverty programs, legal and health departments, would gradually be cut off. The Indians want to be sure their culture, sovereignty, and tribal courts will remain untouched. One man stated that the bill should be amended to include "Indian consent" if tribes are to subordinate themselves to the states.

There was also a little hassle at the seminar over the government's policy of dropping from Indian Affairs rolls those who have less than one quarter Indian blood. What it all came down to was that the Indians had suffered bitter experiences with congressional maneuvers, had watched the depletion of their lands despite federal largess, and were exceedingly wary of benevolence. I found the meeting depressing and left before it ended.

The dancing at the finals on Sunday night was inspired. Not even the superb Moscow folk-dancing troupe has ever been as agile and spirited as those Indians, especially the young men. Shaking gourds, and with ankle bells jingling to the accompaniment of the Indian skin drums' throbbing beat and wails of the men singers, these Indians exhibited unbelievable skill and stamina. Indian dancers are especially alert—to be perfect a dance must stop absolutely on the last beat of the drums. The dance, therefore, becomes a contest, with the drummer trying to outfox the dancer, to catch him off guard—a typically Indian approach to the art of terpsichore.

The costumes were even more magnificent than those of the previous night. Many had ruches, developed from those of porcupine quills and deer hair made by the plains Indians. There were other adaptations of old plains ornaments: explosive shoulder and back bustles that resemble flowers in bloom, made of feathers and downy plumes, often in pastel shades.

There were elaborately beaded breechcloths and chest ornaments, cowry shell and animal-claw necklaces, armbands and gauntlets, wide ornamented belts, knee bells, and angora anklets. The men were the most lavishly dressed, but the women's beautifully beaded deerskin costumes were elegant. The most erotic effect of the male dancers was achieved by leaving their muscular lower backs and thighs completely naked and free of ornamentation.

The greatest moment of this rousing last powwow came with the selection of Miss Indian America by five non-Indian judges. The buildup was terrific, beginning with the presentation of special tribal trophies, awards, and scholarships, followed by an introduction of the family of the reigning Miss Indian America, and then a parading of all the contestants, followed by a display of the horde of gifts to be showered upon the new queen. The selection of Miss Congeniality was announced (a jolly, short, tubby one), and a brief speech was made by the chief judge, a Catholic priest named Father Peter Powell, who, by choosing as his theme the Long Walk, tipped his mitt that the honor was going to a Navajo.

Three of the girls were of that affiliation. Sarah Johnson, my choice, won. The excitement was as great as that usually generated for Miss White America. Amid the squeals and happy cluckings of the 35 also-rans, breathless Miss Johnson exclaimed, "I don't know what to say at this moment. I only wish my mother was here. I want to thank you all so very much. I will do my best for American Indians of this country."

The new queen, her attendants, and the runners-up all posed for pictures then, and in the popping glare of flashbulbs the audience shuffled from the grandstand, many going down onto the track to join the Indians for another night of social dancing.

Ranches for the Dudes

The Sheridan Valley, east of the Big Horns, is often called the bluegrass region of the West. This is superb ranch country. Elaborate horse and cattle estates were established here by wealthy English and Scottish families, beginning in the late 1880s. Some of those ranchmen came as big-game hunters to the American wilds; others were second sons with no place in the ancestral scheme back home—remittance men, sent off by their families to live on an allowance. Ranching then was often on a grandiose scale; ranch houses and hunting lodges were manorial, their interiors finished with expensive woods and furnishings imported from England. There were wine cellars and liveried servants. Afternoon tea was a ritual and formal dinners de rigueur. Hunting facilities and thoroughbred horses usually were considered more important than cattle, men more important than women.

Two of the earliest of these High-West adventurers from abroad were the English Frewen brothers, Richard and Moreton, who, in 1878, a few miles below Kaycee, erected a cottonwood log home they called Frewen Castle. Moreton married the sister of Jennie Jerome, who became the mother of Winston Churchill.

The most important of these English colony ranches was the Quarter Circle A, established in 1893 twelve miles southwest of Sheridan, near the town of Big Horn, by William and Malcolm Moncrieffe, energetic and enterprising young Scotsmen. From the spring of 1901, in one year they shipped 20,000 horses out of the area to be used in the Boer War by the British Army. Malcolm later trained polo ponies and sold them abroad—and fielded his own team on the ranch. He also bred prizewinning Rambouillet and Corriedale sheep.

This 600-acre ranch with 20-room manor was bought in 1923 by Bradford Brinton, a silver-spoon Yale man who made his pile from his father's farm implement business and increased it by being director of six corporations. He turned the place into a gentleman's summer ranch and proceeded to raise thoroughbred horses and to dabble in fish culture and game conservation. He became a devotee of western art, classical music, and rare English and American book editions. Upon his death in

1936, a sister, Helen, carried on at the ranch. When Miss Brinton passed on in 1960, her will dedicated the ranch and contents to public use as a memorial to her beloved brother.

And that's how it stands now—a most pleasant and secluded, manicured and polished, lonely complex, displaying the tasteful acquisitions of a man who never in his life had to worry about where his next dollar, or hundred, or thousand, or ten thousand, was coming from.

We'd never seen a more beautifully situated place—nicely wooded, surrounded by well-kept lawns, with the Big Horns making a splendid backdrop; but it seemed dead, empty, and purposeless, out of tune with the times, a forlorn hideout for a scholarly curator, a drowsy refuge for young ambitionless guides. I couldn't help thinking of those old cracked enamel bathtubs, the rotting ceiling, and caved-in roof at the Indian mission school at Pine Ridge.

We had reservations at the IXL Ranch, situated on the eastern slope of the Big Horns at the mouth of Tongue River Canyon, 23 miles northwest of Sheridan at an altitude of 4,200 feet. It's just south of the small town of Dayton, which elected the first female mayor in the United States, Mrs. Susan Wissler, in 1911.

The IXL is a quiet, simple place, rustic and old-fashioned; the only things we found out of character were plastic flowers in the lounge.

There was a note waiting for us from Jadwega Ziolkowski. "Dear Mr. and Mrs. Ballentine, Tia, Tim & Lulu: How's everyone? We are all fine and kicking hard! Daddy got the tunnel through the mountain! But we can't see it from the house. He feels better now. In school I will be takeing Home Ec, Glee, Socail Study, English & Algebra. Well I bee hearing from ya. Love. Jadwega Ziolkowski, Crazy Horse, Custer, S.D. 57730."

The IXL was started in 1892 by an Englishman named Jack Milward. The water rights go back to 1880. Its name does not stand for "I excel," as I'd first thought, but symbolizes Milward's army unit, the Ninth Bengal Lancers. IXL allowed for an easily made cattle brand, with only one straight stamp iron.

The IXL began taking paying guests in 1910. In 1958, a Montanan, Vic Benson, Jr., and a Chicagoan, M. L. Swyers, teamed up to purchase the place—buying 900 acres and leasing 3,800 more. For a while they dealt in cattle, but now run only about a hundred head. Guests have become a more pleasant way to earn a living (capacity is 50). The dudes come mostly from the Midwest—Minnesota, Illinois, Ohio, and Indiana, though some, attracted by word of mouth, have come from as far off as Argentina, Venezuela, and France.

At our dinner table that first evening we met a young man from Paris, his first time in America. He was heading for San Francisco "to see the heepies." When Tim asked if they pitched horseshoes in France he replied coolly, "No, we are civilized over there."

The grub was good, substantial, and plentiful. The homemade bread disappeared fast. "Whenever it's store-boughten," said our cheery young waitress, "it all goes back to the kitchen."

"But then they use it in the sandwiches for the all-day trail ride," said a sour-visaged gent from Indiana at the head of the table.

After dinner, in the ranch library I discovered why Miss Indian America of 1966 had found the Germans so knowledgeable about our Wild West. They'd had Karl Friedrich May to teach them. While spending eight years in prison he began writing a continuing Western fantasy called *Winnetou auf der Wild West*. The books sold 26 million copies and had a cultural influence equal to that of Johann Wolfgang von Goethe and Thomas Mann. May was read by Albert Einstein, Albert Schweitzer, and Hitler—he used May quotes in speeches. Thomas Mann's son Klaus in 1940 called Hitler's Third Reich, "Karl May's ultimate triumph." Carl Zuckmayer, prominent German playwright, named a daughter Winnetou. This Chingachook Indian character is a nonscalper who reads Shakespeare and Longfellow (favorite: *Hiawatha*) and speaks several languages. He is an eloquent philosopher, expert woodsman, and the epitome of Germanic masculinity—with "muscles of iron, sinews of steel." He has a glamorous complexion: "a dull light brown in color with a breath of bronze floating over it."

Winnetou is not the principal character in May's frontier adventures. The hero is Old Shatterhand, a synthesis of Tom Mix, Hopalong Cassidy, Siegfried, and Christ: a blond, blue-eyed, superman idealist ". . . not broadly built or very tall, his sun-tanned face framed by a dark blonde full beard. . . ."

I'd never heard of Chingachook Indians, and when I went to bed that night I thought I'd discovered another new tribe. On the blankets were stenciled the letters YVANSU. When I mentioned this to Whiskers, she said, "You're looking at the blanket from the wrong side. That's USNAVY."

■||■||■||■||■||■||■||■||■||■||■||■||■||■||■||■||■||■||■||■||■||■||■||■||■||■||■||■||■||■

Tourist Watching

■||■||■||■||■||■||■||■||■||■||■||■||■||■||■||■||■||■||■||■||■||■||■||■||■||■||■||■

A Mountain Mystery

A steep 20-mile ascent, by a multitude of hairpin-turn switchbacks, took us into the heavily wooded Big Horns—a spine-tingle stretch not for the timid, but presenting one superb panorama after another. We'd been told that on a clear day one can see all the way back to the Black Hills, but I never like to look back—so, who knows?

A special thrill of this highway is a startling view straight down 2,000 feet into the solid rock gorge of the Tongue River—flowing so far below it looks like a child's locket chain lost on the canyon's shadowed bottom.

From Cutler Pass, 8,500 feet high, the road runs on for miles across a level plateau atop the Big Horn Range, 4,000 feet above the floor of Sheridan Valley. We were boxed in by heavy stands of white and yellow pine, spruce, and tall firs, festooned with green lichen known locally as "old man's beard." There were mountain meadows where wild yellow roses nodded to the wind in passing.

At Sibley Lake we came onto US Route 14, which gradually squirmed to the summit of Bald Mountain, an aptly named rock dome

10,029 feet high. A geodesic moon perches on top—a lonely radar facility of the United States Army. The narrow steep road leading to it branches off to Medicine Wheel, the High West's most mysterious sight, a 245-foot spoked circle, 70 feet in diameter, of rough rock slabs and boulders arranged on a barren, waterless high mesa, reputedly by a prehistoric race, though some authorities claim the monument is merely a nineteenth-century Indian construction. Wyoming's oldest Indians, however, disclaim knowledge of the crude shrine's origin; archaeologists have likened it to Stonehenge and to the Aztec calendar stone.

The hub is a circular mound of stones about three feet in height. The circumferential stones are piled to form a pattern of six main altars. Whiskers, who'd been reading *Black Elk Speaks,* thought they must have something to do with that Indian's poetic story of the Six Grandfathers in the Flaming Rainbow Tepee, or perhaps they allude to the six nations of the Sioux.

An old gent, who'd brought his son and grandson to examine this curiosity, told us he'd been there in 1906 on horseback before there was a road up the mountain. Then there had been many more rocks. He believed tourists had made off with them as souvenirs. Now a high wire fence surrounds the whole affair. Around it are little piles of rocks built by visitors so they could get a bit of elevation for a better look. A viewing tower is needed, but Medicine Wheel is so esoteric and so off the beaten path that I doubt state authorities will ever authorize such a convenience. Only a fool would try to establish a souvenir concession up there. Mount Rushmore it is not.

Battle or Massacre?

From Medicine Wheel the highway zigzags down steeply along Five Springs Creek. Timber and canyons recede, the road runs into benchlands, then winds through farming country, across a finger lake reaching north for about 30 miles to the Yellowtail Dam of the Big Horn River. At the lumbering town of Kane we were advised not to take the graveled road northward to Custer Battlefield—badly washed out. We were told to go on through Lovell on the hardtop, then north into Montana, turn east at Edgar to go through the Crow Indian Reservation, which we did, and after Edgar it was nowhere—bumpy, dusty, washboard, rutted, few houses in sight, nothing but flat fields and empty horizon, horizon, and more horizon.

The camper's cupboard doors all rattled open and things spilled out—coffee, sugar, and flour screw-top lids worked off. The coffee pot bounced from its tight spot behind the range. The toilet door wouldn't stay shut. The sliding window on the back door got stuck and couldn't be closed, allowing thick dust to be sucked into the camper, covering everything and everybody with a fine powder layer.

We got to the battlefield (a national monument) out of sorts and after it had closed for the day. So we pulled into a small level spot down the road and prepared to spend the night among mosquitoes almost as vicious as those long-legged *zancudos* we once encountered on the Amazon River. Fortunately, our camper had screens. After we'd turned in, we heard others pulling onto our improvised roadside rest, and at daybreak we were a small encampment of four campers, two trailers, and one instant-tent job—suspicious neighbors peeking at each other from behind curtains. As Whiskers fixed breakfast, the Indian driver of a truck whizzing by on the highway leaned from his cab and directed a derisive wild war whoop at us.

By 9:00 A.M. Tim had counted, going past, 21 automobiles (three of them dragging camping units), five house trailers, and one each of camper, panel truck, motorcycle, and jeep, headed toward the entrance to the battlefield. It's popular. We learned, when we got there, that attendance exceeds 200,000 annually.

The place where Custer fought to the last gasp is just a gentle grass-covered rise surrounded by a fence, with small stone markers where each man fell, and a large truncated obelisk, also fenced in, standing over the mass grave of those slain. But the National Park Service has erected a modest little museum nearby, and—by the use of efficiently arranged dioramas, paintings, photographs, maps, artifacts, weapons, documents, and periodic lectures by a live ranger—has done a professional job of bringing into manageable focus the historic event, one of the most significant encounters of the northern Indian wars.

The presentation, however, is heavily shaded on the side of Custer and the Seventh U.S. Cavalry Regiment, which on that fateful day, June 25, 1876, lost 261 officers, men, civilians, and Indian scouts—five complete companies of the regiment's total of twelve, an additional 47 dead from the remaining outfits, and several hundred military horses. A conscientious prober into the Custer occurrence will find serious bias in the legendary retelling by the National Park Service.

Affixed to the museum wall are these words: "Some cried 'fool'; others 'giant.' What say you?" I say, "Fool, blinded by ambition." But the visitor will search in vain at the museum for any hint of this destructive aspect of Brevet Major General George Armstrong Custer. Here, Custer is perhaps not a shining hero, but not too tarnished either.

No mention is made of Custer's activity as a pursuer and punisher of Indians prior to the Little Big Horn fracas. In one brutal raid, against the village of Chief Black Kettle along the Washita River in the Texas panhandle, Custer's cavalry killed 103 braves; captured 53 women and children, 875 horses, and considerable weapons; and either confiscated or made a bonfire of a staggering amount of Indian foodstuffs and equipment. The Cheyennes scornfully called Custer, "Squaw Killer."

Nothing is said either of the disrespect in which Custer was held by his military peers, nor of the men under his command who feared his rashness—brought about, some say, by deeply rooted feelings of insecurity. Custer had been low man of his West Point graduating class of 34 in 1861. That fact is all but overlooked at the museum—stated only at the bottom of a full-length, almost life-size portrait in type so small that it can be read only if one hunkers down to floor level. The National Park Service historical handbook *Custer Battlefield,* sold at the museum, ambiguously places Custer's rating "near the bottom of his class."

The displays give no clues to Custer's political ambition; he coveted the office of President of the United States. Custer was acutely aware that the nation had given its highest office to Washington, Taylor, and Grant because these men had won wars. If he could put an end to the 20 years of plains wars, Custer felt that he also would be so rewarded, for the public seldom will vote against a national military hero.

The Democratic Convention was opening in Saint Louis on the 27th of June, 1876, and Custer thought that a dramatic and successful victory over the Indians would assure him the nomination. If a telegram announcing Custer's victory over the Indians were to be read at the convention on the morning of the 28th then surely his friend, James Gordon Bennett, of the *New York Herald,* and his minions, could stampede the delegates in Custer's favor.

This gnawing desire of Custer's to be America's number one man certainly was a strong factor in causing him to rush foolhardily head-long into battle against the extraordinary number of Sioux assembled at the Little Big Horn—placed at anywhere from 1,600 to 4,000 armed warriors (possibly a total of as many as 15,000 persons in the entire encampment). Custer had 600 soldiers, 44 Indian scouts, and about 20 other nonmilitary people—packers, guides, and other civilians.

Custer's driving desire caused him to ignore all signs that surely pointed to defeat. An experienced campaigner, such as he, must have known from the wide, worn trail made by the Indians that he was up against a superior force—warriors on fresh horses, on their own terrain, who would be defending their own homes and families. He must have known that this gathering of Indians was the annual summer conference of the tribes, the traditional big council of the Sioux with all six divisions represented, plus one affiliate composed of the Burned Thighs, Assiniboin, and Waist-and-Skirt people.

One can assume that it was of the utmost importance to Custer that neither Major Marcus Reno nor Captain Frederick Benteen share in any victory over the Indians. Else why did he divide his already small force—giving Reno command of three companies and sending him to the west bank of the Little Big Horn, and setting Benteen off with three troops on a tangent that led to the rough breaks of the Wolf Mountains, moving from one steep ridge to the next? Additional orders brought from Custer sent Benteen on and on until the bluffs became impassable. Benteen finally turned back.

Custer acted stupidly and stubbornly. He hated to admit that any-one else could be right. Custer denied to his scouts that he saw any Indians at all from the Crow's Nest vantage point overlooking the Little Big Horn. After he'd stared through field glasses for a long time, he'd said, "I've been on the plains a good many years. My eyesight is as good as yours, and I can't see anything that looks like Indian ponies."

Mitch Bouyer, one of the scouts who was familiar with the Sioux and northern Cheyenne summer camps, advised Custer, "Get your outfit out of the country as fast as your played-out horses can carry you." Custer ignored the warning and even closed his ears to that of Bloody Knife, the favorite scout; "There are too many Sioux over there. All the Tetons come together. It would take many days to kill them all." Custer arrogantly replied, "Oh, I guess we'll get through with them in one day."

You will not learn at the government museum all the reasons why the Indians were so up in arms against the white man. A big factor in their belligerence was the irresponsible attitude of the United States toward honoring its treaties. Canada took over her entire region without one Indian battle, by the simple expedient of keeping her treaties, or at least altering them without subterfuge, coercion, or force as conditions changed. The United States government broke most of its treaties with Indians more easily than the chiefs grunted their acceptances.

The wholesale, willful destruction of buffalo, which fed and clothed the Indians and gave them religious solace, was a complicating element in the situation on the plains. Ethically, the great herds on their lands were the Indians' property. Naturally they were angered at having the buffalo maliciously exterminated.

Another reason for the Indian wars was the economic depression of the 1870s, which had put a stop to the financing of railroads planned for Indian territory. It was hoped that by driving the Indians out of gold country—theirs rightfully by treaty—these lands would become safe for prospectors, and the gold strikes then would lure reluctant investors to the railroads.

Also, the Indian conflicts offered a needed battle arena to bolster the army—shrinking since the end of the Civil War—by providing the means of rivalry for advancement of career officers, as well as war profits for contractors and manufacturers. By 1867, the plains had been turned into a hunting ground for military trophies. Warriors were more difficult to locate than peaceable Indians, so usually harmless ones suffered most. Helpless old men, women, and children—made by the military to appear hostile—often were slaughtered in the absence of the more daring, wide-ranging young braves.

Plains officers, spurred by the lure of higher rank, generally were rebellious of authority from back east; they frequently disobeyed orders and acted with selfish expediency. Custer was one of the worst offenders in this respect.

The fact that Custer had not been sent out under battle orders is carefully skirted at Custer Battlefield National Monument. His mission had been to scout the enemy to learn if the Indians were slipping southward to threaten the forces of General Crook. Custer's unit was not organized for large-scale combat. It had no reinforcements of infantry or Gatling guns. Earlier, Custer had refused Gatlings, saying that the condemned cavalry horses pulling them were too slow to maintain his expected swift pace.

When Custer marched on the Indian horde camped at the Little Big Horn, he did so in open defiance of General Terry's orders—he was "cutting loose," as he'd said he would. Terry had specifically ordered Custer to scout a creek called Tullock's Fork and send news of his findings back to the general. Instead, Custer pushed on from there, with caution, despite apprehensiveness of the men and a gathering sullenness among his Indian scouts, who had discovered ominous pictographs drawn by the Sioux, predicting a great fight and certain victory for the red men.

On the day before the 25th—Custer's day to meet death—his men and horses had marched 26 miles, yet after only a brief evening rest (during which the horses stood saddled, the mules loaded), Custer ordered them on again at 11:00 P.M.

The exhausted men were hellishly uncomfortable from long exposure to dust, from dysentery, from saddle galls, and from the day-long attacks by buffalo gnats biting their eyelids and ears. Some of the men's eyes were swollen almost shut. In the morning, many of the riders were too worn out to eat breakfast.

And that was the sort of force that Custer pitted against strong, healthy Indians, who outnumbered it at least five to one and who were primed for the attack by mule brayings, dust columns, horse neighings and stompings, and the cadence of many hooves that any Sioux could feel by touching the bare earth. Indians who were there, questioned years later, voiced their astonishment over the attack, but their accounts have not been drawn upon by the Park Service.

The Indians were insanely angry at Custer for two reasons: first, instead of moving against the warriors, his soldiers had headed for the downstream end of the villages, where women, children, and old people were gathered; secondly, they had attacked the Indians' great summer conference. Both those actions called for the severest punishment by the red men's standards.

Many historians claim the Indian reports are not valid. Yet those of some white survivors and others connected with the affray are known to be not too reliable either. There is not even agreement on the time of day of the battle, conflicting statements varying as much as five hours. (The Indians placed it at high noon.)

We came away from Custer Battlefield feeling that the credibility gap is nothing new.

Our Namesake Town

I'd noticed on the map of Montana a town called Ballantine, about 50 miles northwest of Custer Battlefield, only a little out of our way. The kids were delighted by the idea of visiting a town bearing their family name, and set off on an orgy of postcard writing. "Gee, *wow!* Daddy—to get cards with a Ballantine postmark! *Groovy!*"

I could tell by the type size on the map that it wouldn't be a very big town, not a city with apartment buildings named Ballantine Manor or Ballantine Towers, or a skyscraper called the Ballantine Building—or anything like that. But I did hope to find a little Ballantine Park or Ballantine Square in the middle of town, with trees and flower beds and quaint benches of wrought iron painted white—kilted cupids and intertwined heather motif, no doubt—and maybe a statue of an unknown ancestor in its center, hope not a military one, trusty sword held in heroic erection, and astride bronze horse rampant. I might find a toothless old distant relative who remembered Custer, Crazy Horse, or Sitting Bull. Or maybe one with teeth who is a banker (beware, they bite) and I could borrow five grand, or even ten—well, what the hell, make it twenty just for old times' sake.

The atlas gave Ballantine 350 inhabitants. To that you can add three sheep, seven dogs, a cat, and one horse (didn't see it, but heard it neigh). We actually saw only three inhabitants: the man who runs the grocery market and post office combined, and two teen-aged girls absorbed in the wails coming from a record player on the front stoop of one of the half-dozen dreary houses along the wide, dirt main street.

The place cried out for a dingy poolroom and Bette Davis shooting a lonely game of snooker, one pearly ear cocked for the hoot of the daily express heading for Chicago, Chicago, that wonderful town.

The postmaster told me there are no Ballantines living in town, didn't think there ever were any. The hamlet is a hop-skip from the bigger town of Worden, on the Burlington railroad, and Ballantine was named, he recollected, for one of that line's engineers—didn't know at all why. We bought chocolate ice cream bars, mailed our postcards, and left Ballantine drowsing in the afternoon sun, unmoved by the visitation of five namesakes from back east.

I told the kids the town wasn't really named after me—I'd just made that up.

Yellowstone, Oh Yellowstone

I'd never before come into Yellowstone from the northeast, and it seemed to me that this part of the park is the most satisfying—not glutted with gawking tourists, the scenery splendidly available, uncluttered, on its own, and more rugged than in the south. Of the park's five entrances, this northeast one is the least used—about 91,000 tourists, summer total, compared to more than 500,000 for South Gate; West Gate's 485,000; East, 368,000; and North, 200,000.

At the Lake Hotel, a handwritten card on the bureau in our room informed us that the chambermaid hailed from some obscure college in Mississippi. The card implied: "Don't forget me when you check out."

About 2,300 college students work in summer at the park as room clerks, bellmen, dining room hosts and hostesses, waiters, busboys, chambermaids, cooks' assistants, dishwashers, janitors, and porters. All are nonunion, working an eight-hour day, six days a week, for a maximum $1.20 an hour (the majority at $1 per), plus room and partial board (one serving of breakfast furnished free; other meals $1 each in Staffeteria or at 25 percent reduction in public dining room). Some workers get tips; some do not.

These employees of the park concessionaire traditionally are called "savages." We drew a talkative red-headed one next morning at breakfast—from Bemidji State College, Minnesota. He said the dollar meals in the Staffeteria were "not worth much more than that," and that "frozen eggs and toasted cardboard" were the *pièce de résistance* of the free breakfast.

"But we supplement," he added. "There's never any food goes back to the kitchen from the breakfast buffet trays. We all go out of the dining room with our jacket pockets stuffed." To the staff, he explained, he was known as a "dude-heaver"; the dishwashers were "pearl divers"; the chambermaids were "sheet-shifters."

Sleeping accommodations for the help, he said, were "in dormitories, where you can see stars from your bed and birds fly in and out." Cheerily, he added, "But we all come back year after year because we have such a ball. One fellow I know came for three years, married a girl he met here. They had their wedding alongside Old Faithful, timed so that when the preacher said 'I pronounce you man and wife' the goldarn geyser erupted."

For recreation, the college-kid employees hike, take overnight pack trips, have picnics and dances, go boating, swim in the Firehole River, and go "mud potting" in thermal pools. That last sport is risky, for the mud pots sometimes change drastically in temperature overnight. The previous summer one young fellow foolishly dived into one of those instant cauldrons and was burned so badly that he died soon after being evacuated to a Salt Lake City hospital.

After breakfast a bellman from Ohio State enlightened us about the vagaries of the Lake Hotel's guests. They read the sign saying, "Park Reservation," then ask, "Is this where I register to park my car?" They refer to Yellowstone Lake as Lake Ah-*ree*-ah, because a sign outside reads "Lake Area." They inquire if the bronze Remington statuary is made of plastic. They ask if there is a bridge over the Continental Divide. Occasionally, someone who has never before been west believes a young savage who devilishly identifies Yellowstone Lake as the Pacific Ocean. Most visitors want to see "the trained bears," and some ask, "What time do they turn off Old Faithful?"

That reliable eruption has remained, over the years, Yellowstone's most popular attraction. In season, standing facing it with cameras unleashed, there's always a spread of tourists as wide as the length of a city block. Feeling that it might somehow be considered treasonous to ignore such an all-American classic, I inquired at the travel desk about its schedule. It turned out to be not so old-faithful after all. Eruption intervals average 65 minutes, but vary from 33 to 93 minutes.

The travel agent, Colonel William Smith, Jr., who resembles a plump Buffalo Bill, was in his third season at Yellowstone. Colonel Smith is 75; his wife, Margaret, 69, works with him. They are on duty from 7:30 A.M. to 7:30 at night—"and often later." About Old Faithful Colonel Smith said, "Sometimes I tell tourists I'll turn it on when they get there, and sometimes they believe me. Kids that work over there at Old Faithful Inn once stuck an old steering wheel in the ground near the geyser and when they knew it was going off they'd run out and turn the wheel, pretending it was the valve. We had a Texas tourist once who admitted they had nothing like it back home, but he knew a plumber in Houston who could fix it."

The great geyser erupts after a rumbling prologue that sounds like a roll of distant kettledrums, followed by a great white cloud of steam from which the column of water—like that of a fire hose—gradually ascends to a height of 140 feet. The blast lasts for about four minutes and if you happen to be in the men's room, as I was (psychosomatic suggestion), you miss it. As Nathaniel Hawthorne once said: "My emotions always come before, or afterward; and I can not help envying those happier tourists, who can time and tune themselves so accurately, that their raptures . . . are sure to gush up just on the very spot."

On my way to rejoin the family I walked behind an elderly couple discussing the eruption they'd just witnessed. "It was better forty years ago," said the wife. "They don't make geysers like they used to," agreed the husband.

The kids said that Old Faithful in all its glory looked just like the pictures on their grade school crayon boxes.

I told them my favorite rhyme about Yellowstone:
> "The thing to do in Yellowstone
> Is leave the grizzly bears alone,
> Find a geyser, watch it spout,
> Express surprise, and drive on out."

To the north and south of Old Faithful—along the roaring, deep-cut Firehole River and north of Shoshone Lake—are Yellowstone's principal geyser basins, marked by rising wisps of steam and a strong odor of hydrogen sulfide, a fine smell if you happen to like rotten eggs. Within the park are more than 10,000 "thermal energy features," including about 200 geysers (more than in all the rest of the world) and a myriad of hot springs, mud pots, and fumaroles. Boardwalks for spectators lead past pools of startling blue, water too hot to support any life—even algae. Bubbling mud looks like boiling pewter. Through vents in the silica crust subterranean pressures send forth noisy jets of steam. On shallow rills, swirling patterns of red, orange, green, and sepia are formed by mineral deposits.

After urging visitors not to venture off the official path, signs warn: YOU ARE ENTERING AN AREA OF FRAGILE BEAUTY, SCALDING WATER AND UNSTABLE GROUND.

We shied away from the Fountain Geyser, reputed to spew a scalding 75-foot stream in unpredictable directions at all angles. We also carefully avoided one called Excelsior, which last spouted in 1890—those sly ones are the worst.

Almost as popular as its geysers are Yellowstone's shuffling bears, begging along the highways. Driving about the park, we came, at different times, onto at least a dozen black and brown ones. Each bear sighting causes a traffic disruption that lines up cars for a quarter mile or more. Automobiles slow to a crawl or stop altogether—either right on the roadway or half pulled off onto the shoulders. The park people call these tie-ups "bear jams."

The coy anthropomorphism of "Smokey the Bear," fostered by the Forest Service, has caused people to be less afraid of bears. How could such a true-blue, upright, thrifty, clean, wholesome, and reverent creature be dangerous? Why, he's just like a big lovable Boy Scout. (I happen to think *they're* dangerous, too, above the rank of tenderfoot.)

Despite repeated warnings by park rangers against bears—which are all the more treacherous because they've lost their fear of man—tourists continue to get out of their cars with cameras at-the-ready. Some tourists even attempt to feed the bears by hand. We saw one especially foolhardy father jauntily plunk his infant daughter onto a bear's back and then stand clear to take home movies. My hair stood on end. No one who has been with a circus needs to be reminded to give even well-muzzled bears a wide berth. Backstage there, when these animals are being led to the performing arena, the cry of "Bears! Bears!" scatters all hands to a safe distance.

Yet the visiting public persists in approaching Yellowstone's bears as though they were large live versions of the cuddlesome nursery teddy. Cuddlesome they are not. Bears are the most vicious of all wild animals likely to be encountered by humans, save perhaps the musk-ox, rhinocerous, and crocodile. So, the thing to do in Yellowstone is to leave *all* bears alone—not just the grizzlies.

Beware, too, of wild tourists—especially at Fishing Bridge, where they line up against the log railings—bank to bank, hip to hip, eyeball to eyeball—grimly determined, baiting hooks with reluctant worms, and recklessly, hopefully, flinging lines toward the clear water of Yellowstone Lake, to catch cutthroat trout, windshield wipers, car radio aerials, and on occasion a bouffant hairdo, wig, or a prominent nostril.

What conservationists call "the odor of use" is most apparent at Fishing Bridge; its shabby environs are cluttered and reek of disenchantment and neglect. The Camper Cabin colony there is especially slummy, its Laundromat reminiscent of the sloppy laundry in the memorable French movie of Zola's *Gervaise*. But the repulsive disorder of the frenetic tourist hangs everywhere along the park's main highway, the Grand Loop Road, which reaches most of the great scenic features. This is the trail of the ice cream cone lickers, popsicle suckers, soda pop guzzlers, hot dog munchers, beer can tossers, and other trash makers. It is the territory of spoiled brats, teen-aged screechers, picture postcard bards, fender-benders, crotchety old men with hats, prune-faced women, and yapping, overfed dogs.

This also is the route of the bus package tours; on the porches, balconies, and verandas of the inns and hotels you find the package tourists—collapsed in lounge chairs, grimy with dust, their eyes glazed, their shoeless feet propped on the railings. Every lobby has its great sheepish huddle of luggage—just unloaded or waiting to be reloaded. From the park's five entrances there are about 40 of these junkets, listed—with all their ramifications—in a Yellowstone Park Company folder that is harder to figure out than a Hungarian railroad timetable.

For those who want to get closer to nature, who need to be refreshed and stimulated by immersion in wilderness, there is Yellowstone back country—seven areas in all: Buffalo and Mirror plateaus, Gallatin and Washburn ranges in the north; the Central Plateau; and in the south, Bechler area and Thorofare. All are accessible from the Grand Loop Road—but only on foot, horseback, or in a canoe by people who are not schedule-bound.

Fortunately, the park's most rewarding sight, Grand Canyon of the Yellowstone, is available to even the most casual sojourner. The gorge is 24 miles of twisting sheer rock walls 1,200 feet deep, brushed with shades of yellow, red, and purple—all stunningly set off by the emerald forest border. Looking at it, we experienced a feeling of great serenity and humility. We took in the view from the seething white-foam crest of the Upper Falls of the Yellowstone, a plunge of 109 feet. Then we walked down a switchback trail to the top of Lower Falls, 308 feet high. I offered a two-bits reward for the closest estimate of the actual number of steps. Lulu guessed 2,051; Tia, 1,028; and Tim, 1,025. On our way back, he paced it off and the total came to 937—so Tim won the quarter.

Buffalo Bill's Favorite Spa

The town of Cody is about 50 miles east of Yellowstone on the Buffalo Bill Highway, a drop of 3,500 feet through the grandeur of the Absarokas. Gigantic peaks flank the road, their steep slopes heavily timbered with pine, spruce, and fir. Entrance to the town is through a tunnel 3,300 feet long cut in the solid granite of Rattlesnake Mountain.

The crazy tide of tourists that sweeps in and out of Yellowstone Park all summer long nightly fills Cody's 36 motels, six hotels, and seven campsites from early June to the end of August. The town reels from the onslaught, but even on the worst days, wide streets and the silvery sageland spread on the outskirts give the place a feeling of calm spaciousness.

In spring, fall, and winter, Cody returns to normalcy—just a quiet small town of the sort that puts great store in church socials, lodge meetings, and card parties. It tends to its oil and cattle business and lends loyal support to its high school football and basketball teams.

Cody was platted in 1895 by a group of real-estate promoters and slyly named for William Frederick Cody, the flamboyant, booze-happy showman and buffalo killer (4,280 in 18 months) known as Buffalo Bill. He'd been made president of the realty company to capitalize on the national popularity of his name, whipped up by his famous Wild West Show.

The hotel Cody built in 1902, The Irma, stands as a monument to the joys of the trouping life. Named after Cody's youngest daughter, it is a compact affair of native stone with wide veranda and dark-varnished interior. The hotel's chief attraction, aside from a copious collection of Indian photographs, is a glowing, hand-carved, highly polished, magnificent cherrywood bar that dominates the dining room as a lunch counter. Buffalo Bill had it brought from France, Italy, or Nebraska—depending on which historian you consult. Bill leaned heavily on it many times on returning from his transcontinental and international tours.

Drunk and sober, this westerner from Iowa spent almost 65 years in the saddle—pursuing Indians, fleeing from his wife, Louisa Frederici, sharpshooting (with buckshot) at tossed glass target balls, or chasing after luscious females both here and abroad. In his sunset days, suffering prostate trouble, he had to be helped on and off his horse, but Buffalo

Bill in all his equestrian glory can be seen immortalized in bronze at the head of Sheridan Avenue in Cody, nobly silhouetted against the mountains to the west. The 12-foot statue, a local landmark, romantically depicts Cody as scout, rifle upraised and leaning from the saddle, scanning the ground for Sioux pony tracks, while reining a cow pony named Smoky.

Local detractors of Cody call the statue "Stoned Again." Some say he's looking for a half-dollar he dropped. The work of art, by Gertrude Vanderbilt Whitney, stands on a pedestal of local rock so huge that it all but dwarfs the subject. It is within hailing distance of the Whitney Gallery of Western Art, a severely modern, handsome establishment of stone and glass, built in 1958, the gift of Cornelius Vanderbilt Whitney.

"We've got a captive audience here," claims Dr. Harold McCracken, director of the Buffalo Bill Historical Center, the gallery's principal unit. "They come in, shower, eat, and then look around for some place to go— and by daylight we're the only worthwhile place there is."

He and I chatted in his office while Whiskers and the kids made a tour of the gallery. I found that McCracken and I had mutual friends, the midget Doll Family, formerly of the Ringling Bros. and Barnum & Bailey Circus. Dr. McCracken had met these charming Lilliputians once long ago while making a movie travelogue of Florida. He'd had dinner and gone dancing with them, the circus giant, and a wild-animal trainer, whose names he couldn't recall—had a perfectly marvelous time.

Today, Dr. McCracken is the world's recognized top authority on Frederic Remington, the High West's most eminent artist, and he also knows more than anybody else about Charles Russell, the famous cowboy artist. Dr. McCracken started out in the archaeological field in 1916 in the Arctic, with the New York Museum of Natural History field expeditions.

I found it hard to reconcile this elderly, shy, slim, merry-eyed man with the role of rugged outdoorsman, Arctic huntsman—a killer of Alaskan brown bears (six before he was 23) and captor of walruses and other creatures of the polar wild. He looks more like somebody's nice western granddaddy, snatched from a backwoods cabin rocker and given a soft berth by a more provident relative. Dr. McCracken is aware of his deceptive appearance and frequently uses it to put down sassy eastern tourists who don't realize that they're talking to a sophisticated ex-New Yorker who was a noted movie scenarist and book editor. For those who make a thing out of being ultra blasé about western Americana, Dr. McCracken has an exhibit that never fails to get a rise—a finger-bone necklace made of Seventh Cavalry officers' trigger fingers after the Custer battle at Little Big Horn. The necklace, crafted by Sioux, was acquired in exchange for food by a South Dakota schoolteacher, who had the gruesome ornament for 12 years before she realized what it was.

McCracken will not stand for any deprecation of his gallery. The doughty doctor often locks horns with blustering tourists who object to "paying half a buck to see a goddamned painted sunset." Recently he stood up to Laurance Rockefeller, of the Jackson Hole Rockefellers, neighbors to the west just over the hills, in the Grand Tetons. When Mr. Rockefeller proposed to Dr. McCracken that the National Park Service take over the gallery complex, he was abruptly told that such a move "would mean the kiss of death" to the historical center. "The moment I said it," Dr. McCracken told me, "I wished that I hadn't, but we're still friends, and since then he's given us a generous contribution."

Regarding his Plains collection Dr. McCracken stated belligerently, "I'll match, piece for piece, anything in any museum in this country or abroad for quality, condition, and ethnological importance. Why, we even have plains bear claws, and those animals have been extinct for seventy-five years. We have one bear-claw necklace in mint condition that there's not the equal of in any museum, I don't care where it is."

I was sorry to take leave of such a refreshing gent—a true independent of the High West—imported from Manhattan.

Upon rejoining Whiskers and the kids, they took me to their favorite exhibits. Tia's was the finger-bone necklace. Whiskers admired most a squaw dress decorated with elk's teeth, and she loved the marvelous George Catlin paintings—74 in all—the collection of Paul Mellon, on loan from the National Gallery, Washington, D.C. They are the earliest known pictures of northern midwest Indians: Sioux, Mandans, Blackfeet, and Crows—the most accurate reportage of the primitive High West I've ever seen.

Lulu liked the rare plains Indian pictographs on buffalo hide; feathered war bonnets (especially one of eagle plumage); and an extremely rare sun dance doll used in a ritual that featured self-torture.

Tim took me to see stone knives 600 to 4,500 years old; Yuma arrow points dating from 9,000 years ago; and the mummy of a cave man of the Rockies, a Stone Age citizen circa A.D. 680, found between Cody and Yellowstone in 1963 and dated by carbon 14 method applied to a fragment of his tanned sheepskin parka. Tim had also been impressed by the human scalps.

A great many Cody mementos were on display—among the rarities were young Cody's original Pony Express bag (circa 1860) and a sumptuous fur robe fashioned of wolfskins, a gift to the colonel in 1889 from the Tsar of Imperial Russia, whom Cody had taken hunting in northern Wyoming.

The number of books that have been written about Buffalo Bill is astonishing—nearly a billion words in a dozen languages. As an aficionado of circus posters, I especially relished the flamboyant one-sheets and three-sheets that announced the coming of Buffalo Bill—masterful eight-color lithos that leapt from the walls—especially a French one of a fierce plunging buffalo bearing an oval inset of the colonel in half-profile and the simple legend *Je Viens* (I am coming).

The main gallery contains thundering Wagnerian mountain landscapes of Albert Bierstadt, heroic-size paintings of Indian encampments by Alfred Jacob Miller, and original Charlie Russells by the score—paintings, sketches, more than a hundred bronzes, and more than 50 wax and clay models. An entire wing holds Frederic Remington's studio collection of cowboy and Indian paraphernalia, his finest bronzes, paintings, and illustrations, as well as dozens of revelatory sketches.

It was too much for Tim, who, as the afternoon wore on, complained more and more of a headache. I dismissed the trouble as museumitis. Finally Tim said he couldn't see out of the corner of one eye. We gave him aspirin and an ice pack and put him to bed in the camper. En route back to Yellowstone he became quite ill—developed fever, trembled all over, and was nauseated. We were alarmed. I drove as fast as I dared on the curving rough road. We took him directly to the park hospital's emergency entrance. He was put to bed in a room with a man suffering a broken arm (boating accident). Tim was examined by the resident intern and given two injections of sedatives. We begged rooms at the Lake Hotel, parked the camper in a forbidden place because at that late hour— 9:00 P.M.—there was no other. A worried Whiskers prepared dinner with towels hung over the camper windows inside so that a park ranger couldn't see us flaunting regulations. After checking back at the hospital, we turned in for a night of uneasy rest.

In the morning our camper sported a parking ticket. Tim was much better. When we got to the hospital at eight, he'd already had breakfast. A doctor, who'd been a wartime U.S. Navy neuropsychologist, then examined Tim and judged that he might have had a slight hemianopsia, but said we could safely take him with us in the camper.

The bill came to $84.76, broken down to: laboratory, $7.50; drugs, $11.26; physician, $30; hospital bed, $28.50.

At the ranger station I suffered a mild lecture, but no fine, for parking on the traffic island the night before.

We were almost out of the park when Whiskers added up the hospital bill items and discovered a $7.50 arithmetic mistake. But even so, at $77.26, we figured we'd been badly had. The best double room with bath at the Lake Hotel costs only $14.94—why should a hospital room, shared with a garrulous stranger, cost almost twice as much? How could a doctor with any conscience charge $30 for a five-minute examination and dubious diagnosis? Why should medical service in a national park exploit the tourists' vulnerability?

I wondered how much my son's roommate got nicked for his broken arm, and how much a Band-Aid costs in Yellowstone, an X ray, a splint? How much to stitch up a bear bite? Why should it be so costly to stick out one's tongue and say, "A-a-a-a-ah, wilderness?"

Wilder & Woolier

Earthquake Country

At 11:37 on the evening of Monday, August 17, 1959, in bright moonlight, a tremendous earthquake centered west of Yellowstone within the Gallatin National Forest. Earth tremors sent gigantic waves surging the length of seven-mile Hebgen Lake, sloshing much of it over the top of the dam. A wall of water 20 feet high swept down narrow Madison River Canyon, where 250 campers and vacationers were at dude ranches and three Forest Service campgrounds.

The top half of a 7,600-foot mountain crumpled, crashed down into the valley and cascaded up the opposite canyon wall, flipping huge boulders of quartzite and dolomite back onto the Rock Creek campground. The slide dammed the river and forced the floodwater back. Those campers who'd escaped the crush of an estimated 80 million tons of rock were caught in a fury of tossed trees, mud and debris, upturned and flattened automobiles, trailers, and truck-campers. Large sections of the highway crumpled and fell into Hebgen Lake. Fault scarps, where the earth fractured and dropped, extended along the lakeshore for miles; one was nearly 15 miles long.

After it was all over, 28 were dead and everyone involved had some horrendous story to tell. Heroic and miraculous rescues were made, but some victims of the quake and flood never were found. Many of the fatal accidents were bizarre: a massive eight-ton rock crashed down the mountainside, toppling giant fir trees in its wake, bounded nimbly over a picnic table without disturbing provisions piled there, and neatly crushed a man and his wife as they lay in their sleeping bags, not 30 yards from where their youngsters slept unharmed in a tent. One woman saw her husband grab onto a tree, be stretched out by the fierce wind like a flag tied to a mast—and then he was blown away, sailing off into the sky, never to be seen again.

We entered the quake area from West Yellowstone, where servicing tourists is the major summertime occupation. This town is a High West equivalent of Coney Island, a conglomeration of bars, restaurants, gas stations, and souvenir emporiums—shoulder-to-shoulder, proclaimed by a jarring skyline of flashing neon signs.

Among temptations offered were do-it-yourself cactus lamp kits, a bountiful selection of rustic-framed kitchen and bathroom mottoes, feather flowers, a two-foot-long can opener ("Think BIG!"), Barbie Doll dresses made of buckskin. We paused long enough to fill our gas tanks and to use the small service station's second-story restrooms—a novelty in themselves.

The scars of the monumental catastrophe of 1959 have healed. A Slide Inn Bar & Restaurant now commemorates the tragedy, and the site of the mountain tumble has proven a popular tourist attraction. There, the Forest Service of the northern region (headquarters, Missoula, Montana) has established a new visitor center featuring a bronze memorial plaque. Opened a month before our visit, already 17,000 tourists—at the rate of about 600 per day—had filed through to listen to talks on the quake every 45 minutes from 8:00 A.M. to 8:00 P.M., seven days a week in summer, and to examine assembled photos, maps, and a working seismograph (not a bad idea, since Montana in the last 30 years has experienced almost 3,000 earthquakes).

The Madison River Canyon Earthquake Area—a 37,800-acre tract set aside as a Geological Area by the U.S. Department of Agriculture, Forest Service—expected its three-millionth visitor that week for the anniversary of the giant landslide. The area's main points of interest include buildings and roads destroyed by the quake, a knoll where quake survivors gathered, a first-aid station set up by the Forest Service, evidences of drastic changes in the bottom and shoreline of Hebgen Lake. Additional attractions offered are scenic campgrounds, lakes, trails, a boat-launching ramp, and excellent fishing.

According to the Forest Service, "Natural beauty, lots of fishing, and the easy-to-see effects of one of the world's stronger earthquakes makes this one of the West's outstanding attractions."

The Way It Was

We turned north, away from the Continental Divide. From just below West Yellowstone, it stretches west and northwest for more than 200 miles to form a natural boundary between Montana and Idaho. At about 60 miles southeast of Anaconda, the great divider comes back into Montana and cuts through it up to Canada, splitting Glacier Park in twain.

At Ennis we turned west for Virginia City, sole survivor of the stampede cities of an 1863 gold rush in Alder Gulch to the west, and once capital of Idaho Territory, which included all of present-day Montana. The town is heralded by its most ardent boosters as "The Williamsburg of the West." It is not that, albeit an interesting place for those who are amused by such quaint items as wasp-waisted corsets and display dummies attired in period costumes. The town's stately, still serviceable County Courthouse and the weathered façades of several unrestored shops, however, are gems of nostalgia. Three free museums—one of them in a drugstore's spacious basement—have photos, documents, and household appurtenances that clearly show what the benighted, bewhiskered life really was like back when boys played in silver cornet bands and righteous men stretched ropes with desperadoes.

Not far out of town we passed Robber's Roost, where back in 1862 a gang of highwaymen known as The Innocents plotted stagecoach ambushes and murders. Known to each other as the Plummer gang, because their chief was a sheriff of that name, this outfit killed 102 persons before their flagrant lawlessness sparked the organization of Montana's first vigilantes. In one month they hanged 24 of the worst baddies and drove away the others.

Though no doubt they served a purpose in perilous times, vigilantes have been overglamorized. Little note ever is made of the anguished pangs of conscience suffered by the families of those men who participated in hangings. Nothing much is said of the influence vigilantism has had in shaping and narrowing the western mind. Throughout the High West in general there is too much admiration for the barbarity and ruthlessness of the territory's early buccaneers, whether vigilante or villain. Historic precedent too often is cited as reason enough for present-day brutality and injustice. Instead of romanticizing the frontier, could we learn from it? Historic people and events ought to be viewed not only for their derring-do and color, but in terms of the consequences of their acts. They ought to be judged by standards that recognize a sense of responsibility that largely is absent from the celebrated tales of the wild-and-wooly.

The displays at Virginia City, like those of so many western museums, simply add to the uncritical making of myths that lock westerners to their brief violent past. The historical markers that spot Montana's highways also take a blithe view of the rough old days. Cowpunchers, miners, and soldiers are presented as "virile persons as a rule . . . quick on the draw and used to inhaling powder smoke." Funerals are regarded flippantly. In one typical coy treatment of a victim of violence, a hanging is described as having "tamed him down considerably." However, these legend boards are so different from the usual cut-and-dried ones erected by state highway departments that their originator, Robert Fletcher, is to be commended. The inscriptions are flavorsome, have wit—at times cloying—and, although the viewpoint lacks consistency, they contain odd bits of information and advice.

Regarding the chaperoning of pack mules: "Never maltreat them, but govern them as you would a woman, with kindness, affection, and caresses, and you will be repaid by their docility and easy management."

Extermination of the buffalo: ". . . Some Indian legends say that the first buffalo came out of a hole in the ground. When the . . . buffalo were wiped out there were Indians who claimed the whites found the spot, hazed the herds back into it, and plugged the hole."

The naming of Missoula: "Funeral arrangements were more or less sketchy in those days even amongst friends, so naturally, enemies got very little consideration. In time the place became so cluttered with skulls and bones that it was gruesome enough to make an Indian exclaim 'I-sul,' expressing surprise and horror . . ."

On some of the boards the Indian is treated with understanding and dignity; on others, he is looked at with clownish condescension. An example of each: "Many years ago the Blackfeet ranged from north of Edmonton, Alberta, to the Yellowstone River. They were quick to resent and avenge insult or wrong, but powerful and loyal allies when their friendship was won. . . ." "Back in the days when Indians were industriously wafting arrows white-manward instead of playing college football and being white men's wards . . ."

The Richest Hill

It is said by the commoners of Butte that a local cat cannot drop a litter without the sanction of what they call "The Company," meaning the fabulously wealthy Anaconda Corporation, which not only has a constrictor-like grip on the city's activities, but lays strong muscle on matters of state regarding hydroelectric power, public development, taxes, and especially politics.

This city, built over and sprawled around a great mound of copper ore, long was regarded as the world's richest, roughest mining camp ("A mile high, a mile deep, but still on the level"). Street names have a metallic ring: Copper, Gold, Platinum, Galena, Antimony. More than $4 billion worth of mineral riches—copper, zinc, lead, silver, and gold—have been clawed from the earth underneath Butte. It is estimated that enough copper ore is on hand to last 70 years more.

The Butte workings have produced more nonferrous metals than any other mining district in the world. Butte's mines include almost 12 miles of vertical shafts, more than 2,600 miles of winzes, tunnels, and other passageways. Total length of the various underground workings is about 10,000 miles.

Granite, very hard igneous rock—still cooling from the volcanic age —forms Butte Hill. It is studded with gallowslike shaft frames standing amidst dilapidated homes. Work clothes hang drying on front porches and children listlessly play TV cowboys in dusty, treeless streets. Except for the lavishly illuminated sleek building of the Montana Power Company, even downtown Butte is in such a neglected state that the sight of fresh paint is startling.

On the city's other hill, at Broadway's west end, stands the world-acclaimed Montana School of Mines (380 students), fronted by Augustus Saint Gaudens' statue of Marcus Daly—insouciant, standing hat in hand, overcoat slung carelessly over one arm. Daly was a principal warrior in the bloody battles for possession of Butte's mineral riches. A magnetic

Irishman who'd fought his way savagely from rags to riches with miner's pick and shovel, Daly had as opponents storekeeper-cum-banker William A. Clark (described by John Gunther as "one of the most tidily ruthless men who ever lived") and German Brooklynite F. Augustus Heinz, a graduate of Columbia University's School of Mines. He broke into mining as a $5-a-day surveyor. As a poacher on the rich vein of the Boston and Montana Company, Heinz was a leader in the most memorable of the copper mine wars, in which rival factions fought brutally in the underground corridors with guns, dynamite, smoke, steam, flooding, fire hoses, and electrified turnsheets; they even poured lime into opponents' ventilating systems.

Butte's more responsible citizens are struggling to alter its image as the bawdiest brawler of the West, for the city no longer is a place of unbridled Babylonian temptation. It now claims to be an important transportation and distribution center, as well as headquarters for hunters and fishermen. Many neighborhoods once bereft of any vegetation now have shade trees and flowers. Third-generation miners and their families have been updated culturally at a million-dollar Civic Center by visiting symphonies, lecturers, and theatrical companies.

The city's first step toward respectability wasn't made until just after World War II, with the dumping of corrupt city officials who long had countenanced open gambling and prostitution. Children used to play slot machines while their mamas tried their luck at keno; 234 prostitutes stalked the streets or leaned aggressively from front windows along Mercury Street, a few blocks from the city's most progressive high school. (A hard core of about 30 professional hustlers still is available on the fringes of town.)

In Butte, Saturday evening is called "the devil's night." To sniff the brimstone we needed to go only a few blocks from our hotel, up Broadway into a neighborhood known as Finntown. We selected the middle one of three juxtaposed bars: The Alaska, The Broadway, and The Helsinki ("Steam Bath, Grill & Fishing Tackle"). Upon entering, we were witness to one of the swiftest, most silent, one-punch differences of opinion I've ever seen, including some dandies in the circus backyard. The victim thudded to the floorboards in front of the bar. Bleeding at the mouth, he stumbled past us out into the street. A good beginning.

"Put something on the bar besides your elbows," snapped one of three female bartenders, all slinging beer and pouring shots as fast as greased lightning for their rough trade of Finns, Poles, Irishmen, Mexicans, Indians, and recently imported Appalachians. A good third of the patrons—including the women—were staggering drunk. The men all had powerful shoulders and slim hips; the women's ample bottoms mostly were zipped into gaudy tight slacks. I remarked to a beefy bar neighbor that it seemed pretty drunk out that night.

"A man wants to go into the twilight zone," she shot back, "that's *his* business." I decided I'd better button my lip or I might go home with a fat one.

A sign on the wall warned: NO DANCING! Everyone danced superbly to music roaring from an electrified accordion and a set of uninhibited drums. Some of the dancers were shoeless; others were toothless. Several of the men wore their hats. We had such a delightful time I don't recall exactly when Whiskers and I stumbled off wearily to bed.

In the morning, we drove out for a look at the great earth scar called the Berkeley Open Pit, where 150,000 tons of copper ore are scooped each working day and loaded into gigantic ore-hauling trucks that cost $100,000 each and are so immense that alongside them their drivers look like undernourished midgets.

We also saw from the outside Anaconda's fully automated, but then idle, Clyde E. Weed Concentrator. Its reputed cost ranges up to $64 million—the company is reluctant to release an official figure. This industrial monstrosity, named for Anaconda's chairman of the board, is an enormous complex of 14 buildings housing the latest equipment for extracting copper from raw ore (about 800 pounds produce one pound of the metal).

A 26-mile line of 34-inch steel pipe brings water to the Weed Concentrator from the town of Anaconda to the west, and to pulverize the ore there are 12 large autogenous (or rock-on-rock) grinding mills, as well as six conventional rod mills and the same number of ball mills. When they all start pounding away at the same time there is one hell of a racket —enough to waken Marcus Daly, wherever he may be.

Practically every step of the process is operated from an enormous electronic nerve center, and the work is observed by closed circuit television. Not many human hands are involved—and that's what gripes the men of Butte.

A fledgling Butte tourist attraction that has laudably ambitious plans for future expansion is a grubby World Museum of Mining, situated on the western edge of town and marked by the Nordberg Hoist, a heavy-timbered structure towering over the defunct Orphan Girl Mine. The establishment, depending on contributions from the public, is being run on a shoestring by a group of mining enthusiasts headed by a local dentist. We found its exhibits confused and badly in need of a professional curator. Still, the modest buildings contain much that is fascinating and significant about the dirty business of wresting minerals from the earth. I'd say the most inappropriate item is the "Log Chewed By A Beaver," or perhaps the modest sign in the downstairs lavatory: "These fixtures donated by Sears-Roebuck." Dr. McCracken would be aghast.

Grizzlies
and Forest Fires

On a previous visit to Butte, I'd met Dr. Robert Kroeze, a surgeon, a leader in the citizens' committee that braved the hoodlums and managed, despite all threats, to get the city operating on a more respectable basis. On our way west we stopped off to see him and his family at their summer place on Echo Lake, west of Anaconda, adjacent to ruggedly beautiful Anaconda-Pintlar Wilderness.

"I wish," said Whiskers when we left, "that I could be an elk with a newborn calf and live there maybe forever." I felt that way too, except I'd rather be a mountain goat.

With typical Montana hospitality, the Kroezes loaded our camper with chunks of elk meat, fresh rainbow trout, venison steaks, elk sausage, elk liver, an enormous homegrown zucchini, and a large bouquet of fresh-cut sweet peas.

Dr. Kroeze recommended that we drive to Missoula over Skalkaho Pass, and I'm glad we did, for it is an exceptionally beautiful road—narrow, shaded by stands of willow, quaking aspen, cottonwoods, and evergreens, and graced by rock slabs and waterfalls. At noon in a woodland glade by a chuckling stream we stopped, and Whiskers cooked six of our trout with brown rice and squash. I bathed in the stream and felt glorious splashing naked in the cold water. During lunch a chipmunk came and diligently nibbled on our rice sloppings, grain by grain.

The highway just south of Missoula was under repair, making our entry into that city less than triumphant. Hot, dusty, disgruntled, and well shook-up, we checked into a three-story motel right downtown built around an outdoor swimming pool. After we'd all enjoyed a cooling dip,

Whiskers whipped up a venison dinner in our camper, and the kids carried it, under towel cover, right past the coffee shop and up to our blessedly air-conditioned third-floor room. At the desk I picked up a local newspaper. The headline was a shocker: "Glacier Grizzlies Kill Two Girls, Maul Youth."

Bears had slain two teen-aged park employees in their sleeping bags in separate incidents at Glacier National Park early Sunday and seriously injured an 18-year-old young man, also a summer employee. The girls were the first people ever known to be killed by bears in that scenic park to which we were heading. There was also a front-page story about forest fires raging in northern Montana, but, as we went to sleep that night, bears were most on our minds.

"In Glacier Park, Dad," Lulu asked quietly, just before we turned out the light for the night, "will we be sleeping in the camper?" "I hope not," Tia whispered hoarsely. Tim said nothing, but he didn't go to sleep for quite a while. Neither did I.

The next day we visited the new Aerial Fire Depot of the U.S. Forest Service, a research and training center for prevention, retardation, and control of forest fire, the greatest enemy on the western side of the Great Divide. Out here Smokey the Bear is no joking matter.

It was too late in the season to observe actual training of smoke jumpers (parachutists who drop in on fires). The beginning of fire-threat time in mid-July terminates the program, which involves annually 175 college men eking out their education funds—not only forestry students and premeds, who are the greatest seasonal repeaters, but majors in foreign relations, law, and theology. Each year 1,200 to 1,500 applications are received for about 60 vacancies.

In this northern region of the Forest Service, comprising 16 national forests in eastern Washington, northern Idaho, the western Dakotas and Montana, as well as some grasslands in Wyoming—a total of 28 million acres—1,123 fires were raging, compared with only 857 fires at the same time the year before.

Nearly 2,600 fire fighters were on the job, including smoke jumpers and 200 Zuni and Apache Indians imported from New Mexico. By the end of that day, more than 30,000 pounds of equipment and supplies would have been channeled from Missoula to the various fires and 28,000 gallons of retardant dropped on them. In the past three days smoke jumpers had made 207 jumps. There then were only 65 of these specialists on hand in the Missoula depot compared to the 200 usually available.

Fifteen of the fires were in Glacier National Park—three of them out of control—all in remote areas; the worst there in 30 years had blackened 2,000 acres, and smoke enveloped much of the more accessible scenic parkland.

Lightning was causing most of the fires. To date that year, 905 fires resulted from lightning and 218 were man-made; the year previous, in the same time period, the totals had been 649 and 208 respectively.

The current rash of fires was temporarily giving Smokey the Bear a bad name, but this anthropomorphic character that symbolizes forest fire prevention (the creation in 1945 of Albert Staehle, a *Saturday Evening Post* cover artist) has been very effective. Pre-Smokey, fire annually devastated a scandalous total of 30 million acres of America's forests and rangeland, a timber area almost the size of New York State. Since the advent of Smokey the Bear, there has been a drop in forest fires in the United States of approximately 31 percent—from 210,000 to 145,000 annually.

The Other Side of the Divide

On the day we left Missoula, the Montana big sky had never been bluer, the breezes from the mountains never more lovely. It's not always like that. In winter the sun goes away from Missoula and stays hidden for days on end—in 1966 there were only 48 hours of sunshine during January—and then overcast skies hold down the stink from the paper mills, and the smoke from the lumber mills lingers to pollute further that air which Montanans claim "has never been breathed before." Out here the unspoiled mountains, forests, and waters aren't always all-important. People listen for the rustle of money as well as the wind in the trees—just as they do back east.

The trials of civilization are not confined to the canyons of New York, the freeway plains of Los Angeles. We passed through the town of Garrison, and I remembered that its residents had been aroused by the pollution of their air. They blamed it on the smokestack of a phosphate plant, billowing waste material into the sky at a great rate, and according to a *New York Times* story, spewing "an almost blinding quantity of heavy gray dust . . . carrying sulphur dioxides and fluorides that coated the grass, ruined car finishes, and irritated skin, eyes, nose, mouth and lungs."

Not far beyond Garrison, at MacDonald Pass, we crossed over the Continental Divide, heading east. More than four-fifths of Montana lies east of this great upheaval. The more cocky Montanans claim that only there do you get the true feel, color, and smell of this state that has only 700,000 people—not quite five to each of its 147,138 square miles—yet is bigger than Italy or Japan. Montana is the fourth American state in area —though 41st in population—and is almost three times the size of New York, which is inhabited by over 18 million people (eight million of them in New York City alone). Positively boggles the mind.

The Montanan finds it hard to imagine any place crowded, or glutted with skyscrapers that cut the sky into small patches. A New York subway train at rush hour would scare the boots off a Montana native.

In its history, Montana has belonged to six other states or territories and has seen more than its share of violence and bitter rivalries—industrial, political, and cultural—but none has exceeded in bitterness the one that exists today between the two factions of Montanans who occupy opposite slopes of the Continental Divide. A. B. Guthrie, Jr., dean of Montana's authors, who makes his summer home in Choteau, has said that the western slope belongs more to Idaho and Oregon.

"Men are known to raise cherries there," he says, "and apples, which may be the finest in the land but still aren't wheat or beef or mutton. It is hard to think of a Montanan as a cherry picker or an apple knocker. He needs to have wheat straw in his hair and cottonseed cake in his whiskers. He needs to have the print of wind in his face and the mark of the saddle on his pants or the smell of sheep in his Mackinaw."

At about 6:30 in the evening we arrived in Helena, which natives accent on the first syllable. The only sleeping accommodation we could find was a vintage-1935 cottage, one of the original units of a more modern motel. It was clean, had a stall shower but only one bed, so the kids agreed to sleep in the camper out on the street. We checked in and then drove up into the wooded hills above town to cook an elk dinner. While driving back through the main street, the kids did the dishes and unplugged the drain as the camper went along—giving it the appearance of a large peeing turtle.

The city's main street, a long, narrow, gently climbing, zigzag affair, quaintly named Last Chance Gulch, was allegedly so constructed to re-duce shooting range during Helena's hectic $2 million gold-digger days.

This main drag is a neonized hodgepodge where you can find almost anything from a bicycle to a secondhand bidet, diamond bracelets or a hand-me-down, double-breasted, chalk-stripe suit—at the Capitol City Rescue Mission, Inc. "Jesus Saves."

Along hilly streets on the west side of town are moldering mansions once the epitome of bourgeois opulence and elegance. Helena abounds in quaint and bizarre structures. The prize is a Moorish temple (formerly the local Shriners' headquarters), now being used as the city's government center. It is a gaudy affair of tapestry brick ornamented with mosaics, with barrel-vaulted roof and skinny minaret—from which the mayor does not summon his council at sundown. (I inquired.)

The most startling sight in the skyscraperless city is the extravagant Saint Helena Cathedral, most impressive of the city's 29 churches, a Gothic-style building modeled after the Votive Church in Vienna, with spires 230 feet tall, at least 50 enormous circular stained-glass windows made in Bavaria, and a lavish altar of Carrara marble. No doubt, some guilt-ridden soul's ticket to heaven. I thought the baptismal font (brass? copper? *gold*?) looked like an Italian espresso machine. Whiskers said no, a magnificent pressure cooker.

Overlooking the downtown area is the most vivid reminder of hell-raising days, a well-preserved, squat wooden fire tower from which alarms were sounded on a large metal triangle. Fires were greatly feared and respected in these pioneer towns, built mostly of wood.

The sandstone and granite state capitol is sturdy, stodgy, graceless, and proper, with a marvelously old-fashioned all-copper dome topped by a replica of the Statue of Liberty. In the antiquated house chamber an immense painting depicts Lewis and Clark on an expedition seeking the Pacific in 1805 and meeting their first Montana Indians in the Bitterroot Valley. It is the largest work (25 feet in length) of the state's most beloved artist and sculptor, Charlie Russell. He got so carried away by the pageantry of the Indians, whom he adored, that he almost didn't have room in the composition for the two explorers. Lewis and Clark are off to one side in the middle distance.

Russell is the High West renaissance man. He participated in range life—as hunter, trapper, cowboy, and squawman—and so could capture graphically the old-time ways before they slipped away. Two art galleries devoted to Russell's untutored genius are in the ultramodern Veterans & Pioneers Memorial Building on the capitol grounds. There we saw

Russell's earliest extant sketch (1882); a small watercolor landscape notebook; and also his most famous work, "Waiting for a Chinook— Last of 5,000," a portrait of a gaunt, starving steer, made for a ranch foreman during the terrible winter of 1886/87 to advise the absent owner that his herd had perished. Russell, an early booster of racial tolerance, would have been delighted by the sight of a lean-hipped young visitor— pride of Montana shining from his eyes—explaining the paintings and drawings to his radiant pregnant wife, a Japanese girl.

The capitol's Museum of Pioneer Relics features an unusually complete firearms collection and also a gallery of dioramas that illuminate earliest Indian days of this wild land. One shows how the then-horseless Indians obtained food, clothing, and shelter by means of the *pishkin,* an ingeniously contrived stampede of buffalo off a high cliff onto crippling rocks below. (Montana archaeologists have mapped hundreds of *pishkin* sites—some placed, by carbon 14 method, at the time of Christ.) The buffalo furnished the Indians with sled runners, tools, thread, fly whisks, powder horns, spoons, cups, ladles, stirrup covers, tobacco pouches, moccasin soles and linings, drumheads, shields, luggage, religious objects, saddle padding, clothing, blankets, and food (especially the hump and tongue). At the *pishkin* diorama was this disheartening comment: "The elimination of the buffalo and the Indian was necessary, but perhaps it could have been done more humanely."

On display also is a large stuffed white buffalo named "Big Medicine," an animal sacred to the Flathead Indians. It died in 1906 and the Flatheads are still waiting for another (fat chance—white buffaloes come only once in five million births; if Barnum were alive he'd bleach one for them and nobody the wiser).

Mountain Man's Love Affair

For dinner on our second day in Helena we drove west of the city to a unique establishment atop the Continental Divide called Frontier Town, perhaps the best representation of pioneer log construction in all North America. It was built practically singlehandedly by one man, John Quigley, a most original personality of the High West.

I suspected Frontier Town would be just another of those places that claim to re-create pioneer times and fail miserably. I'd about had my fill of pseudo frontier forts and villages. This one, bearing the unmistakable stamp of its creator, gave us a pleasant surprise.

At the highway entrance was a group of jerkily animated life-size carved wooden figures—a growling trapped bear, surrounded by hunter and dogs barking weirdly and continuously. The kids couldn't stop laughing, or barking over the camper's intercom.

The place—with 46 rooms—is relaxed, pleasant, rustic on a monumental scale. The bar is a single split log of Douglas fir just over 50 feet long; the width of its polished flat top is the length of a gorilla's arm. The barstools are well-broken-in saddles. At one end of the room stands a stuffed 500-pound bear—big for a black—shot by Quigley one midnight after it had broken in by ripping through the kitchen wall of corrugated sheet metal. A heavy split-log door leads to a large upstairs dining room. Its focal point is a fireplace in which elephants could be staked out. The stone mantel is six feet thick and eight wide at its center.

Much of the charm of Frontier Town lies in the unexpected gracefulness that Quigley has managed to impart to massive timbers and huge rocks. All of the log doors, for instance, are so beautifully balanced that they open and close at the touch of a finger. But the man himself is the most winning attraction—a true High Westerner, lean and rawhide-tough. A grandson of a Wisconsin merchant who in 1863 set up an emporium at a gold camp named Blackfoot City (now not even a ghost town), John Quigley, the third, was reared on his father's cattle and horse ranch at Avon, west of the Great Divide between Helena and Missoula. His wife, Sue Whittier, a descendant of the poet John Greenleaf Whittier, is from back east in Michigan. She met John while he was a bartender-lifeguard-busboy at a Florida resort.

Quigley has the sort of openhanded, modest pride that easterners expect to find out west. When complimented on his accomplishment, he says, "I worked like heck for it. It took twenty-one years. See those calluses?" When asked where he got all the fascinating relics displayed in every nook and cranny, he says offhandedly, "Oh, I been pack-rattin' this stuff since I was a little kid." When something nice is said about his excellent wood sculpture, he responds, "It's lousy carvin', but I'm just a hillbilly, never took a lesson. It just comes out of my fingers."

He is a likable fellow, yet always ready to disturb the ingenuous surface is deep-rooted prejudice that flaws the fabric of so many mountain westerners, especially those of this state. There is a strongly bigoted attitude here toward non-Anglo Saxons. Odd, when one realizes that in the earliest days along the Great Divide, French and Scottish fur traders integrated sexually with Indians—but then, so did our deep-southerners with blacks.

Montanans like to think they have no social stratification—that a man here is accepted as an equal whether rich or poor. And this is true—unless the man happens to be an Indian, a Negro, or a Hutterite, of an agrarian, socialistic sect that originated in South Dakota but some of whom have drifted down from Canada. Indians are paternally tolerated and there are not enough Negroes ("jigaboos" here) around to matter much, but the Hutterian Brethren hold to clannish seclusion, and their beards, uniform dress, dowdiness, and sobriety go against the grain of hearty, two-fisted Montanans. Anyone defending Hutterites is likely to be regarded as a malicious, meddlesome rascal.

While we were at Frontier Town a party of Cree Indians visited, from the Rocky Boy Reservation. The older of the two men—a really *red* man—wore long braids tied together in front. Quigley got to chatting with this patriarch, bought him a beer, and for his amusement generously turned on the animated miniature figures in the diorama behind the bar (usually takes a quarter to get them moving) : Indians and soldiers fighting, a stagecoach holdup, a buffalo *pishkin,* a soaring eagle, an Indian sending smoke signals.

"Cost me a dollar," said the old Indian laconically, "to come in and see my grandfather make smoke signal." Quigley pointed to the miniature pitched battle.

"Hear them war whoops," he said. "See them rifle shots. They're shootin' up the white men."

"Didn't shoot enough of them," said the Indian.

I asked Quigley how he'd gotten dogs to bark so strangely for the come-on display out front on the highway.

"They're not real dogs," he explained. "I tried real ones, but I couldn't get it continuous, which it has to be—you got a ten-second gap and three cars'll go by. So I practiced until I could imitate dogs real good, even good enough to fool a real dog. You should see them sometimes trying to jump out the car windows."

We hated to leave this haven of the old West, but had to cut loose since we were going to Helena's Old Brewery Theater, a 250-seater occupying the former malt house of the Capital Malt & Brewing Company, makers in the 1880s of Old Rocking Horse Brew. A resident company, The

Bandit Players, was presenting a musical, *The Unsinkable Molly Brown*, the story of how Denver's socialite world was set on its collective ear by the hoydenish wife of a common miner who became a millionaire by discovery of the Little Johnny Gold Mine at Leadville.

The performers were from 11 states—29 from the West, 12 from the East. The play, in two acts and 21 scenes, had commendable production, with good lighting and amazingly professional costumes, but it was just too much for these neophytes to pull off. There wasn't a good singer in the lot. But after rationalizing that this was just the sort of performance that people had to suffer back in gold rush days, we began to enjoy it—clinker notes, ham acting, dubious choreography, and all.

The worst scene was that of Molly Brown in the lifeboat after the sinking of the *Titanic*. There was no illusion at all. The lifeboat flat was so small that the audience could see Molly's feet behind it as she stood on the stage, and this killed what little drama Meredith Willson, the show's author, had put into the lines. How much better to have written the scene closer to the way it really happened.

Just before the ship hit the iceberg the real Molly Brown had been walking the promenade deck attired—from the skin out—in a suit of woolen long underwear, heavy Swiss walking bloomers, two woolen petticoats, a walking dress of Scottish cashmere, heavy-woven golf stockings, flat-heeled shoes, knitted mittens, and over all a $60,000 chinchilla evening cape. She carried a $4,000 Russian sable muff in which there was a Colt automatic.

"If anyone was dressed to meet an iceberg, she was," Gene Fowler wrote of the event.

To clothe others in the party who were inadequately dressed for the chill night, Molly peeled her various layers, then rowed to keep warm. Brandishing her Colt, and ignoring the fact that it was pitch dark, she screeched at the slackers, "Row, you sons of bitches, or I'll let daylight into you."

Poor thing, like Baby Doe, her ill-fated sister in mining history, Molly ended up broke—in a furnished room of a New York City women's club, where she intimidated the other inmates with her Lady Du Barry crookcane, her polished profanity, and muttered snatches from classic French dramatists.

"I have a heart like a ham," she used to say. "I'll never die." She was wrong on both counts. She did die, and she was *all* ham.

Charlie Russell's Bailiwick

To those High West enthusiasts biased in favor of the Rockies' eastern slope, Helena is acceptable but Butte is not, even though it straddles the Divide. In fact, they'd like to deal Butte out of the deck completely.

The true love of those who live within sight of the Rockies' front range is Great Falls, created not by gold or copper benificence, but a city that grew slowly, carefully planned for its industrial possibilities. It lies in a bend of the mighty Missouri and at the mouth of the Sun River, just east of where the plains break into the Continental Divide. With an estimated population of 62,600, it is the largest city, not only in Montana, but in the four-state area including Wyoming, North Dakota, and Idaho.

Hydroelectricity made Great Falls the giant it is today. It has five of Montana's 17 major dams (the state is said to have America's greatest hydroelectric potential, although this is disputed by Idaho). In Great Falls also is the world's largest freshwater spring, which pours out 388.8 million gallons daily.

The Chamber of Commerce likes to include in its listing of mileages from Great Falls those pertaining to Canadian cities, for it is this area's biggest metropolis near the border. There are 36 motels, 32 hotels, and Canadians drop down to weekend or vacation from Alberta (Lethbridge is 187 miles and Waterton Park, 204) and from Saskatchewan (Swift Current is 357 miles and Regina, 515). New York City, we learned, is 2,247 miles away—almost as far as Anchorage, Alaska, 2,525.

On his first day in this area the famous explorer Meriwether Lewis was chased by a bear, detoured by a herd of 10,000 buffalo, and terrorized by a rattlesnake. The menaces here today are less personalized but vastly more destructive and infinitely more subtle. Great Falls harbors the Malmstrom Air Force Base, the largest intercontinental ballistic missile complex in the world, covering an area almost the size of Maryland. Air force people in Great Falls make up about one-seventh of the population of the metropolitan area and annually spend more than $28 million in the community. In addition, other military spending brings this figure to $40 million a year. Besides that golden flow, the only outward sign of power held in abeyance is an insistent, periodic radar beep that we heard coming over our camper's radio—sounding like the staccato punctuation of a jazzman's trumpet. "Pray it's not Angel Gabriel tuning up," said Whiskers.

Military installations, dams, refineries, and other industries contribute most to Great Falls prosperity—still education, culture, and compassion have not been neglected. The city has an excellent, modern public school system; a liberal arts college; a magnificent new library; symphony orchestra; community choir; four public swimming pools; and a hospital that is the first in the nation to introduce a revolutionary system of specific billing in which a patient's costs are itemized instead of being lumped together, and where meals are ordered a la carte. If Tim had been ill in Great Falls instead of in Yellowstone Park, our bill, exclusive of the doctor's juicy fee, would have been $12 less.

From answers to my inquiries I gather that the young people of affluent Great Falls are not much concerned with matters beyond the city's Elysian fields, and the town's military personnel are not inclined to express social opinions. About the only blacks in town are those at the base, so Great Falls is in little danger of racial rioting. The only really pressing social problem is that of landless Indians who live in dilapidated shacks in a district called Hill 57.

The greatest cultural influence of Great Falls is a man named Charlie Russell, dead now for 40 years. He wrapped up all the characteristics that Montanans most admire: perspicacity, common sense, orneriness, honesty, robust and convivial living, and a dry wit. (He once said of a teetotaler farmer who'd welched on a ranch deal and made off with most of the outfit's equipment: "It looks like the only thing that honest prohibition farmer won't take is a drink.") Great Falls is proud of its small but magnificently modern Charles M. Russell Gallery. A fund of $350,000 is being raised for much-needed expansion, as the present building is barely large enough to contain the abundance of Russell artwork and memorabilia—three-quarters of a million dollars' worth (there's even a livery stable's iron safe door embellished by a red-blanketed Russell Indian). Lots of postcards and illustrated letters written by Russell to friends are exhibited. I copied part of one that concerned a bear attack.

"Well, Bill, there ain't much doing up here, but I heard there was a man up on the mane range that mixed up with a lady grizzley and they pulled off the genuine grizzley bear dance. They say the man wasen't strong on round dances but he couldent refuse a lady an you know everybody's doing it an I guess before that dance closed he thought pretty near everybody had done it to him. The folks that arrived after the ball didn't find much. A belt buckle, some buttens, things a bear couldent use. Well, Bill, I will close with regards to yourself and the bunch, your friend C.M. Russell."

Of Russell, Will Rogers once said: "He not only left us great living pictures of what our West was, but he left us an example of how to live in friendship with all mankind . . . and with Nature and all of Her creatures."

Charlie Russell was privileged to know intimately mountain men, fur traders, frontier explorers, gunmen, dance-hall doxies, tinhorn gamblers and all sorts of ranchers, cowboys, and Indians.

Some of the best of the work in Great Falls depicts Indians. These paintings and drawings are long on respect, for Russell regarded Indians as "Nature's noblemen." He was attracted to Indian women; the sexiest works in the gallery are the bare-shouldered portraits of Keeoma, his favorite terra-cotta beauty.

About drinking, Russell once wrote: "I drank, but never alone, and when I drank it was no secret." His favorite Great Falls saloon was The Mint, long gone. Its proprietor grubstaked Russell in return for paintings, and the walls were casually covered by original Russells now mostly in museums and worth thousands of dollars.

Adjacent to the gallery is Russell's skylighted cabin studio, built of split telephone poles; the fireplace clock is stopped at 11:15—". . . when Russell changed ranges." A *Cabin Studio Catalogue* lists all the furnishings and things Russell worked with; to me the most interesting item in it is a short piece he wrote, which sums up Charlie's philosophy: "To have talent is no credit to its owner; what man can't help he should get neither credit nor blame for—it's not his fault . . . Any man that can make a living doing what he likes is lucky, and I am that. Any time I cash in now, I win."

Continuing north along the western edge of the oceanlike Great Plains, the road wound between vast grazing lands and wheatfields oddly striped by alternate bands of plowed and fallow land—to thwart soil-robbing winds. Some of these strip-farmed stretches were ten car-lengths wide. There were quail, ducks, horses, and well-nourished cattle galore, but not many people—aside from fellow motorists and a few stragglers in roadside hamlets through which we passed.

Once we met a car coming slowly toward us, driven by a girl, with a child leaning from it bearing a large red flag. We stopped and were told that they were "only flagging the combines."

Soon we met two of these great green-enameled monster machines of the wheatfields, each with a stony-faced farmer standing stoically behind the steering wheel. We got nary a nod, smile, nor wave of hand—strictly business those fellows were, no time for silly tourists in a plastic camper.

A hazy blue silhouette, ahead and as far left as my head would twist, reminded us that Montana truly lives up to its name as a land of mountains. From Rogers Pass just north of Helena to Marias Pass, the lowest in the Rockies at 5,216 feet, no road crosses the Great Divide. The concentration of lofty peaks in that 150-mile stretch is amazing—more than two dozen recognized giants. The highest, Sphinx Peak, is 9,510 feet above sea level; the lowest, Trinity Mountain, drops to a mere 7,535 feet. This sort of geography brings to a Montanan the element of peril that sets him apart from other High Westerners. The weather here can range from 50 below to 110 above. People of the Great Divide pay dearly to live here.

Just outside Dupuyer (from *depouille,* back fat of buffalo—a delicacy of this area's Blackfeet Indians), great piles of uprooted trees and log debris strewed the fields, mute evidence of the force of a flood several years back when dams on Birch and Medicine creeks burst due to the coincidence of snow runoff and 30 hours of continuous rain.

When the unbroken sweep of mountains, sky, and boundless plains began to overwhelm, I pulled onto the road's shoulder, stopped, got out, and, much to my wife's amazement, examined closely a single blade of grass—helped put things in proper perspective.

The vastness of this country so hypnotized me that we almost ran out of gas—just barely made it into Browning at dusk on a pint and a prayer.

Blackfeet Stomping Ground

Browning, a drowsy small town (population 2,011), about 40 miles from the Canadian border, is the metropolitan center of those Indians generally known as Blackfeet. Up here many people prefer the plural "Blackfoots."

A.

A. *Oglala Sioux Indian chief Iron Shell, officiating at Frontier Days, Cheyenne, Wyoming.* / B. *The Gay 50's Kitchen Band performing at Frontier Days, Cheyenne's annual week-long celebration and rodeo.*

B.

A.

A. *Main Street, Cripple Creek, Colorado.* / B. *Tia crawling out in the morning: "the hardest part of camping out."* / C. *Korczak Ziolkowski, sculptor of Crazy Horse Mountain, South Dakota.*

B.

C.

A.

A. *Toby and Tim with the engineer of a steam locomotive in South Dakota.* / B. *Toby, Tim, and the Ziolkowski boys pushing boulders off Crazy Horse Mountain.* / C. *Crow Indian Baptist Choir, Sheridan, Wyoming.* / D. *Indian boy dancers, All-American Indian Days, Sheridan.* / E. *Navajo woman in the grandstand, All-American Indian Days.* / F. *An elder statesman, All-American Indian Days.*

B

C.

D.

E.

F.

A.

B.

A. *Bob Scriver and his clay model for statue of rodeo star Bill Linderman.* / B. *Approaching our namesake town in Montana.* / C. *Mary Ground, a Blackfoot matriarch of Browning, Montana.* / D. *The emancipated life in Clinton, Montana.*

D.

C.

A.

A. *Whiskers and the girls.* / B. *Buckskin Billy, hermit and freewheeling lord of the middle Salmon River (Idaho).* / C. *Wooden Indians carved by Cherokee Irishman Ralph Gallagher.* / D. *Effect of the Salmon's rocks on riverboat propellers.* / E. *The rocky road to Supai, Arizona.*

B.

D.   E.

A.

B.

A. *Navajo hogan, Arizona.* | B. *Ancient petroglyphs, Monument Valley, Arizona.* | C. *Navajo trading post, Tuba City, Arizona.* | D. *Emerson Whitney Kaytso tucked into his cradleboard.* | E. *Bessie Kaytso making squaw bread.* | F. *Mother and child, Navajo style.*

C.

D.

E.

F.

A.

A. *Sheep-watering hole, Monument Valley, Arizona.* | B. *Stone-pocked petroglyphs, Monument Valley.* | C. *Abstractions, Mesa Verde, Colorado—windows in ancient cliff dwellings.* | D. *Artist Peter Hurd at his San Patricio ranch, New Mexico.*

B.

C.

D.

A.

B.

C.

A. *Artist Georgia O'Keeffe at her Ghost Ranch desert home in New Mexico.* | B. *A poor man's piece of land, New Mexico.* | C. *Billy the Kid Museum in Fort Sumner, New Mexico.* | D. *Reies Lopez Tijerina, champion of the Spanish land-grant claimants.*

D.

A.

A. *Old Indian man, keeper of the kiva, San Gerónimo de Taos, or Taos Pueblo, New Mexico.* / B. *Resurfacing an adobe wall, Taos Pueblo.* / C. *Back entrances to "apartments" in Taos Pueblo.*

B.

C.

It is contended by such linguistic authorities as gas station attendants and short-order cooks that one reason the culture of these Indians never approached that of the Sioux or Crows was that the Blackfeet simply didn't have enough words to describe what was going on around them—couldn't even say, for instance, "White man speaks with forked tongue." Best they could get off was, "White man plenty big mouth," which I think is close enough. The Blackfeet also are supposed to have had little understanding of smoke signals. I doubt this. Probably there wasn't much firewood available, and after tedious hours of gathering buffalo chips the Blackfeet likely forgot what it was they wanted to say.

At least one resident of Browning doesn't agree with this superficial wiseacre appraisal of the Blackfeet—young Bob Scriver, born and reared there. He looks on all Indians with respect and admiration, but he's especially fond of his friends the Blackfeet. Scriver is stocky, his round face finished off with trim goatee. He dresses cowboy style. An accomplished cornet player, for some time he was a music instructor in Montana schools, where he organized Indian brass bands that were phenomenally successful.

Scriver gave up music to become a taxidermist and did so well at it (it was he who mounted the sacred buffalo, White Medicine, in the Helena Historical Society Museum) that eventually he built his own wildlife museum in Browning and placed on display full mounts of his own hunting trophies.

Taxidermy was but a step to sculpture; now he even casts his own bronzes, and art experts compare him to Charlie Russell and Remington —a notion that embarrasses Scriver considerably, for he grew up in awe of those master portrayers of the old West.

"We lived right across the street from Russell at one time," Scriver told me when we stopped at his museum, "and my mother wouldn't let me go near him. He was considered a bum, not fit company for the son of a proper middle-class store owner, which my dad was. He still owns the big mercantile store here in town, but now my brother runs it for him—Dad's retired. Even after Russell became famous, Dad never would admit that he was any good—'Charlie never amounted to much,' Dad says, 'just painted a few pictures.' " Scriver chuckled.

"He'd paint a spoon or some such thing, some trinket, for the whores that he knew and they'd put a ribbon on it and hang it on their wall. When the pictures began to fade out or chip they'd bring them back to Charlie to be touched up, and by this time he was off the sauce—his doctor had said either stop drinking or stop painting—and was living a fairly respectable life on a paying basis, thanks to his wife, Nancy, who was pretty proper. She used to burn up when the girls brought these things back for reconditioning, but Charlie did it just the same—always for free. To him, a friend was a friend forever.

"The pictures of his I'd really like to have are some of the sketches Charlie made for bars to put in their movieolas—those machines you crank to make moving pictures."

"Pornographic?"

"Well, not really. Let's just say they were for adults only—a little rough, but a lot of fun. My mother would've had fits if she'd known I was sneaking into the saloons to see them. I regarded them as educational."

When Bob took us around to meet his mother at the mercantile store, I asked her about Charlie Russell. "Why, I lived right across the street from him," said Mrs. Scriver, a pleasant placid lady with wavy silver hair, "and he was a real fine gentleman."

Our kids took well to Scriver and were struck dumb by his mounted large animals—buffalo, timber wolf, Rocky Mountain goat, antelope, grizzly bear, and more—all displayed without cases, spotlighted in a large, dimly lighted room which smelled of pine.

"I never like to see a mounted specimen behind glass," said Scriver. "We get a good many blind visitors, and this way they can feel the animals to know what they're like. We give them a stepladder for the moose."

"We have to vacuum them all every day," said Mary, Bob's wife, a buxom, pretty blonde.

Scriver settled us into his living quarters behind the museum, a large skylighted room that seemed more an outdoor man's den than family living room. A Persian rug on part of the floor had a hole cut into it irreverently to allow access to a floor plug for an electric fan. Buffalo-hide rugs were scattered elsewhere. Indian artifacts were tumbled about and hung on the walls, along with paintings of the old West done by modern followers on the Russell-Remington trail. Over a massive stone fireplace was a fine set of elk horns. Under them hung a Kentucky squirrel rifle (muzzle-loader with octagonal barrel), a Sharp's buffalo gun, and a rifle marked "S. Hawken, St. Louis."

"Only thirty of them in existence," said Scriver. "The famous gun of the Mountain Men."

By the hearth stood a bronze casting of a grizzly's left foot track. My hand measured against it reached from its heel to base of toes; the claw marks were almost as long as my little finger.

There were many Scriver bronzes, including a remarkable small Christus on the cross.

"That's my brother-in-law, Maurice Chaillot," said Bob, "from my second marriage—professor of French at the University of Montana. After I'd got the commission, I took one look at Maurice and said 'Lordy Moses, there's my Christ!' He had just the right face and skinny figure for it, and he was willing to strip down and be roped up so I could model him in clay."

The room lights could be dimmed automatically so that a midnight-sky blue flooded the ceiling while soft music played.

"This was built for bachelor quarters," said Scriver, smiling at the playboyish mechanical seductiveness. "I never meant to get married, but I couldn't chase Mary away." She smiled delightedly.

"We used to have a big collection of mounted songbirds," Scriver continued. "About a hundred and fifty, all taken—after they were already dead from cold, hunger, and what not—by Indians on the reservation. A nice display—had it for ten years and an Indian had it for two years before that. Schoolkids especially used to love it. It gave them a look at wild birds they didn't have much chance of ever seeing.

"I had to get rid of them all because of the regional federal game warden. He threatened to fine me for having them. The law is very strict about songbirds. You've killed a blackbird, haven't you? Well, it's a two-thousand-dollar fine. If a songbird hits your car and gets stuck in the radiator grill and you cross a state line with it, it's a fine.

"But it wasn't the law so much as this guy bore a grudge agin me, because once I wouldn't let him in free to the museum with a large party of friends. Not long after I'd turned him down, one winter day another guy came and said he wanted to see the museum, and he paid the usual. It was bitchin' cold in there, but I figured if he wanted to go in and tough it out, he's welcome. After a while he didn't come out and I thought he must be freezing, so I went in and he's standing there with a little notebook, writing down a list of all my birds. He said they were illegal. Threatened to arrest me, close up the place, confiscate the specimens, and fine me two thousand dollars. We argued quite a bit and finally I come right out and asked how much it was he wanted. At my suggesting that he could be bribed, he blew up and stormed off, and pretty soon my federal taxidermy license was revoked without a hearing. And now I even have to have a fishpond permit for those five little trout I've got in that little fountain up front."

Scriver sat back for a moment reflecting on the pettiness of the bureaucratic mind. "I burned up the birds," he finally said. "I'm thinking seriously of getting a domestic goose from some farmer and mounting it to look like a swan, which it is very illegal to have a specimen of. Then when the game warden nails me for it I can make him look silly, and all the Indians will have a good laugh."

"Tell them about the buffalo," urged Mary.

Scriver laughed heartily. "Oh, the buffalo," he said. "Well, Tom Kehoe, who was director of the Museum of the Plains Indian just across the way from here, shot one hell of a big buffalo during rut season and asked me if I wanted to come out, skin it, take the hide to mount, and then make the bones into a skeleton for him. After I skinned the animal we hauled it in here to make casts of it. Plaster heats when it hardens, and this made the buffalo meat cook and stink to holy heaven. You could smell it all over town; everybody thought the main sewer line had busted. We just kept mum. Had to. The Indians would have run us out. Prisoners from the jail come and boned out the carcass for us. The bones are still over there in the basement—all varnished and numbered; but Kehoe left the post, so he never did get his skeleton put together."

We intended to sleep in our camper overnight—and the kids did just that—but Whiskers and I ended up bunking on the Scriver's foldaway sofa bed. "It's something we don't tell anybody we have," said Mary, "unless we really like them, and I can't think of anyone we've enjoyed more than you folks."

Every 15 minutes all through the night the electric clock atop the bookshelves chimed its jaunty little musical phrase. Drove us wild.

"Disconnect it," whispered Whiskers.

"Haven't the right," I whispered back. "Not our home."

"Put a pillow over it, or a pishamore or something. Won't get a wink of sleep," muttered Whiskers.

But we did—a lot of them. In the morning I noted the clock's face was cracked. Someone probably threw a shoe at it. Whiskers?

"Our fox did that," Scriver explained at breakfast. "He got up there one night and kicked a bronze over onto it. He also chewed on the piano and several picture frames, so we had to turn him loose."

The Scrivers once had a pet bobcat that purred like a contented motorcycle. Now, they were harboring an eagle—but not in the house. The bird was kept in a backyard pen, was six years old and called Iggie. "He's a legal eagle," explained Scriver. "Fell out of its nest and would've died but for us taking him in. Have to catch a gopher every day to feed him; he eats all but the tail. For an eagle, he's a little peculiar—once he hatched a goose from an egg."

In his sculpture studio Scriver proudly showed us his latest project, a portrait statue of the famous rodeo cowboy Bill Linderman (all-time biggest money winner), who'd been killed in an airplane accident. It was one-fifth bigger than life-size and had been commissioned by the Rodeo Cowboys' Association for the Cowboy Hall of Fame and Western Heritage Center at Oklahoma City.

At first Scriver had agreed to take whatever was collected from the membership—he felt "they'd be square about it." But then a purchase price was arrived at: $12,000 f.o.b., with Scriver having the right to sell 12 facsimiles. He wasn't sure yet whether the work could be cast in his home foundry and had gotten estimates from professional ones on the East Coast and in Mexico. They varied widely—from $1,800 to $7,110.

Bob said he'd kept careful track of the hours spent on the project and to date he'd put in 435; the 1,000 pounds of clay—worth about $3,000—had been borrowed from another sculptor, a woman living in Chinook, 190 miles to the east. It looked as if this project would be a labor of love.

"The cowboys on the committee," said Bob, "are very particular about details. They look at the model and say, 'His ears were much farther back'—things like that. They know exactly what they want. The set of the hat, the way the rope is made has to be just right; they want all the stitching to show in the saddle. I took a Turtle Association saddle apart and made a pattern of every piece, actual size, and then scaled them up one-fifth for the big clay model—made myself a one-and-a-fifth measuring stick for the job. Nobody had any exact measurements on Linderman; I had to guess from photographs and by asking questions."

We saw the small clay model. It had hundreds of pins stuck into it. Looked like the voodoo doll of someone especially vindictive.

"They're like surveyor's grade stakes," explained Scriver. "The pins on the little model correspond to the matches stuck in the full-scale one. It's my way of enlarging. Sure puzzles tourists, though. They look at it and say, 'Oh, the matches are holding it together, eh?' or, 'Oh, you're going to light the matches and bake the clay, eh?' Sometimes they can be pretty dense."

Scriver casts his bronzes in a homemade foundry out back, using the lost-wax method, a technique that has come down basically unchanged from the Bronze Age. The small hoist for lifting the castings is modeled after a giant crane hoist of the Anaconda Company at Great Falls. "I went in on one of the regular tourists' tours and studied it until I knew it by heart."

Out in Scriver's backyard stood a futuristic life-size buffalo made of welded sheet steel for the Great Falls High School. "I took what the kids could pay—$1,500," said Bob.

"If they get tired of it," commented Lulu, "they can always plant geraniums in the stomach."

I was anxious to talk to some Blackfeet Indians, so Scriver offered to drive Whiskers and me around town in his jeep to look in on a few of his friends.

Instead of coming with us, Tia, Tim, and Lulu decided to give our camper its first bath. Scriver told them when they'd finished they could take turns riding his horse in the Tribal Ceremonial Grounds across the stream—just be careful crossing the narrow bridge. I was sure the camper would get a very fast washdown.

The Blackfeet nation consists of three tribes: Blackfeet, Bloods, and Piegan, or Pikunis. The three tribes formed—with their allies the Gros Ventres (big bellies) and Sarsi—a sort of loose confederation, speaking a common language (an Algonquian dialect), sharing customs, inter-marrying, warring against common enemies. The tribes, however, were independent—each with its own chief and its own Sun Dance, the great annual religious ceremony surviving from aboriginal days.

The Blackfeet are proud of their lineage—no Indian nation ever exceeded them in bravery—yet today no one living on the reservation has sufficient knowledge of the Sun Dance to be able to lead its complex series of rituals and songs.

The Piegan were introduced to agriculture by a sudden and complete break with their nomadic past—the elimination in 1883 of their buffalo, the last of those great plains beasts to go. In 1830 some 40 million bison were grazing in the West. Forty years later, in spite of constant hunting by both Indians and white men, the number remained nearly the same. Then in 1871, a tanning process was developed that could convert buffalo hides into a tough and durable leather suitable for machine belts; the demand for the hides became insatiable. Twelve years later the buffalo was virtually extinct from unparalleled slaughter.

The winter of 1883 was a starvation one for the Piegan. Their reservation Indian Agent John Young had tried since 1880 to warn federal authorities that increasing scarcity of game was leading to an impossible situation. He repeatedly urged the teaching of crop-raising to the Piegan. Nothing was done. When the buffalo disappeared in 1883, those Indians became destitute. Congress tragically underestimated the necessary appropriations for relief, and freighting in emergency rations during the winter through the snow-filled coulees proved to be nigh onto impossible.

The Indians wasted away; 600 died. Young angrily resigned, and when his successor arrived in spring he found, in a tour of inspection of 28 lodges, only a rabbit cooking in one, and a steer's hoof boiling in another. Not another bite anywhere. Probably ate all their horses. Pitiful —and shocking.

Summer finally brought relief, and by fall of 1884 the starvation epidemic was under control. From then on, the Piegan have been dependent upon the white man for their very existence. Although the country around Browning—except for a few modern roads, campsites, strip-farming, and the east-west track of the Great Northern Railway— remains as it was when early fur traders first found it, the people have changed greatly. The Blackfeet tribal rolls number about 8,500, mostly Piegan (in 1895, barely 1,800), more than one-third of Montana's Indian total of 24,100. Due to the warring nature of these Indians, women used to outnumber men three to one. Today, there are a few more males. About nine-tenths of these Indians are mixed bloods. Many have surnames of French, English, Scottish, or German origin, Gallic ones being most prevalent.

Full bloods have such picturesque names as Chewing Black Bones, Weasel Head, Bear Medicine, Rides at the Door, and Fast Buffalo Horse. Sign language still is extensively used among them, but nearly all can write their names in English, which most modern Blackfeet are able to speak, read, and write.

The reservation originally covered a million and a half acres. Now, due to fee patenting and selling, the Blackfeet Indians' land is down to 944,879 acres, held in trust status. Not the largest of Montana's seven

Indian reservations, it is exceeded by the Wind River (1,887,372 acres—Shoshone and Arapahoe), Crow (1,574,231), and Fort Peck (1,025,100 —Sioux and Assiniboine).

Sixty percent of the nearly 900 Blackfeet families have agricultural incomes; the others work for wages in private businesses or government service. About half the population is employed off the reservation; many men are in the armed services. Some tribal members receive income from oil, gas, timber, titanium, and coal. I asked Scriver if the Indians here benefited much from the tourist influx.

"When tourists come West, first it's like a flood," he said, "then rivers, then it trickles into streams and cricks, and by the time they get this far they're just moisture sinkin' into the ground."

As we started off to meet his Indian friends, Scriver smiled and said, "My nephew come out from back east, and the first Indian he meets he says, 'How!' I had to tell him, don't do that—these aren't TV Indians; they're civilized same as we are." Yet I noticed that when Scriver subsequently greeted Indian friends, while he didn't actually say, "How," aloud, he did give each an uplifted palm salute.

The first Blackfoot we met was a young modern one, Hughie Welch, living in a neat, well-organized prefab house. He operates a television and radio repair business. He was three-eighths Indian; two of his daughters also were on the government's Blackfeet roll, but the youngest girl was not, since she'd been born after the passing of the regulation requiring a recipient of federal Indian aid now to be at least one-fourth pureblood.

I was curious about the Indian sense of humor.

"One thing I know," said Hughie. "Indians laugh at their own troubles more than anyone else does. They're not stoic, like everyone thinks. It's just that when they don't know what to do, they do nothing— just hold still, and let you do all the talking."

Hughie told us a story. A man buying a horse from an Indian selects one, and the seller says, "He don't look too good." The buyer retorts, "Well, he looks all right to me; I'll take him." The deal is made; the horse turns out to be blind. When the new owner objects, the Indian simply says, "I *told* you he don't look too good."

We next visited an aging carpenter named Mike Oscar who lives in a government-built shack of three rooms. A very red man, he was tidying his not-too-miserable household before taking a trip to Yakima, Washington. After much personal chitchat with Scriver, the old gent brought out a handmade, handsomely decorated buckskin shield with spotted eagle feathers attached. Then, feeling obliged further to entertain his guests, he sat on the couch and offered a ghost story. Once as a child he and nine other boys were swimming in a river at dusk and saw lights approaching from the distance. They all hid in the rushes on the bank, then saw a naked man come running by with his feet four inches above the ground and lights shining from his breast through exposed ribs and also through from the knee bones.

After that dramatic recital, the old Indian hauled out of a drawer a handkerchief-wrapped copper medal, much bigger than a silver dollar. It was dated 1789, and bore the likeness in bas-relief of George Washington on one side, clasped hands on the other commemorating friendship between Indians and white men; the old Indian obviously cherished the token.

As we were leaving he told Scriver that a friend had just signed a contract for an H-bomb shelter. Bob was incensed. "It's criminal," he stormed to us, "how people take advantage of the Indians. What possible need would anyone—especially an Indian—have for a bomb shelter up in these wilds?"

The only reading matter that I'd seen in the house was a late copy of the *Police Gazette* with articles on: "War Swingers Go For Bargain Abortions," "Mystery of Al Capone's Millions," and "Why Stalin's Daughter Fled Russia."

The old Indian's goodbye was poignant. "Glad to see you," he said amiably, "if I never see you no more."

Scriver took us then to a small bakery-coffee shop and there phoned the police chief, Albert Flammand, who soon appeared with his wife. We all had maple sticks and coffee as we talked about law enforcement on the reservation, where the job is handled by three city and eight tribal policemen, the county sheriff and five deputies—besides the immigration patrol, the FBI, the state highway patrol, and state, tribal, and federal game wardens. Chief Flammand blamed welfare for most Indian delinquency.

"It's the worst thing that ever happened to the Indians," he said. "It keeps them living on handouts—idle. Why should they work when they can get everything they need for nothing? Used to be, beginning in August through September, you'd see these big wagons loaded with wood for the winter. Now only one family here in town gathers wood;

everybody knows that when they run out the government will supply Presto logs. Why work?"

Chief Flammand's jail consists of four cells (two for juveniles, one for men, another for women) and two "tanks"; usually the occupants are drunks.

"The smell of the cork," said the police chief resignedly. "We can't buck it."

According to him, the town's young people have not yet embraced narcotics; there has been no rioting in the bumpy, dusty streets, although long-endured bigotry and neglect might stand the Indian as close to the threshold of violence as the Negro.

We went to a dismal colony of tumbledown houses and to newer ones built by the government as compensation for homes supposedly damaged in the 1964 flood—a piece of political chicanery, for high waters hadn't touched this part of Browning, though the city did have eight inches of rain in two days. Scriver took a dim view of such hypocrisy.

We stopped to chat with braided-hair full bloods basking in the sun on benches in front of commercial establishments along the main drag. Few had any notion about what strikes an Indian as funny. His sense of humor seems mainly to be a macabre one—rather oriental in concept.

Nearly all with whom we spoke considered the red man advanced over whites in social relations with animals and other living things. Indians respect the land more than anybody else does. "When an Indian cut hay," one old Indian said, "it's like cutting his own mother's hair."

The Indian treats every creation of Nature as a member of a particular family, or nation, having its own characteristics and way of life. Tolerance is a strong point among primitive Indians, and although most Indians today are archconservatives, nonconformity still is admired and respected.

At the tribal office we met a suave, fleshy Indian named Joe Show, who told us the tribe was anticipating employment for about 200 at two factories and a sawmill soon to be established on the reservation. One plant was to manufacture electrical gadgets; the other, mechanical cherry pickers that grab a tree, shake it, and box all its fruit in a matter of two and a half minutes.

As examples of other forward steps, Mr. Show mentioned that the tribe had just been granted $50,000 for an economic development survey, and that a contractor wanted to come on the reservation to employ Indians at nonunion scale, beginning at $1.85 an hour, in the manufacture of prefabricated houses, 55 of them to remain on the land as part of the deal.

I asked if there were any Negroes around.

"No," said Mr. Show, "we float them off the reservation."

As we drove on down the street Scriver spoke of wage scales for Indians.

"I can't pay more'n one-fifty an hour because I have to make a profit, and they won't work for that, because they're spoiled by the government paying three-seventy an hour for a two months' job—then they quit and take unemployment.

"The Indian's logic is to live today and let tomorrow take care of itself. It's not just 'the hell with tomorrow,' but more, 'don't worry about tomorrow when you're working on today'—one thing at a time, more or less."

Our last stop was at the modest home of Mary Ground, a slim, tall, blue-eyed matron of 81 with braided, wavy gray hair. She was wearing a long, old-fashioned, high-necked housedress—a flower print, mostly blue—and on her wrists some ancient copper bracelets. Mary, the wife of a rancher, had been widowed 15 years ago after producing 12 children, who'd brought her a cluster of grandchildren, who'd begat great-grandchildren, who'd gone on to great-great-grandchildren—more than 80 in all, she told Whiskers.

"How can I even know them all?" she asked. We sat with her in the yard on a pile of long tepee poles, a fragrant herb called "turkey feet" growing all around us. The talk mostly was between Scriver and Mary about mutual friends and local happenings.

Her evaluation of the tribal agency: "They got twelve clerks down there, do nothing. All full of holes like gopher holes—you don't know which one to go into. A person could be dead and nobody care."

When I asked Mary Ground if she ever felt like moving off the reservation, she answered, "I'd die with grief out there."

About marriage Mary said, "You are tied to a man's suspenders. When you go away you get permit, when you come back you get questions."

This Indian matriarch told us without rancor a saga which indicated how casually home ties were regarded by priests recruiting for the early missions. According to Mary, some Indian lads out swimming were invited by a traveling priest to come along with him in his wagon. The boys washed the mud from their naked bodies, dressed, pulled on their moccasins, and all those who could got aboard the wagon; the others trotted alongside. They went through Marias Pass, over the mountains, and south along Flathead Lake. The boys' footgear soon wore out and their feet had to be protected with canvas strips torn from the wagon's top. It was many days before they reached Saint Ignatius Mission, 200 miles away, and more than a year went by before some of the boys' parents learned where their children had gone.

Mary hadn't responded to our interest in Indian humor, but as we were leaving she brightened and said to Scriver, "You better go see Charlie Undermouse—he's feeling pretty low." The line was thrown away in the best vaudeville tradition, and I suppose we'll never know if there really *is* a Charlie Undermouse—it's possible—or if the remark was Mary's attempt to please her guests with something funny.

The afternoon was getting on, and we still hadn't been to Browning's renowned Museum of the Plains Indian, so Scriver dropped us off there—we could easily walk back to his place.

This museum is proud of its archives containing Blackfeet Agency records from 1874 forward; in the basement vaults are priceless costumes and trappings of all Montana's Indians east of the Great Divide.

Every museum director of the High West realizes how difficult it is to entertain and enlighten tourists. They come in first to use the restrooms and by the time they've examined a half-dozen displays they're not even trying to read the captions on the cases—their attention span is not great. We were no exception.

Perhaps we were suffering from overexposure to museums, but soon the stilted, coldly designed displays—their legends couched in language of the initiate in terms that promptly alienate the layman tourist—became intolerably tiresome. We did, however, admire the fresco secco murals of a bison hunt, painted in the entrance lobby by Victor Pepion, a deaf-mute Blackfoot Indian also known as Black Shields.

In late afternoon we left Browning for East Glacier, as we wanted to spend the night at Glacier Park Lodge, reputedly one of the High West's most splendid inns. "It'll have to go some," said Whiskers, "to come up to *chez* Scriver."

She came away from Browning with a recipe for Blackfoot *pemmican,* a meat preparation that lasted Indians through winter (and well into summer, for the less squeamish). To make pemmican, first find a dead buffalo, cut from it strips of meat, and dry them in the sun. Pound the meat into a flaky mass and mix this with wild berries or chokecherries and buffalo fat, and pack the result into a skin bag to create something that looks like an Italian salami.

Pemmican might even be good, but it sounds to me like solidified haggis, which my Scottish grandmother made me and my cousins eat every New Year's Day.

In lieu of buffalo meat, salty dried chipped beef could be used; canned bing cherries and hog fat make a fair substitute for wild berries and buffalo suet; and instead of a skin bag a lady's large leather purse could be utilized. At worst, the stuffed bag could be carried as a weapon to be used against metropolitan muggers.

Glacier's Pinnacles and Beyond

At East Glacier, we bought gas. I asked the pump man if business had fallen off since the bear attacks.

"If anything," he responded, "it's better since the bears."

I ventured that people seem to have a morbid streak.

"Yup," he agreed, *"they* do." And that was that.

When we registered at Glacier Park Lodge, the college-boy clerk gave us the once-over, then said pleasantly, "We require a deposit."

"How much deposit?"

"Seventeen dollars."

That, it turned out, was the room rate for two persons. (We planned to sleep the kids in the camper.) Some deposit!

The hotel is 50 years old and looks it, although the lobby is spectacular—framed in huge Douglas fir pillars claimed to be more than 800 years old, each of them 40 feet in height and about one yard in diameter.

At first we thought there must be a convention of embalmers or computer programmers at the lodge, but then Whiskers pointed out that those men dressed sedately in dark suits, white shirts, neckties, and shiny black shoes, contrasting eerily with the barefooted casually attired tourists, were merely the lodge's corps of security men.

Our room was big but tacky—one measly little throw rug on the floor, a dingy bed lamp, one wobbly chair, the only picture a small calendar-reproduction of a Winold Reiss portrait of a Blackfoot Indian (24 for $2 at any souvenir counter), and there was a clumsy, wide, stone fireplace. I called the manager's office to be told haughtily by a clipped Canadian male voice that "no one *evah* has used the *fiah*place, so far as we know."

We soon rectified that situation. Whiskers and the kids promptly rose to the challenge and went out searching for kindling and faggots. After laying the fire they went swimming, and a young bellman, at my instigation, augmented the one towel that was in the bathroom and brought three sheets of stationery and two envelopes. I could see we were going to have a real luxurious time of it here.

In conversation with the bellman I learned that Glacier Park's grizzlies had been especially active due to a seasonal scarcity of their usual diet of roots and berries and a shortage of water. "They claw out deep trenches looking for food," the young man said. "Lots of hikers and campers around here have been treed by grizzlies. Not too long ago three of them killed seventy-two sheep in a meadow just out behind the lodge."

That evening I went to the lobby for some postcards and learned from an off-duty park ranger that there are about 100 grizzlies in Glacier's more than a million acres.

"A bear," he said, "ain't too much different than a man. You step on his toes and he either fights or runs. And if somebody walks up and feeds him, why should he spend all that energy turning over logs and rocks to get food?"

The grizzly has come under considerable study of late, notably by Frank and John Craighead, twin brothers and eminent ecologists (both have Ph.D.s), who for some time in Yellowstone Park have been gathering knowledge about *Ursus horribilis*. Using tranquilizing darts they've immobilized these fierce bears in order to tag and outfit them with radio-transmitter collars weighing only two ounces, so that the bears' habits can be studied. The brothers are learning how long a grizzly lives, how much land he needs, his migratory habits, weight, pulse, and the chemistry of his blood and the females' milk. Such facts will aid in the preservation of this great wilderness prowler, actually a very social animal, a doting and protective family creature.

The bears' radio signals can be picked up at 20 miles, ideally over a period of six years. To date, more than 200 grizzlies have been marked and observed by the Craigheads. Some specimens weighed half a ton. The program has enabled the brothers, for the first time, to track a grizzly to its winter home, which this particular bear always enters during a snowstorm so as to leave no telltale footprints.

Bears are a headache to foresters and lumbermen. The animals love to strip bark to get at the sweetish cambium layer and sapwood beneath. The trees are left so badly peeled—even 30 feet above the ground—that they rot and are ruined by fungi and insects. Coming out of hibernation a bear can kill 20 trees a day for the next two months. Douglas fir is the favorite.

Whiskers and I didn't sleep well that night. She kept saying, what if the bears come and claw their way into the camper? Nonsense, I'd say, and then I'd remember that sheet-metal kitchen wall that the bear busted through at Quigley's place.

Our mental tension was aggravated by light pouring into the darkened room from the porch through the flimsy window drapes (even after I went out and unscrewed a couple of bulbs) and also through a crack under the door big enough to peel a banana in; a lawn sprinkler outside the window phut-phut-phut-phutted all night long; someone tried turning his key in our lock; and at 4:00 A.M. a long, noisy freight train clattered by right on the edge of the lodge grounds. "It's going through the lobby!" said Whiskers.

I think I even heard a rooster crow, but Whiskers said, "Don't be ridiculous. It's probably a bugling lovelorn elk."

"I didn't know elks could play bugles," I said, which made her madder than she already was.

Red-eyed, we checked out just after dawn and struck north 32 miles to Saint Mary. The ranger at the park entrance there jumped to attention, sleepy-eyed, hastily put on his official hat, checked our Golden Eagle Passport (a $7 permit admitting bearer and party to all federal recreation areas), and waved our camper on.

Almost immediately we were abreast of a magnificent command of four mountain peaks: Red Eagle, Mahtotoba, Little Chief, and Citadel—lined up shoulder to shoulder, reflecting handsomely in the still water of Upper Saint Mary Lake. The sudden sweep of grandeur was overpowering. The mountains, miles away, seemed practically in our laps, with Little Chief rising 5,000 feet above the lake's surface. We stopped often to gasp at innumerable picture-postcard views. Looking up the Red Eagle Valley, we could see Triple Divide Peak, an 8,000-footer from which water starts on its way to the Gulf of Mexico, the Pacific Ocean, and Hudson Bay.

Glacier Park is noted for its rich variety and abundance of flora and fauna. From spring to early autumn there are flower displays somewhere within the park. Southern forms mingle with northern, eastern varieties contrast with western—in all, over 1,000 species of wild flowers and trees. The showiest bloom is bear grass, usually considered the park flower, a strikingly peculiar and very stinky member of the lily family.

Whiskers had bought a book that identified Glacier's flowers, and I was overawed by the fancy names until she told me that the lambs-tongue fawnlily, "also known as the trout or glacier lily," was nothing more than a dogtooth violet, that we had butter-and-eggs toadflax growing by our mailbox at home, and that thimbleberry grew along our driveway.

Within the park is every species of animal known to the region except buffalo and rattlesnake—57 kinds of mammals, 216 different birds.

White mountain goats and bighorns are common. The most unusual birds are the osprey, the slate-gray water ouzel, the scarlet-crested pileated woodpecker—big as a crow. Bald eagles are numerous, especially in the Lake McDonald area. There, naturalists have counted as many as 352 of them—plus a few golden eagles and snowy owls—during the annual run of kokanee salmon (landlocked sockeye).

The naturalist John Muir once said of Glacier Park, "Give a month at least to the precious preserve. The time will not be taken from the sum of your life. Instead of shortening, it will definitely lengthen it and make you truly immortal."

We didn't have the time to be made immortal but had to confine our visit to a drive on the only motor road that crosses this high park between east and west, the Going-to-the-Sun Highway, 50 miles of mountain splendor.

Glacier is one national park more rewarding to hikers and trail riders than to motorists. The finest natural features are well off paved road: towering snowcapped mountain peaks by the score; long, skinny, blue-green lakes; high flowering meadows; and the great glaciers from which the park gets its name (about 50 still remaining within its borders). Yet, while the Going-to-the-Sun offers only tantalizing glimpses—a sample, really—of the thrilling wonders beyond in the park's rugged interior, that which can be seen here from an automobile is vastly more spectacular than the sights available along Yellowstone's Grand Loop Road.

Pauses can be made en route at such natural wonders as Lost Lake (great fishing); Baring Falls; and Jackson Glacier, one of the few visible from roadside. The kids wanted to stay and see it move, until I explained that these frozen masses crawl only a few inches a day.

As we climbed steadily, pure, evergreen-scented air spilled down from the heights. We passed Pollock Mountain, which each winter creates the impassable "big drift"—at times 80 feet deep—that must be plowed through to open the road in early summer. (In the past several years sonic booms of jet-fighter aircraft have been used to start snowslides to get the big highway open earlier than its usual June 15th date.)

By long, comfortable switchbacks and through tunnels we moved along to Logan Pass, a summit point of the Divide (6,664 feet).

"All there is to see is scenery," complained a tourist in the modern visitor center to the ranger on duty, who gave this boor a long cool look, then drawled, "Waaal, that's what we *mostly* keep in stock, but there is a little geology, too—about a billion years of it."

From Logan Pass geology-minded hikers can go by a six-mile trail to Grinnell Glacier, the park's largest, with a surface area of more than 300 acres and a maximum thickness of 500 feet (average about 73 feet). Grinnell Lake is especially beautiful, its water an incredible blue-green made by the absorption of glacier-ground rock flour called *Gletschermilch* (glacier milk). Tourists who brave trips to glaciers come back smugly babbling about moraines, névés, firns, *Bergschrund,* and moulins, and are easily able to put down the sneakers-and-binoculars set.

The winding descent from Logan Pass was sensational and scary, with only a low log barrier at roadside between us and oblivion in gigantic dished-out glacial valleys, now barely visible because of the hazy blue forest-fire smoke that lay all over this part of the park. After dropping from the heights the road meandered along McDonald Creek. From Lake McDonald Lodge—Alpine-style, shaded by cedar and pine—a ten-mile trip by hike or horseback can be made to Sperry Glacier, the park's second largest (285 acres). The trail is steadily upgrade—a 3,356-foot ascent in the first six and a half miles. At that point an overnight stop is advisable at stone chalets, where often it is possible "to walk in clouds up to the waist," as Charlie Russell once put it.

As we drove along through forest-bordered swampland we could see orange flames licking wickedly at timber high overhead. In a blackened patch of woods, scar of another season's fire, a crow perched atop a pine tree skeleton and screamed.

We hated to leave the park and face again the rigors of civilization. I understood why the ranger at Logan Pass was so nettled by the insensitive tourist. I imagine that it is only the beauty of the natural surroundings that keeps national park rangers from going mad due to their constant exposure to the Great American Tourist. En masse, we are a vile, noisy, untidy lot—vandals, graffiti scrawlers, and feckless bear lovers. Ordinary nuisance makers are legion and all in the day's work to a ranger, but the ones that cause him really to shudder are the foolish explorers who get themselves hung up on cliffs, wedged in crevasses, tumbled over waterfalls, crippled on the ice of glaciers or in snowfields, buried in snowslides, drowned in frigid lakes and swift streams, struck by lightning while hiking along a high ridge during an electrical storm, or lost forever on a mountaintop.

While people for whom national parks were established make the most trouble for rangers, their peace of mind also is disturbed by those who would exploit this scenic land that is being held in trust for the public. Commercial operators try to get hold of park timber or mineral resources. Someone is always clamoring for permission to slaughter a park's elk or deer for meat, or to open park areas to cattle-grazing. Concessionaires want to introduce such tourist conveniences as tramways to mountaintops, helicopter services to canyon bottoms, the floodlighting of beauty spots, or musical broadcasts at "inspiration points."

The National Park Service turns down such hucksters, for its stated intention toward natural areas is to "provide for all appropriate use and enjoyment by the people that can be accommodated without impairment of the natural values"—in other words, to keep things as wild as possible within the range of comfortable public use. Wildness is described by the National Park Service as "a whole environment of living things dependent on a continuing interrelationship free of man's spoilation."

To the Park Service, a fallen tree represents an incident in the unending living process which the park was created to protect and preserve. If the tree does not obstruct a road or trail it is allowed to remain where it has dropped, a part of nature's wilderness. A roaming mountain lion or grizzly is regarded as a natural citizen with rights equal to those of all others inhabiting the park, including motor tourists, hikers, horsemen, campers, and rangers. The animal is a predator only in the scientific sense. Strictly speaking, a park ranger cannot set a trap for mice in his cabin without getting permission from his Park Service bosses.

Driving south, we came to Hungry Horse Dam, which was supposed to change the face of Western Montana by offering cheap power to attract new industry. The project, on the south fork of the Flathead near Columbia Falls, cost $101,824,000. It has brought in only one major new industry—a sizable aluminum plant operated by the Anaconda Company.

Some Montanans smell a very old rat. We paused there only long enough for a look at "the world's biggest glory hole-type spillway," a circular shaft 35 feet in diameter, which lets out overflow through bedrock at a maximum rate of 53,000 cubic feet per second—just like water going down a bathtub drain. The drop is almost 500 feet. I would hate to fall in the drink anywhere near—just one more thing to have nightmares about. Move over, grizzlies.

We continued along the east shore of 38-mile-long Flathead Lake. Residents there favor doghouse-sized mailboxes having such architectural details as log siding, shingled roofs, towers, belfries, verandas, rainspouts, pillars of rock, and bay windows.

After leaving this lush fruit-growing country, roadside towns ahead to the south were hardscrabble, dispirited, and unkempt—seeming like places where impulses take precedence over dreams. Many stunning views of the mountains were marred by foreground piles of rusting, crumpled, junked autos.

Lumbering is the big deal here; 77 sawmills in the area process ponderosa pine, western larch, spruce, and Douglas fir. We frequently overtook gigantic, heavily loaded logging trucks. A million and a half Christmas trees are harvested each year.

It was a mournful afternoon with heavy-laden clouds languishing on the horizon. Occasionally the sun broke through and danced bright patches on distant foothills.

After skirting Mount Harding, 10,000 feet, we came upon the town of Saint Ignatius, where we visited the tall, dignified, red-brick church of the Jesuit mission established there more than 113 years ago to convert the Flathead, or Selish, Indians.

I wanted Whiskers and the kids to see the church's lavishly decorated interior, featuring dozens of large murals, most of them circular, about ten feet in diameter, and all painted by a Coadjutor Brother of the Society of Jesus, J. Carrignano, who was also the mission's cook. In my opinion he was darn good on the flames of hellfire, but his celestial clouds look a little like steamed cauliflower.

We rang the bell at the parish house, and a swarthy, jolly, short man in rumpled work clothes answered and immediately put one arm around me as though we'd been lifelong buddies. Said he was Brother Gallant. I thought he said Gallon, but was corrected. "No, not gallon. I no drink that much."

The church is light and airy, and the semiprimitive paintings and *trompe l'oeil* show off well. Brother Gallant rattled off the titles of all the panels for us. When he passed in front of the altar he didn't genuflect but heartily slapped the top of the altar rail much as you would a faithful old horse.

"Fifty-eight color paint they sayed," he said. "I heard maybe fifty-*nine*. No is marble, just painted. Wood is no wood, just painted. All painted to look like real."

We thoroughly enjoyed the brief tour, and I offered him a dollar for his trouble. "I cannot take," he protested, as he took the bill. "I cannot spend." He moved toward the donations box, but I'm not sure he made it.

We jogged west to the National Bison Range at Moiese, a grassland sanctuary for about 500 of the 20,000 great shaggys remaining in the United States and Canada. Also on the wildlife preserve, one of the oldest in the country (founded 1908), are mule and white-tailed deer, elk, bighorn sheep, pronghorns, bobcats, coyotes, badgers, mink, beaver, and an occasional visiting bear. The famous sacred white buffalo, Big Medicine, lived here until his death at the age of 26. In the high-fenced exhibition pasture, 30 or so morose buffalo were at dinner.

Upon leaving the place we ran into a light drizzle. Suddenly the sun shone and smeared against the glowering cobalt clouds ahead the most marvelous rainbow I've ever seen—the colors looked like thick tubes of fluorescent light. By rights, Judy Garland should have been at one end, accompanied by John Philip Sousa and his band at the other—a fitting glorious climax to our stay in Montana.

A State of Wilderness

Through Lolo Pass

Say "Idaho" to an easterner and he'll snap back "Potato!" but a native Idahoan likely will respond "Mountains!" A good two-thirds of the state's area is perpendicular, or close to it. The people out here say Idaho would be the biggest state in the union if it could be flattened out. All of Idaho's mountains are violent—old, but not slouch-shouldered and submissive. They are defiant and erect, sheer, with jagged and challenging peaks that few men care to dare.

Flowing from the heights are torrents so swift and highwalled they've taken a terrible toll of the most professional of boatmen in the sturdiest of boats. Its highlands give Idaho more running water than any other state—35,000 miles of rivers, most of them nonnavigable or only partially so, and largely unharnessed for power. There are more lakes than have ever been counted or named (and nobody knows how many undiscovered).

We entered Idaho through the Bitterroots at the same point as did Lewis and Clark in 1805, the first white men to lay eyes on this stupendous territory. Our route was through Lolo Pass, named for a Nez Percé traitor. (One of our children kept referring to it as Lulu

Pass.) The new Lewis and Clark Highway parallels an old Nez Percé buffalo trail which was the road of those two early explorers.

En route, we paused to chat with a carver of wooden Indians, a muscular, half-Cherokee Irishman named Ralph Gallagher, who'd come up for the summer from Montana in his house trailer. He was chopping resolutely at a near-life-size pinewood buffalo. About the clearing stood 20 or more wooden warriors, ranging from six-footers down to some only a yard high, which resembled circus dwarfs costumed for the *Grand Entrée*. The figures had been shaped by chain saw from big logs and were painted in the most gaudy, raw colors imaginable. Gallagher told us that he'd learned the craft from his father, who'd picked it up from *his* father.

The wood-carver's wife, a comely young full blood, was bent over a prone totem pole, swabbing it with bright enamels; the couple's two children regarded us much as they would have any other strange animals. In the shade of a small shed lounged two beer-guzzling cronies, already well into the twilight zone, though the sun was still pretty far this side of the yardarm.

Lewis and Clark took about nine days to travel the 100-mile stretch from the pass to the village of Kooskia; we did it in less than three hours. Of course we didn't have to stop to kill and eat a horse, as their journals indicate they did. At that time there was a great deal more unspoiled wilderness to relish, but the route still goes through some extraordinarily lush and fragrant forestland, and threads along the charming Lochsa River. In the wooded seclusion of one of its feeder creeks, at dusk before dinner, we all became rollicking skinny-dippers.

We put up for the night in our camper just outside Grangeville, on the south side of a very beautiful valley. In the morning we drove down the many switchbacks of White Bird Hill, through brown grass and sunflowers—almost 3,000 feet in 12 miles—over a sweeping mass of great lumpy hills. "Just like driving over a giant potato," said Tia, our ever-hungry one. As the road descended, the panoramic view gradually closed in—letting go first the vast canyons southward, the forested backbones, and then the low brown and green foothills. Finally it entered a defile leading to the village of White Bird.

Near here was fought the first battle of Chief Joseph's Nez Percé Indian War of 1877, a crushing defeat for the 100 U.S. cavalrymen who were wiped out by about 80 Indians, with not one red man lost. Joseph's fighting tactics were good enough to be later introduced into the curriculum at West Point.

Idaho is the most peculiarly shaped state of them all. It measures north to south 500 miles, as long in that direction as its two western neighbors, Washington and Oregon, together, and almost as long as the combination of Montana and Wyoming, the states to the east. Yet Idaho is only 50 miles across its top, while its southern frontier measures 330 miles.

Its mountainous wilderness middle splits the state in two, culturally and economically. North Idaho, largely wheat, timber, and mining country, regards Spokane, Washington, as its natural citadel and market. Southern Idaho, dominated by agriculture, looks to Nevada and Utah.

The central barriers also prevent Idaho from having a direct north-south railway. Traffic within the state between the two areas can be only by highway or by air. It is an arduous day-long journey on the train—by way of both Washington and Oregon—between Boise, the capital, and the seat of the university in the north at Moscow (named for an Indian tribe, the Masco, not for the Russian city).

Yet for all the inconvenience they cause, Idaho's mountains are regarded with reverence by the natives. "They can yap all they want about the atomic age," an Idaho Basque sheepherder once remarked to me, "but in them mountains the *real* power is stored up—the spiritual power."

The mountains are loaded with minerals, too, that have made Idaho an important mining state. It produces more silver, zinc, pumice, and antimony than any other state, and it's second only to Missouri in the production of lead. Idaho holds the greatest known reserves (268,000 acres) of phosphate rock in the world, 85 percent of the U.S. total. Besides the major minerals, the state has asbestos, bentonite, cinnabar, cobalt, copper, feldspar, graphite, limestone, nickel, sandstone, thorium, and tungsten. Idaho's gems include agates, jaspers, onyxes, opals, rubies, and sapphires.

The most magnificent range is the Sawtooth, a rugged barrier of jagged, snow-snagging pinnacles that jab skyward to heights reaching well over 11,000 feet. It is the southern boundary of the Sawtooth Primitive Area, Idaho's most spectacular but smallest, a mere 200,000 acres of forested wilds, largely unexplored. Two others, Idaho and Selway-Bitterroot, each cover well over three million acres.

Idaho has more primitive, or wilderness, areas than any other part of the country, but oddly, there's no national park and only one national monument. More than a third of Idaho is wooded; there's more timber than its entire logging facilities could process in a century.

Approximately 73 percent of the state's 83,557 square miles is publicly owned. Sixteen national forests total more than 20 million acres; there are 13 parks and recreation areas.

Nowhere in Idaho is a fisherman ever more than an hour's drive from a clear-water, fly-fishing stream. The angler take is over ten million trout annually: steelhead, rainbow, kamloops, cutthroat, Dolly Varden, and mackinaw. There also are salmon (chinook, kokanee, and sockeye), giant sturgeon, bass, perch, channel catfish, and sunfish.

It's the ideal place for anyone who has become disenchanted with civilization and wants to take his chances with the solitude, serenity, and raw challenge of nature.

River of No Return

It's an easy drive from White Bird to Riggins, at the mouth of the Salmon just north of He Devil Mountain, a whopper at 9,393 feet.

My instructions were: "Go to Doug Crump's Chevron Station, right side of main street; he can direct you to shortwave radio on which you can talk to Paul Filer."

There are no telephones along The River of No Return. We were to go up the Salmon by turbojet, with Filer as our pilot and host. We contacted our man, who said he'd pick us up at eleven "at the top of the road, upriver." It was then 9:00 A.M.

I was anxious to meet this intrepid riverman, for I'd heard much about him. It was he who unblocked the lower part of the Salmon so that ordinary boatmen—not just daredevils—can now shoot its rapids upstream. Filer had pulled himself out on a cable over Dried Meat Rapids and blasted a passable channel through that notorious troublemaker.

Born in Spokane, Filer was a dropout from the University of Idaho. On his first job, as a restaurant kitchen flunky, he married the cook's daughter. He started a little general store at Orogrande, a gold-camp village back of the river, leased it to go into the Seabees during the war, accompanied by his wife, Marybelle, a registered nurse. When they got out in 1945, Orogrande had become a ghost town due to government restriction on gold, so Paul opened a second store in Elk City. Five years later he bought the Shepp Ranch on the Salmon, and with a "mortgage, a prayer, and a hunk of bailing wire," decided to be a cattleman.

A beef price slump caught him short. ("I was pea-green; thought all I had to do was turn a bull in loose with cows and wait for the dollars to roll in.") Within a year, he was out of the cattle business. Then he began to take in hunters and fishermen, and now his principal occupation is hosting them and organizing and operating pack trips into the wilderness.

Filer turned out to be a short, wiry, wide-mouthed, friendly buzzsaw of a man. We met him at the end of a dirt road that follows the river for 25 miles east from Riggins. Suddenly there he was, standing in his bobbing jet boat at the skid dock, looking up at us quizzically—carefully, but not offensively—taking our measure as he checked his pile of timothy hay bales stored at riverside under a big oiled canvas.

He helped us leap aboard. We'd restricted ourselves to the clothes we wore, bathing suits, hats, and sweaters. We stood, sat on the engine housing, or leaned against the boat's side. The pilot had the only real seat. He made us put on orange life jackets. The kids thrilled at that promise of danger.

The speed of the river flow, I judged, was about 12 miles per hour; bucking against it, our speedometer registered 36. A spectacular tubelike wake of white water spewed out behind as we shot forward, skimming over green, glassy, clear water on a cobblestoned bottom. Frequent little white sand beaches appeared on either side of the narrow river; cliff walls came down straight and gray.

Dozens of water ouzels skittered over the water or perched on rocks— Filer called them "teeter asses." We followed a band of wild ducks that would rise, fly ahead, land, and rise again as we approached. Some beaches had footprints of animals—deer and something that had dragged its tail, possibly a porcupine.

We went through several stretches of rough water before we got to the first real rapids. "Dried Meat," Filer called casually over his shoulder. He didn't have to tell us to hold tight. Deftly, Filer put the boat into a rockbound channel just about wide enough for it. Suddenly we swung madly, skidding so close to the rocks that I thought we'd had it, but then we bucked up a steep little falls that dropped at least three feet—literally leaped it like a determined spawning salmon—and we were in the clear.

I could no longer be blasé about shooting the rapids up the Salmon. It was wild. I was scared. I'm a lousy swimmer.

We continued upriver, skirting scrappy waters on their less turbulent edges, worming slyly around others, and after about 14 miles we sheared into a quiet little bay at the mouth of Crooked Creek and disembarked at Shepp Ranch, Paul Filer's home.

It was about as peacefully pretty a spot as I'd ever been to—accessible only by jet boat, or by airplane for about three hours a day when the wind currents are right. Nearest neighbors: 18 miles downstream, 10 miles up. The ranch house and outbuildings stand well back from the water, behind a long, wide beach of fine white sand, and are shaded by tall evergreens and a huge walnut tree. We were in a little pocket of steep, rounded, and wooded mountains.

This spot once was a base for Tukvarika and Nez Percé Indians. In the late 1880s a Nez Percé family named Mallocks lived here. The present ranch house, built in 1910, has whipsawed logs. The nails were fashioned by hand; the windows have their original putty. Floors are tongue-and-grooved by rabbit plane; the roof has handmade shakes. The place no longer is lighted by coal-oil lamps, but by a hydroelectric plant that Filer said cost $50,000 and took him five years to build. The cement had to be brought in by air, 400 pounds at a time.

"They sent the first batch," said Paul, "with the sand already mixed in—when there was all this sand right at my front door."

We stayed several days with the Filers, bunking in a two-bedroom-and-bath primitive log cabin and taking our meals in the main ranch house with family and two ranch hands, Albert Crawford and Roy Evert, the first genuine cowboys the kids had ever been close to.

The children and Whiskers swam in the swift current of the river—floated, really, wearing life preservers at Filer's insistence. His Newfoundland dog had to be confined during these sessions, otherwise he rushed into the water and tried to save everyone in sight by grabbing whatever he could get into his big mouth—an arm, an elbow, a leg, a head. There was horseback riding for the kids, and Tim went fishing several times happily and bravely by himself.

One morning just after sunup we watched the hands load eight sleek black mules with bales of hay and blocks of salt, and then with three plodding horses clop off over a narrow wooden bridge that had been built by Italian prisoners of war ("They sure was afraid of Indians") and up into the highland to one of Filer's hunting camps.

There was a little excitement one afternoon when a small forest fire broke out on the high mountain behind the house. A Forest Service plane came over and bombed it with red-colored borate; then Filer and one of his hired hands rode up on horseback to spade out what was left of the blaze.

"It'd take the Forest Service 24 hours to get a man on it," Paul said, grumpily. "We can get to it on horseback in two."

It was the first hint I'd had of the grudge river people have for forest rangers.

In the evenings there was no television to entertain us, but there were jigsaw puzzles, books and the Sears catalog to read, and records to play—even an album of *Music of the Bullring* (the Filers winter in Baja California). In the dining room the shortwave radio, on constantly, also was a source of entertainment and gossip.

"In the old days we were all linked up to the ranger station by a party-line telephone," said Paul, "and those who could play musical instruments would give concerts over it for all the others."

"That was fun," said Marybelle wistfully.

Mostly, during our visit, we talked to each other. Paul told us things about the old gent from whom he'd bought the ranch, Peter Klinkhammer, who, at 82, rode horseback a good many uphill miles in a blizzard from the ranch, over the mountain, to vote in a congressional election at Dixie, a five-house community with neither jail nor church. "Didn't have a jail," said Paul, "because there was no church to tell the people they were sinful."

We heard the legend of Polly Bemis, who'd lived just across the river until she'd died in 1933 at 81. Polly, a Chinese dance-hall girl (real name, Lalu Nathoy) was brought to Warren, a gold-rush town south of the river, by her owner, an elderly Chinese, in a packtrain from Portland, where she'd been bought for $2,500.

Some say Charlie Bemis won Polly in a poker game. Others claim he paid off her original owner and married Polly because she was the only one in the camp who'd help him after he'd had his cheekbone shattered during a gun brawl over a gambling account. Polly is supposed to have fished the bullet out with a crochet needle.

Paul Filer often spoke bitterly about the Forest Service, accusing it of deliberately trying to run off outfitters like himself. "They want to take over the outfitting themselves," he said. "They're closing in on us. When they take out that checkbook be ready to give up and sell out to them, because if you don't they'll keep at you until you do. It's getting so there's some new regulation every week almost. We have to pack out all the garbage now from our hunting trips—used to be we could just bury it. But do they bury theirs? Heck, no—not on your life. They just throw it.

"Now it seems they want us to pack in all the stock feed—and you just can't do that without making the operation prohibitively costly. You've got to allow for some grazing. I've got a permit—they're hard to get—to graze a certain number of my horses on Forest Service land, and they're always after me about them. I'm sure that Smokey the Bear has got more to do besides count my horses."

Paul blamed the Forest Service for the slipshod work being done in the forests by the Job Corps.

"We haven't had any Negroes in here at all until the Job Corps program," he said, "but we're getting them now. And if they don't want to work they just walk away and quit. You got to have a leader if you want these boys to work and the Forest Service just doesn't have the leaders. The old CCC was under army discipline. If you didn't work you went to the brig. That's the sort of thing we need in here to get something done."

We spent one full day on the river, going upstream 50 miles and stopping off to visit a half-dozen or so of Paul's neighbors. We met fellow outfitters—both new and experienced—and listened to their shoptalk. At a resort called Mackay's Bar (sand, not liquor) we were surprised to find a real-estate developer entrenched, blithely peddling Salmon River sites for fancy prices to people who want to rough it but still be comfortable. There was an elegant broad airstrip and a jet river cruiser with cushioned *seats*. It all looked painlessly prosperous.

We met one of the big orange rubber rafts that make regular float trips down the Salmon, carrying vacationers. Some of these rafts are quite luxurious—equipped with railings and canopies, two-man kayaks for side excursions, propane refrigerators, deep freezers, and bars. On one such super-floater, for six days on the river—floating by day, camping by night—the fare per person runs to $400 (meals and cocktails included).

At Campbell's Crossing we climbed a hot, sweet-smelling trail dotted with dried horse droppings to an old cottage on a bluff well back from the river, with fields and an orchard behind and a government weather station near the kitchen, past which there flowed a swift and sturdy little stream.

A knock at the door and a holler from Filer brought out a paunchy elderly man clad only in a pair of pants—he had rosy wrinkled skin, disheveled white hair, and pale blue eyes. He invited us into a cluttered living room. He and his wife, Frances Zaunmiller, a lively, healthy looking, and pretty woman who writes for a weekly newspaper, had been sleeping out the heat of the day. The fireplace held a cat-litter box for a pair of Manx; there also was a large gentle dog. We were served ice water from a cut glass pitcher.

"I just poured it in the pitcher to brag I have one," Frances said.

Her clock contrarily was on Pacific Standard time instead of Mountain Daylight Saving.

"I don't think the sun pays much attention to what the brain trusters do," she said.

She exchanged river gossip with Filer and passed on some Salmon River lore to her visitors from the great beyond. She told us of the Dudley kids, who put on their annual Christmas pageant for an audience of one, their father. Told us of Harry Guleke, who used to run a freight route down the river on an 8 x 18-foot wooden plank scow, using 24-foot sweeps with six-foot blades operated from a raised platform amidships. At the end of each run the boat was knocked apart and the boards made into furniture, floors, and doors. Captain Guleke then walked back up-river by trail about a hundred miles to build himself another boat for the next trip down. Told us about her friends the bears that come to the orchard and fight "with punches, just like men, except that men don't bite each other's necks." I could see she'd never been to Hollywood, the East Village, or on a circus.

Our most interesting stop that day was just above a humdinger rapids called Ludwig. There we met the fabulous Buckskin Billy, known from one end of the Salmon to the other. He strolled out of a stockade gate and across a narrow stretch of sand to greet us—a stubby fellow in Scotch plaid shirt, dingy broadfall pants that stopped several inches above the tops of his heavy workshoes. He wore trifocal glasses, a grime-blackened conquistador helmet made of leather, and sported marvelous chin-whiskers—white at the chin, straw-colored tips—accompanied by bushy red sideburns. He had Irish features, sun-weathered complexion with rosy cheeks, and bad teeth, and a bath wouldn't have been out of line.

Paul had told us that Billy's real name is Sylvan Ambrose Hart, 61 years old and baching it on the Salmon for about 35 years—with a short time out during the war, when he worked in Alaska with the air force. Some say Billy is a squatter on an old mining property; he claims to own

50 acres bought at $1 each in 1932, and to be one-sixteenth Apache, born in the Indian Territory of Oklahoma, with ancestry that traces back to John Hart, a signer of the Declaration of Independence.

Billy has a nasal, reedy speech that turns O's into broad A's (sparrow into sparrah, for instance). He talked incessantly but not foolishly. About people who slave at regular jobs: "On weekends they open all the cemeteries and all those dead people march out—all the same sickly shade of hide, all sunken-eyed, but not really seeing anything, just walking about because it's a weekend. Poor human ciphers, they lead such pitiful circumscribed lives, caught up in their own chains."

About city life: "It's a jumble, like facts scribbled in a college freshman's notebook."

About Harris tweed (his dress-up jacket): "The louder the pattern, the better, in my opinion. It never shrinks because they cure the wool in urine."

About trifocal spectacles: "I can see eagles with them, read, and also look at tourists."

About patriotism: "Oh, I'm patriotic all right. Every time a bald eagle flies by I take off my hat."

But what truly is remarkable about this hermit of the Salmon is not his loquaciousness but his craftsmanship. His cozy establishment, built Spanish-style around a small patio and architecturally rampantly eclectic, consists of a kitchen with food-storage loft, a blacksmith-machine shop, and a tall narrow building with stone first floor and frame upstairs balconied bedroom. It has a back bay window made of the Plexiglas bubble canopy of a B-18 bomber. The buildings are stuccoed in pink, made by the addition of iron oxide to the plaster.

The patio held a table made from heavy oak flooring hauled down from Dixie; a chair made entirely of elk horns; and a rocker said to have come around the Horn. (Out this way, nearly all antique owners claim that route to the West for their favorite possessions.)

The doors have elk-horn handles; the kitchen utensils and receptacles are handmade of copper and wood, and a champagne bottle is used as a rolling pin.

We were shown some pickled mountain lion kittens in a large jar, and Whiskers was instructed in the making of a mince pie with whiskey, plum preserves, raisins, dried apples, treacle, and gamy meat. She also learned how to can elk and to make bear cracklings. On a pantry shelf,

I noted 15 kinds of tea, including Argentine *maté* and Japanese pan-fried. Nearby were the *Larousse Gastronomique,* Irma Rombauer's *Joy of Cooking,* a sheaf of late copies of the *Wall Street Journal,* and a magazine photo of Emmett Kelly, the famous circus hobo clown.

Billy told us that for meat he shoots a bear one year, an elk the next— renders the fat in his homemade Dutch oven, and smokes the meat. He catches fish—bull, cutthroat, rainbow, steelhead trout, and whitefish. He also bags grouse, fool hens, and an occasional mountain lion. ("It's light meat, just like turkey.") He makes his own goat cheese, and on occasion he relishes a few rare insects. For sweetening he uses birch syrup, and from that tree he also makes vinegar.

For some peculiar reason known only to Billy, he imports potato flour from Peru. "Once when a box busted," said Billy, "the post office thought they had me on a marijuana rap. What would I want with that up here? Just nature is more'n enough for me."

Billy's favorite gun is a .45 caliber flintlock rifle he fashioned himself of fine Swedish steel on a primitive rotating helix. The gun took a full year to make. He demonstrated for the kids how the flint-topped hammer struck the frizzen to make a spark which drops white-hot into a charge of priming powder—the size of a grain of wheat—causing a fire that slips down the just-right slope of the firing pan into the main charge. "I can drive a tack with it," said Billy. "It kills birds."

He also makes his own bullets and hunting knives—dagger, Indian crooked blades, and bowie knives, on the blades of which he engraves such mottoes as "Liberty or Death," "Kill or Be Killed," and "Nuts." His tools, too, are homemade—of copper, silver, and other metals culled from abandoned mountain moonshine stills, mining machinery, griddles, skillets, and gold-ore pans.

We were served lapsang souchong tea brewed in an elaborate samovar of Billy's design, and we met his houseguest—slim, large-eyed, middle-aged, and ladylike. She was wearing jeans, a heavily ribbed, expensive blue sweater, and a silver cross on a neck chain, and she was introduced as "Lady MacDuff, from Virginia." After reading about Billy in a national magazine, on impulse she'd written him asking permission to visit. Billy is not equipped to take in guests, but he'd been intrigued and said come on. She'd been there eight days and was taking voluminous spidery little notes in a large spiral-bound book concerning the daily life of this hermit. He'd taken her on excursions in his rowboat, named Charon—once to the orchards across the river—and guided her on a three-day mountaintop hike. She told us it had been more rigorous than she'd expected, but she was glad to have taken the dare. I admired her insouciance.

As we sipped tea and chatted, a young woman came drifting in from a hill path. She was oddly dressed for the wilderness—in flowered bucket hat of straw and a crisp, big-sleeved pink dress, almost a mini. She looked ready for a ladies' club garden fete. The newcomer was introduced as the wife of Buckskin Billy's nephew. She was a psychology instructor at Columbia University working for her Ph.D. Her husband, who soon appeared, was studying at Columbia for *his* Ph.D. They both told us how *marvelously* exhilarating it was to be in the wilds reading in the original Latin from "thirteen hundred pounds of books."

Billy took us to see his lovely, picket-enclosed, spring-irrigated garden in which he grows all manner of vegetables and fruits, as well as Oregon grapes, squaw cabbage, dandelion, shadbush berries, currants, rose hips, gooseberries, brodiaea roots, oyster plant, and little purple Peruvian potatoes.

Then we were taken way out back through the woods, across a stream on a wobbly log bridge, and up a little draw to an ancient Indian overhang cave which had blackened petrified smoke on its roof and a fine-ash floor scattered with remnants of mussel shells. "I give them to my chickens," said Billy nonchalantly, but knowing full well that he was using kitchen midden 5,000 years old for poultry roughage.

In late afternoon, after telling Billy we'd return someday soon, we took off downriver for the Filer place. En route we saw a baby elk at water's edge. Paul said that it was an orphan; he'd often seen it in that spot. We were fairly exhausted by our long day on the water under the sun, and by all the short takes we'd had of the lives of those loners who live along the most remote river of the High West.

Paul had promised to take me for an airplane ride over the wilderness in the morning, so he turned in early that night.

An aerial view of this part of Idaho is a privileged one. At times the trees of the steep-sloping evergreen forests stick up like bristles of a brush. Then again, the sweeps of lodgepole pine, fir, and spruce seem more like tangled, impassable jungles—forests where the sound of an ax has never been heard. Small lakes of unbelievable tranquility tuck away in the hollows. Silver streams hide in the shadows. There are rolling high meadows where a man, if he were able to get into them, could walk knee-deep in wild flowers.

The trees below thin out and soon are no more, and you are flying over raw jagged rock—mountain peaks jabbing up all around. No roads here. Wilderness area. Go down, and chances are you'd never be found.

We flew close to a forest fire, circled above its smoke while a Forest Service plane, a lumbering big thing, dropped a couple of smoke jumpers dangling from orange chutes. Pretty, but scary. Every once in a while Paul would lose sight of the bigger plane and ask me to find it for him— me, the less than lone eagle, who can hardly find the sky from an airplane. Suddenly Paul located what it was he'd been looking for—glancing all around like a nervous turkey hen—and we began to descend. He's mad, I thought, there's nothing down there but trees, trees, trees, but there it was—the landing strip of a remote wilderness ranch on the Selway River.

When we entered the main lodge the hi-fi was playing—I swear it— "Home on the Range."

"We heard on the squawker that you was up this way," said the ranch boss, "and was hopin' you'd be droppin' in on us."

After a brief visit we took off again. Flying back, I was calm until we got close to Filer's place. I didn't know that we'd approach by following a curling stream at tree-top height, bending the plane around trees and high boulders. I recommend it for those who like to run with the bulls at Pamplona.

But we didn't overshoot the landing strip.

After a hearty breakfast, we all said good-bye to Marybelle and boarded the turbojet to go back to our camper. The trip downriver was a lot less exciting than the one we'd had coming up, and so we had more time to admire the gorgeous cliffs and the trees. I don't expect to see so beautiful a river ever again.

Forest Men

After our short stay with the loners of the Salmon we moved out of the camper into ultra-motelegant rooms at the Downtowner in Boise (from *boisé*, wooded, but now pronounced *boy'-zee*).

After the kids went to bed, Whiskers and I took a spin to sample Boise night life. We encountered some convivial Basques, who clued us in on these most hardy of all Idahoans. There are about 10,000 Basques in the Boise Valley. They are great sports enthusiasts; their feats of strength are astounding. A Basque weight-lifting champion once hoisted 305 pounds 27 times in 15 minutes. A popular Basque sporting event is a weight-carrying contest, in which a man carries in each hand a 105-pound rock fitted with a handle, and walks as far as he can; the Boise record is 960 feet. Basques like to dance—*la jota, parrosalda,* and *aurresku,* to drum and flute (*tambor* and *txistu*).

Basques came here about 1877 as seafarers, to escape being Castilian-ized in Spain. Because they were highlanders, they ventured inland from the West Coast and established a small colony in eastern Oregon, from which they drifted into southern Idaho. Sheepherding was open to them because no knowledge of English was required for that job.

"I hated sheep," said one old man we talked to. "I still do. They're stupid and they stink. But my granddaddy was a sheepherder and so was my father, and no one in our family could speak English, so what else was I to do?"

The Basque tongue is Euzkera, a very old and difficult language, not related to English, Spanish, French, German, or Latin. Basques claim it was the original language spoken by the Creator, but I think that is pushing it a little.

The next morning's papers were full of forest fire news. Blazes continued to lap up valuable timber; weather forecasts indicated no immediate relief. In fact, lightning that would start more fires was expected, and high winds were predicted that would fan the flames. The outlook was not good.

At least six major fires were burning out of control in the Nez Perce and Clearwater national forests of northern Idaho. One fire in that region had raced through 750 acres of timber before crews were able to reach it.

Up in the Idaho panhandle a 2,000-acre timber and brush fire was threatening a hamlet of 185 residents. "They figure if the wind shifts we'll have to evacuate in five minutes," reported the owner of the store there, estimating the fire to be three-fourths of a mile from the town limits.

About 60 miles east of Grangeville more than 1,000 acres were ablaze. Three other fires raged in that area, and two bad ones were east of Riggins. We'd gotten out just in time. The largest of those fires—at Brushy Fork, 75 miles east of Grangeville—covered 2,400 acres of remote land, and was being fought by only 50 men. I'm sure this was the one I saw the start of when I was flying with Filer. Many smaller fires were reported.

Borate planes had been grounded by the pall of smoke. Going-to-the-

Sun Highway in Glacier was closed to through traffic. "We're wearing out," said the fire control officer of that park, where flames had blackened 5,000 acres. The total fire-fighting force there now was 1,100.

Fires had been burning steadily in Idaho forests for the past 11 days. The governor had declared a state of emergency. National Guardsmen had been mobilized to provide mess halls, transportation, communication facilities, and first-aid stations for more than 3,000 fire fighters; ten new fires had started since we'd left the Salmon.

The cost was tremendous. The state of Idaho alone, in less than two months, had spent for fire control and emergency services more than one fourth its two-year appropriation. The actual daily expenditure for fighting Idaho's fires was estimated at $12,000. In all, about 80,000 acres were charred in Idaho, Montana, Oregon, and British Columbia.

Professional caterers were hard put to find enough food for feeding the men on the fire lines. At one blaze 3,000 meals were needed daily. One small-town cafe owner had been flabbergasted by a sudden order for 300 sandwiches.

In contrast to those efforts of man to preserve nature, the *Idaho Daily Statesman* carried a front-page story and three-column picture concerning a New York City police raid on a right-wing terrorists' cache of arms, an informal arsenal that included 18 sticks of dynamite, two cans of black powder, one plastic bomb, 102 blasting caps, 45 rifles, seven shotguns, 14 pistols, one antitank gun, one submachine gun, one gun disguised as a cane, three hand grenades, one machete, 250,000 rounds of ammunition, and 12 hunting knives. The Wild *West?*

After breakfast, while Whiskers and the kids went swimming in the motel pool, I dropped around to the Department of Forestry, housed in an old assay-office building built in 1870, where more than $75 million worth of gold and silver had been appraised.

An interesting exhibit there was the trunk of an Idaho white pine that had started growing in 1642. Its rings were marked to indicate the tree's diameter at the time of certain historic events. When the first post office was established in the United States the tree was about eight inches in diameter. At the time of the Declaration of Independence it was 18 inches through, and there were two inches more when Lewis and Clark came to Idaho. In 1890, as Idaho became a state, the tree was only six inches less than its present diameter—three feet, eight inches.

A placard on the wall announced: "61 fires yesterday; 452 to date."

There was a drawing of a curious bug labeled "GUBERIF"—which turned out to be FIREBUG spelled backward, the creation of one R. A. Trzuskowski, which if spelled backward is Ikswoksuzrt.

You can see I didn't have much to occupy my mind while waiting to talk with one of the forestry officials about the controversial problem of public use of government land versus private use. I was told that the rangers base their actions entirely on the Multiple Use-Sustained Yield Act of Congress of 1960, a mandate for management of national forests, which directs the Forest Service to operate them for outdoor recreation, range-timber watershed, and wildlife-fish purposes. The rangers oppose anything that exerts a negative influence on any of those areas. From this office I was sent to the Boise headquarters of the Forest Service Intermountain Region, where further intricacies of the problem were delved into.

A pleasant young officer there referred to the Salmon River people as "savages and renegades" who "have a philosophy all their own and want everything their own way to benefit their particular business of outfitting and guiding." I was shown the manual of *Forest Land Special Uses,* surprisingly about five inches thick. I didn't dream there were so many uses to which a forest could be put. It was explained that a use can be commercial only if it serves a need of the public.

"We don't give out permits just because the land is there to make money from," this man said emphatically, but not unkindly. "We permit the outfitters and guides to make a profit from the use of national forests only if by so doing these men serve the public."

Then he led me through the ramifications of owning property and living within a national forest. I asked about bona fide landowners being forced off their properties by the Forest Service and was given a long, involved explanation that was in the kind of stiff convoluted prose that lawyers use.

"Not so," said this fellow. "There has been a great deal of abuse of public land by squatters, but anyone who could legally claim national forest land as a principal place of residence for seven years prior to passage of the Church-Johnson Act in 1964, could apply—if there was no interference with public land use—for a land-use permit, nontransferable and nonrenewable, that would allow lifetime use or use for a period of time sufficient to amortize his investment, after which he'd have no proprietary interest and must therefore be obliged to sell out to the government . . ."

It's no wonder the river people and the forest rangers don't get along. They don't even speak the same language.

This official said further that the government is making a great effort to clear up land records.

"A lot of these old knotheads have a paper that they got from someone in Grover Cleveland's administration or some such, and they've thrown it into a strong box without putting it on the public record. The land maybe is rightfully theirs, but no one knows about it officially. Aside from the aforementioned private use of land in national forests, there are only two other categories: patented, meaning the government has issued title to the land through mining or homestead survey; and lease, in which there is ground use only for purposes of mining."

The battle goes on, with neither side conceding the other's viewpoint. One riverman had told me, "Anything that's Democratic, we always vote against it." The Forest Service people insist that recreation is only one of the many uses of the national forests, that all other resources must be wisely used, and that the need for farsighted development programs is especially evident today with population increasing and land diminishing.

Valley of the Dollars

Our next stopover in Idaho was at famous Sun Valley. It is not a resort in a resort area, but one splendidly alone, with no competition for miles and miles around. There it sits, beautifully sheltered in a superb 7,500-acre mountain bowl—proud, self-assured, aloof, and serene, self-styled queen of them all, for this is the original ski resort, the world's first to be created exclusively for winter sports.

Sun Valley was begun in 1936 by W. Averell Harriman, who'd become board chairman of his daddy's railroad, the Union Pacific, after inheriting about $100 million from old E. H., familiarly dubbed "the little giant of Wall Street." The railroad was looking for a way to attract passenger traffic to the West, and, the story goes, Averell's second wife, Marie, was fed up with packing off to Austria or Switzerland every time she wanted to ski.

The scouting for a suitable skiing spot was done by a Count Felix Schaffgotsch, who spent months looking at mountains all over the High

West before settling on the enchanting, windless basin where Sun Valley now stands—surrounded by totally treeless slopes with pine-covered Baldy Mountain towering at the western mouth of the valley.

When word first got around that an Austrian count was snooping around the mountains on skis and talking of building a million-dollar hotel, the residents of Ketchum (pop. then, 270) weren't much impressed. "Don't cash any of his checks," cautioned one prominent sheepherder.

Promotion of the resort was given over to that shrewdest of all tub thumpers, Steve Hannigan, the man who turned a sandbar into Miami Beach. He immediately injected S-E-X into all the ads with a shapely cutie skiing in a bathing suit and a handsome young male skier stripped to the waist and sun-bronzed.

A big assist was given the resort by a musical extravaganza called *Sun Valley Serenade,* in which Sonja Henie twinkled her blades and Glenn Miller's orchestra tootled its horns (theme song: "It Happened in Sun Valley"). That was before skiing had become a popular sport, when only rich, glamorous people took to the slopes. To the ordinary working man, Sun Valley meant really living it up, to dream the impossible dream, the epitome of a resplendent winter spa for celebrities.

Gary Cooper went there, Ingrid Bergman, Clark Gable, Ann Sothern, Rosalind Russell, and countless other movie luminaries. In those halcyon days of Sun Valley, Eddie Duchin played piano in one of the cocktail lounges; Hemingway wrote part of *For Whom the Bell Tolls* on the balcony of Room 206, overlooking the skating rink.

Then came the jet age and the great mass ski boom. Thousands of skiers bloomed overnight and went skittering about the country discovering new winter sports areas. Suddenly Sun Valley was old hat. It slumped, as Aspen, Squaw Valley, Vail, and many other more modern resorts stole its thunder. Jet travel enabled the ski set to skip from Saint Moritz to Stowe to Breckenridge; office workers flew to the High West for weekend ski holidays, but to the newer spots—not to Sun Valley. It was considered a relic of the past and too remote.

Then a couple of enterprising ski enthusiasts, Edwin and Bill Janss, took a fresh look at the doddering dowager, bought the place, and today, through their efforts, Sun Valley has recovered much of its aplomb and offers a wider range of accommodations than ever before without loss of the unique character that once made it irresistible. The golden people are drifting back from the nation's glamour gardens—the famous, the beautiful, and the wealthy, of Hollywood, New York, and Washington, D.C. The Henry Mancinis have been here, as well as Janet Leigh, Art Linkletter, Charles (*Peanuts*) Schultz, the Leonard Bernsteins, the Shah of Iran, Robert McNamara, Andy Williams and wife, Jimmy Stewart and family. All the *best* people, meaning those with money.

Idaho's liberalized divorce laws, which make the residency requirements six weeks—same as Nevada's—have encouraged many of the more gilt-edge divorce-bounds to sit it out here instead of at more commonplace Reno or Las Vegas. Among the carriage-trade types who have dispensed with their mates in Sun Valley are Mrs. William Rockefeller, Happy Murphy (now Mrs. Nelson Rockefeller), and Patricia Kennedy Lawford.

Sun Valley isn't impossible to get to, as some of its detractors claim. It's merely difficult. Actually, a New Yorker can reach Sun Valley in twice the time it would take him to fly to Paris or Zurich. But then, Sun Valley boosters like to say, "Shangri-La was not an easy commute."

Commercial airlines operate from Boise, Salt Lake City, and Idaho Falls into Hailey-Sun Valley Airport, which is about 15 miles from the resort. The Union Pacific Railroad stops at Shoshone, about 55 miles south of Sun Valley, with connecting bus service. For motorists there is an excellent, direct road from Boise.

Much the prettiest way to Sun Valley is a roundabout north-and-west swing through the Boise National Forest to Idaho City (center of Idaho's 1860 gold rush, which produced more gold in an 18-mile-square basin than all the Yukon), and on to Lowman, and then up the south fork of the Payette River, crossing valley lands and forested foothills contrasting strikingly with a backdrop of jagged, snow-streaked peaks of the steely-blue Sawtooths, and on to the Stanley Basin, an area I'd stack against anything Switzerland has to offer.

The Stanley Basin is one of Idaho's finest sportsmen's paradises and source of the Salmon River. The metropolis here is Stanley (population 35), a sleepy town—one dusty wide street, one block long, lined with a nondescript slew of low-slung log and board-and-batten buildings plus one lone stone garage. Perfect setting for a horse-opera showdown shoot-down. The gas station attendant, likely having us on, said that the garage changes ownership maybe a dozen times during the continuous poker game that goes on all winter while the town is isolated by deep snows.

"Never do know when you break through in spring jest who in heck's gonna be in charge," he quipped.

Below Stanley are a number of gemlike lakes. Sawtooth, Hell Roaring, Yellow Belly, Toxaway, and Alice are not readily accessible from the road, but Redfish, Petit, and Alturas can be reached easily on unpaved spurs. Redfish is especially beautiful—crystal clear, mirroring perfectly the surrounding mountains; in many places a wall of trees forms the shoreline. Past Galena Summit (8,701 feet), the road threads through a broad valley punctuated by clumps of evergreens and hemmed in by distant snowy mountains. A sheep trail right-of-way as wide as a six-lane highway parallels the road in part, but more often lopes across gently rolling hills.

In late afternoon, at Ketchum, turnoff point for Sun Valley, a local friend took us to see the grave of Ernest Hemingway. He'd wanted to build a home up in Sun Valley, but by the time he'd arrived all available property was gone. So, like other latecomers who love this hilly high country, Hemingway had to be content with a house in Ketchum.

Hemingway's burial place is in an unpretentious roadside cemetery. Across its graveled entrance lane a chain looped dispiritedly. A stepladder leaning against it called the barrier to the attention of motorists. We heisted ourselves over the chain and, after waiting for a revolving sprinkler to make its spraying round past us, scampered across the wet grass and walked past graves decorated with bouquets of gaudy plastic flowers—practical, well-intentioned laments. There were none at the man-size polished gray granite coverlet that lay flush with the grass stubble marking the last bed of Ernest Miller Hemingway—July 12, 1899 . . . July 2, 1961.

I said to the lady who'd brought us, "It must have been an accident —he was always so dramatic, if he'd wanted to kill himself, wouldn't he have waited for his birthday?"

"Oh, I don't know," she said. "When you're sick and blue, all days are alike. Birthdays don't mean much." She was silent a moment, then said, "I'm glad they got a stone now. Last time I was here there was only the dirt, and tourists were carting it off by the handfuls—even the pebbles and stones. Won't anyone be able to lift that chunk of granite."

Beside Hemingway rests his longtime friend, John Taylor Williams, who inherited the hand-corrected manuscript of *For Whom the Bell Tolls*. Just behind lie the remains of another crony, Gene Van Guilder, one of Sun Valley's first sports directors, reputedly buried with his favorite saddle. His stone inscription is by Papa Hemingway: "He has come back to the hills that he loved and now he will be part of them forever."

At the head of Hemingway's grave stood a chunky white wooden cross, firmly planted, looking like one on a battlefield, its simplicity seeming just right.

"The sun also sets," said the local lady.

Sun Valley Lodge is massive, built of concrete scored and stained to simulate the herringbone timber siding of a Swiss mountain chalet. The interiors have been described as "Depression Moderne," a style that employs much indirect lighting, handcrafted copper, and lots of mirrors. To these staples have been added Polish rug hangings and American Indian artifacts.

Clark Gable wouldn't have been content in our quarters; there was no balcony such as Hemingway enjoyed. From our window we could see neither Baldy nor Dollar mountains, where all the skiing takes place in winter; nor the Olympic-size all-season skating rink, where Sonja Henie once twinkled across the ice; nor any of the three glass-enclosed swimming pools, nor the golf course, nor the boardwalk shopping mall, nor even the hospital. We did have a dandy view of a bank of windows of other rooms; we could watch the hired help coming and going from their work. And there was a very nice tree just outside our windows in which there lived at least a hundred cheery blackbirds—early risers. They started talking to each other at about 5:30 A.M. (Tim reported that one baby got up even earlier, but his mama soon hustled him back to bed). Still, our rooms were much the nicest we'd had thus far—spotlessly clean, everything substantial and in excellent taste.

Neither Whiskers nor I rise well to the thrill of a mammoth commercial playground such as Sun Valley, where there is nearly every sport and pastime to satisfy the ego—except a tattoo parlor. The management stands ready to gratify the guests' every whim. Mind you, I don't knock this sort of thing. Many people enjoy being catered to—actually need it— and are willing to pay a premium for such attention. To them, salaam. It's just that I'd rather work things out to my own style and pace.

Not all the recreations in the world would have pulled Sun Valley out of its doldrums. What did it was the transformation of this plush resort into a vacation village of condominium apartments, ateliers (or studio apartments), and single residences. The condominiums, at $54,000 each, sold like hotcakes; they are rentable when the owners are not in residence;

the ateliers, also rentable, are priced up to $24,000; and the private homes being built are in the luxury class and tucked along Trail Creek or facing the golf fairways.

Dorice Taylor, Sun Valley's veteran publicist, took us on a brief tour of these new facilities and also to Trail Creek Cabin, a romantically situated rustic inn that is favored for weddings by the resort's hired hands and many guests. Troth-plighters apparently place no significance in the fact that the dining room chandelier is a bear trap four feet across.

"Our climate is the best thing we have to offer," said Mrs. Taylor. "Very little wind and plenty of cool shade in summer. We're over a mile high. There's no air pollution, which is why we're getting so many Californians—they're popping in by droves. We've always been known for our clear air. Steve Hannigan never would allow any photos of the place to be released for publicity if they showed any smoke coming out of our high stack." .

Back in the village a large landscape diorama gave us a wintertime look at Sun Valley's 4,300-acre spread nestled in the shelter of a sun-abundant natural bowl. Lulu sagely pointed out that the uniquely designed chalet that Whiskers and I admired so much in this miniature model really was a very dead beetle.

The kids bought ice cream cones at Poor Richard's Konditorei (three for $1.05), and then Lulu and Tim went for what turned out to be a dreary horseback ride—one hour of ambling through a sun-hot shadeless field eating dust.

Whiskers and I had a beer at the slyly named Ore House and met its young owner, Teddy Teren, from Portland, Oregon, who'd come to Sun Valley from the Bay area near San Francisco, where he'd operated a real-estate business.

"I was coming up ulcers at twenty-five," he said, "so I'm a rat-race dropout." Besides this restaurant and bar, young Teren organizes float trips down the Salmon, makes wildlife films (with his wife), and operates a river-frontage real-estate development on the Big Wood River near Ketchum. Adjoining us at the bar was a group of young people being entertained by a plump, brassy-mouthed girl telling vulgar stories about the Pope, LBJ, and Ladybird, and rapping minorities ("An anti-Semite is someone who hates Jews more than he should," was one of her cracks). She told me that trying to find out all about the High West was like trying to write the Kinsey Report in two days. Her comment on Hemingway: "He blew his mind here."

The bartender apologized for her crudity, saying, "She's not such a bad sort. You should see some of the heirs and heiresses that come in here."

We were glad to push on from Sun Valley. Our kids had felt a little out of place there—sort of like Liliom's barefoot daughter among the fat, smug Snow children, prancing in their Sunday best. We reentered Wyoming via Teton Pass, the most famous route of early fur trappers. The first wagons hauled over it took 11 backbreaking days. Bill Sublette, famous mountain man, wrangled his packtrain of 78 men and 150 horses over the pass early in July 1832, on his way to that year's monster rendezvous at Pierre's Hole. In 1895 Negro soldiers, ordered west during an Indian fright, tugged and pushed their own wagons across after their horses failed. The first automobile over Teton Pass on its own gears was a Hupmobile, driven by Ed Burton on July 23, 1914.

I don't know how long it took Ed and his Hup to wheeze up and over, but we made the climb and drop in less than an hour.

The Grand Tetons

Skiing in the Sky

Wyoming's northwestern corner is that state's most attractive spot. To avoid as much as possible the honky-tonk hustle of Jackson, the area's tourist-trap metropolis (pop. 1,437), we holed up at Teton Village, a burgeoning $7.5 million Alpine skiing community located in a secluded, sunny valley and snuggled against the base of craggy, 10,445-foot Rendezvous Peak. It was delightful there as well as convenient—only 12 miles north of the town and just on the edge of Grand Teton National Park.

The place was established by Paul McCollister, a Californian who retired from the advertising business and came elk hunting to the Tetons. He fell in love with the mountains, bought 21 acres in 1950, built a summer home on them in 1952, and four years later moved in permanently, prepared to settle down for the rest of his life. He didn't reckon on the High West casting its spell. Now, with a partner, Alex Morley (retired from a construction business in Wyoming), McCollister reigns over what promises to be the most exciting resort of America's 118 major and more than 500 other developed ski areas.

Being still in its growing stage, this ski village hasn't yet achieved the busyness of more established resorts, nor does it have the elaborate summertime attractions of Sun Valley. Therefore, we found Teton Village a little easier to live with. Its visitors weren't so determinedly bent on getting the utmost out of every living minute, weren't relaxing so anxiously.

Teton Village already has three attractive, but unpretentious, Alpine-style lodges, an automobile service station, and the nation's longest aerial tramway (2.4 miles), plus a building housing its machinery, the resort's offices, and a cafeteria. Two additional luxurious inns are planned, along with 36 shopping chalets and 700 condominium apartments; 101 home-sites were for sale. Eventually the village will sleep 6,000.

Between our lodge and the gas station a half-dozen young men, bearded and bare-torsoed, were at work with hammers, longhandled axes, and crosscut saws on a wierd construction which looked like a peeled forest—a hundred or so upright tree trunks all bolted together by a maze of crosspieces. When finished, the boys said, it would be the Mangy Moose Saloon, Spaghetti Emporium, and Opera House, and would cost $65,000. It was the property of a 28-year-old man from Cleveland, Ohio, who was giving up law practice there to settle into the High West.

One of the builders was a "drop-up" from Laramie University; when he learned we were from New York, he said he'd been there and met the hairy East Villagers, liked them immensely (". . . they're very nice people . . . "), but didn't think many statesmen would develop from among them. "They're as *crude* as politicians," he said, "but they ain't grabby enough."

The mountain dominates the village and offers six square miles of ski terrain. The massif is six and a half miles across, from the gigantic shoulder called Ship's Prow to the subpeak named Après Vous. The bowl, three miles across its top, is a tree-studded immensity with headwall and sides so steep that the shallowest of traverses produces the kind of breath-grabbing speeds that rouse dedicated skiers to hosannahs. Jean-Claude Killy, the world's greatest skier, called this mountain the best for skiing he has seen in America.

Snaking off its top is a 3,275-foot vertical drop run that could be the trickiest, fastest downhill run in the United States. In all, at this Jackson Hole Ski Area, there are 24 trails—55 miles of them—around eight major ridges, 13 bowls, seven canyons and gullies. The lower slopes' ski runs are served by three double-chair lifts, though one is reserved for students at the ski school, headed by a boyish 29-year-old Austrian Olympic champion, Pepi Stiegler.

Skiers are taken to the really tremendous drop—the one that separates the men from the ski bunnies—by an aerial tramway that can haul 63 people at a clip (standees with skis) up a 4,135-foot vertical rise. The cable car goes so high that often in winter it passes from bright sunshine at the base, through clouds floating at the route's midway point, to a snowstorm at the top.

The tramway trip, a big summertime draw at Teton Village, proved a thrilling way to climb the mountain effortlessly, though we had to suffer a wiseacre making nervous jokes about impending disaster as well as a lady who considered herself an authority on aerial cable cars because she'd ridden the one at Disneyland. Afraid to look out the windows for awhile, I fixed my gaze on a point above the door and so the car's place of manufacture is forever imprinted on my brain: *"Traunsteinwerkstatten Josef Swoboda, Schloss Oberweis Ob. US. Austria."*

We found the ski terrain overwhelming—not for sissies. At the gravelly summit it was frightfully cold. A sign there bore a picture of a cannon shell and said: "ATTENTION! This is a High-Explosive Dud. DO NOT TOUCH IT. Report it to the Tram Attendant *Immediately.*" Must have something to do with the reveille barrage of 105-millimeter mountain howitzers that shakes avalanche-prone slopes in wintertime.

"What happens to you if you hit one when you're skiing?" asked Tim.

"You don't have to report it," said Lulu.

"It reports you," said Tia.

To the north, lording it over us, were the majestic Tetons: the Grand, 13,766 feet; the Middle, 12,798; and the South, 12,505. Eastward, the dropoff is abrupt. Far below lies Jackson Hole, fantastically lovely, looking like a bit of blue-green paradise stolen from the Land of Oz, guarded by mountains on all sides. Through the valley the Snake River is a silvery twist.

That evening we drove to Jackson to take in the show at the Pink Garter Theater, a fixture for the past nine years, operated as an educational and cultural nonprofit corporation by an enthusiastic group of young professionals under the wing of an energetic entrepreneur named Paula Jeffry. On tap was their musical adaptation of *Tom Jones,* with a cast of 11 and played clownesque in broad *Comedia del Arte* style. Action and lines were brash and brazen, and a slow-motion scene—traditional with this company—of a free-for-all fight was a marvel of split-second timing, perfectly disciplined control, and comic choreography.

During intermission the kids bought sarsaparilla and Old English treacle from cast members in the rococo lobby. When the play was over we rocked with the capacity audience to a rousing olio. This musical-comedy approach was a refreshing change from the usual frenetic parodies of musty melodrama that are endemic throughout the High West.

Next day before driving into Grand Teton National Park we visited the Jackson Hole Museum in Jackson to see what these parts were like before the age of the affluent skier, when the Mountain Men were here, diligently trapping beavers to make felt stovepipe hats for dandies back east.

The kids were enchanted by such exhibits as the world's record heads of moose (score: 205 4/8 points) and elk (441 6/8 points), branding irons of cattle rustlers and horse thieves, hand-forged traps and fur-finishers' tools, crude dolls found along the Oregon Trail, a fiddle made from a lard can, and a horsehair bridle fashioned in the Wyoming State Peniteniary.

The museum is one of the few establishments in Jackson where the tourist gets an honest shake. A horde of scruffy shops and large stores lure visitors with gaudy souvenir junk, overpriced resort wear, and other tourist merchandise.

There are bars aplenty. By far the grandest, at the old-fashioned Wort Hotel, is a serpentined mirrored stretch, its polished top imbedded with 2,032 silver dollars. It is the longest bar in the Rockies—85 feet. A burnt leather fascia behind it depicts episodes of Jackson's lusty past. In the old West, a long bar was a mark of prestige, something for a local to brag on when away from home. There aren't many of these super-lengthy bars left from the old days. Westerners today are more interested in boasting of the length of their ski runs and about the number of beds they have to accommodate tourists.

A favorite, long-established eating place is Ed Hodgson's Old Wyoming Chuck Wagon, out at the edge of town, with a superb view of the Sleeping Indian Peak of the Gros Ventre Mountains. For a modest price a hungry tourist can eat all he wants of a ranch-style breakfast, consisting of sourdough hotcakes (served with plenty of butter and maple syrup), ham or bacon and scrambled eggs, orange juice, and coffee, in one of two large canvas tepees or in an open-sided dining room. A vast meadow in view across the highway is an elk-grazing refuge of 23,754 acres. In winter, upwards of 10,000 of these wild Wyoming creatures are fed there.

A pleasant way to escape the claptrap of Jackson is to take one of Phil Kent's float trips in a large rubber raft on the Snake River—where the rapids are just rough enough to be fun, where silverberry bushes glisten on the sandbars, cottonwoods grow along the banks, fields glow pale with wild buckwheat, and an occasional bald eagle can be seen feeding her young in a treetop nest. It doesn't take much trying then to feel like a young, starry-eyed pioneer come to tame the West.

Mr. Rockefeller's Park

But for the tenacity and generosity of John D. Rockefeller, Jr., there would be no Grand Teton National Park. He is the area's greatest single benefactor, having supplied approximately $2 million for land acquisition and given nearly 25 years of effort to influence the congressional action that preserves this spot as recreational territory.

In 1926, John D. bought 34,000 acres of private lands with the intention of presenting the tract to the nation as a scenic monument, but pressure from Wyoming congressmen thwarted the gesture. It wasn't until 1943 that the Rockefeller holdings, together with 170,000 acres of federal land and 17,800 privately owned acres, were joined to form the Jackson Hole National Monument by President Franklin D. Roosevelt, citing as authority the Antiquities Act of 1906. Local cattlemen, although promised full compensation for their lands and no loss of grazing rights, bitterly opposed the edict and campaigned against it. The state of Wyoming even filed suit against the federal government to test the validity of the presidential proclamation. Congress passed a bill nullifying the whole thing, but FDR killed it by a pocket veto.

After seven years more of opposition shenanigans, Congress in 1950 finally consolidated the monument with Grand Teton National Park, which had been created in 1929 by President Calvin Coolidge out of land previously in the Grand Teton National Forest.

Compared to Yellowstone, its big sister to the north, Grand Teton National Park is small—only 485 square miles. The level valley floor of Jackson Hole, which makes up the eastern half of the park, accentuates the western part, which is all mountains—sharp ragged cones, sheer, unrelieved, and rising abruptly, without benefit of foothills, from beautifully timbered lakelands. The east face of the Tetons is one of the steepest fault escarpments in the world, the result of a geological uplift along a great fracture in the earth's crust. The Tetons were ripped out of an ancient part of it, thrust upward by tremendous forces from within, and then carved by erosion. They are a 50-mile range, jagged and harsh, moody and treacherous, streaked with glaciers and caressed by envious clouds.

From the shoulders of the larger peaks rise little spires and turrets. In morning light the massive rocks are clear-cut and mastodonic; in afternoon, their long, pointed shadows creep across the valley floor and the pinnacles have shimmering edges of light. At sundown, the glittering glaciers hidden in shaded basins and chasms become a luscious pink, catching the reflections of the sun's rays spilling through the gorges like wildfire.

We thought them much the most exciting mountains we'd yet seen, never out of sight from any of the park's roads—a skyline formed by ten major peaks, each over 11,000 feet, and five each reaching a height of about 1,000 feet less.

The park is bordered on three sides by the Teton National Forest, of almost a million and three-quarters acres. In these highlands are 38 peaks ranging up to 12,165 feet and also the headwaters of five rivers. The Teton Wilderness Area, in the northern part of the forest, has 2,000 acres of mountain lakes and 1,420 miles of trails. To the east of this vast, high, wooded area are Shoshone and Bridger national forests and the South Absaroka Wilderness Area—all of it rough high country.

Between the two distinct areas of Grand Teton park lies Jackson Lake, nearly 20 miles long. On its southeastern shore is Jackson Lake Lodge, a pretentious, resplendent, $6-million creation, its coldly impersonal interior remindful of a large bus station. The sparkling lake and Mount Moran can be viewed from overstuffed lounge chairs through an ostentatious three-segmented picture window. "The view of the Grand Tetons is so spectacular," states the Grand Teton Lodge Company's advertising brochure, "guests have been known to applaud when particularly beautiful sunsets color the mountains with splendor."

In the dining room there are excellent murals, large gesso panels painted in polymer (a plastic medium), which faithfully reproduce, in large scale, historic water color sketches made by Alfred Jacob Miller, official artist of a wagon expedition that penetrated the Wyoming wilderness in 1837.

Just below Jackson Lake are Jenny, Leigh, Emma Matilda, and Two Ocean lakes, like children around a mother. Jenny Lake, second largest in the park, is shallow and clear enough along its rocky shoreline to show stony bottom, but it deepens to 226 feet. In the morning

Jenny is so still that it mirrors distant Teewinot (meaning "many pinnacles"), the only Teton peak that rises to a pointed summit—no bigger than a man's thumb.

Jenny Lake was named for the Shoshone wife of "Beaver Dick" Leigh, from Manchester, England, one of the last of the old-time Mountain Men; he trapped the western Teton canyons. His marriage was the first in this region of white man and Indian woman to be sanctioned by white man's law. Jenny and their six children all died in 1876 of smallpox during an epidemic after the Leigh family had given aid to a young pregnant squaw, who with a three-year-old daughter was fleeing the plague in terror, unaware that she already had been infected. (Historical note: in pre-Revolutionary America, unscrupulous European traders—and later the U.S. Cavalry—used to give blankets infected with smallpox germs to Indians in order to impair their fighting strength.)

William "Uncle Billy" Owen, first surveyor of Jackson Hole, gave his wife's name to Emma Matilda Lake.

Between Jenny and Leigh lakes is a skinny meander called String Lake, which seems more like a river. It is very good for swimming, even if the water is as cold as a pawnbroker's heart and bathing suits are obligatory.

Grand Teton seems to quiet folks down, which, after all, is appropriate for the world's only park named for a mammary. Everyone seems less up-tight, less prone to agitation—perhaps it's those steam things popping off up there that gets Yellowstoners running around like frustrated rabbits. Tourists at Teton settle in primarily for the enjoyment of nature—to camp, hike, ride horseback, go fishing and boating. And they climb mountains.

The Tetons are regarded by mountaineers as the prime climbing area in North America. Teton rock is solid, noncrumbling, piton-holding granite. There is variety in climbing terrain and the summer weather is the most consistently good of any climbing region in the world, dependably dry—often six weeks without a drop of rain. The Grand Teton has the same profile as the Matterhorn and a similar climb of 7,000 feet.

Three days before we'd come to the park a 26-year-old climber from Mahopac, New York, ascending the north face of the Grand with his girl friend (from Sandwich, Illinois) had tumbled 20 feet when a rope snapped. He landed on a ledge, breaking a leg, and had to be peeled off the mountain by a rescue team which included four park rangers—probably the most difficult rescue attempt ever made in the park.

Apparently the accident hadn't dampened the ardor of the Tetons' climbers. At the ranger shack three parties were registering their proposed climbs, the wall chart indicated many climbs in progress, and the bulletin board was loaded with scrawled messages of climbers to other climbers.

Sunshine High & Low

Mountain Bewitched

There's a time in every long motoring trip when the principals must get away from each other. This is especially true if five are traveling in a camper built for four. We felt a need to be lifted out of ourselves. We'd been gone from home about six weeks and had to catch our breath, realign our perspectives. Our plan was to get off the road a few days before the Labor Day weekend. I'd no desire to become a traffic statistic during that time of merry mayhem. I figured the highways then would be real slaughter alleys, judging by the customary speeds of westerners.

So we waited out the holiday at the home of a friend, snugged up against the Wasatch Mountains at the edge of a quiet village near Salt Lake City, after sending the kids by air to visit their grandmother at Capistrano Beach, California. Then, in a week, we picked them up again in Las Vegas, an easy plane hop from Los Angeles. From Vegas we headed east, and when we reached the Arizona border, three-quarters of the High West was behind us. Only New Mexico lay beyond.

The whole northern part of Arizona is an almost level, arid, and picturesque high plateau, marked by isolated, colorful buttes and gigantic stone monuments and gashed by deep, twisting canyons. In the northwest the Colorado River cuts through 200 miles of gorges before turning south to form the state's western boundary with Nevada and California.

Best known of Arizona's mountains are the Superstitions. Somewhere in their deep recesses, reputedly near a great volcanic upthrust known as Weaver's Needle, is supposed to be the Lost Dutchman Mine, a romantic High West legend for almost 100 years. Before the Gadsden Purchase in 1853, when this part of Arizona still belonged to Mexico, a young Mexican lover, fleeing the wrath of his sweetheart's irate father, hid out in these mountains and found a great gold deposit. Subsequently, the people of his village formed an expedition and mined as much gold as they could carry out. Apaches ambushed and killed all 400 of them, except two youngsters who hid in the bushes. About 1870, when the children were grown, they returned to the mine with a third partner. They'd hardly begun to dig when they were surprised by a prospector, the Dutchman Jacob Walzer (or Walz or Wolz). He became friendly, learned of the rich mine, and killed the three Mexicans. From then until his death in 1891, the mine was his. But he took to his grave the secret of the mine's location.

Literally thousands of prospectors—professional and amateur—have searched for the famous lode without success. Since 1900, Lost Dutchman expeditions have been responsible for almost 50 deaths—an average of one every 16 months. Some men disappeared mysteriously. Others had violent ends. A headless, roped body was found wrapped in a blanket; another, with temple pierced by a bullet; a third, shot square between the eyes; a fourth, with guts blasted out; a fifth, with head severed and widely separated from the body—and gorily on. The victims were from both East and West, and from as far away as Austria and Hawaii.

Some say these mountains are cursed; others claim that an unscrupulous prospector has found the mine and kills anyone approaching it. There also is a theory that pigmies or Apaches guard the mine.

The town nearest the Superstitions is Apache Junction, 35 miles east of Phoenix at a Y in a six-lane superhighway. The northern branch of the Y, known as the Apache Trail, is a favorite scenic drive of natives and travel-wise tourists. It climbs steeply to Tortilla Flat, through Fish Creek Canyon (weaving up sheer, bronze-colored walls, allowing views 2,000 feet straight down) and goes on to Roosevelt Dam and Lake, namesakes of Theodore Roosevelt. Teddy, taking in the view here through his bottle-bottom spectacles, called it: ". . . the most spectacular, best worth-seeing in the world . . ." Bully for him. It's a good view, but I know of many better ones.

Apache Junction is a tough little burg, right out of the rip-roaring past and completely under the spell of the Superstitions. There are more pistols and high-powered rifles per capita here than in any other town its size (1,000 population). Residents think nothing of finding up in the mountains a skull ventilated by a bullet hole, nor of someone bringing a rattlesnake into one of the local cafes to be broiled into a meal. All sorts of picaresque characters abound: fools and foxes, amateur con men, secret gamblers, serious hermits, and, of course, hopeful prospectors by the dozens.

Nearly everyone in town has some sort of crude map purporting *positively* to show the location of the Lost Dutchman Mine. The last time I was in Apache Junction I'd run across a real-estate dealer, as sensible and level-headed as ever I'd met, but sure enough, on the last day of my stay he broke down and, after swearing me to secrecy, brought out *his* map of the lost mine. It was on waxed paper, scratched by fingernail. The paper had been the wrapping of a sandwich carried into the Mexico City archives, where pencils and paper are forbidden (according to this chap) to prevent visitors from copying the ancient Spanish and Mexican maps kept on file there.

I congratulated my friend and cautioned him about misinterpreting mustard stains. But, who knows, maybe it *was* an authentic map of the famous mine and my friend will become rich as Croesus. It's the sort of outlandish thing that can and frequently does happen out in the High West. It's a most peculiar place.

The Long Walk

Ever since learning of Indians living on the floor of Grand Canyon I'd wanted to visit that Shangri-La, America's most remote reservation. So we headed in that direction.

We got to Hilltop, 60 miles north of Peach Springs, about noon—truly, in the Arizona sun, a time for mad dogs and madder easternmen. But fortunately the sky was overcast, a storm brewing. It was plenty warm, but not blazing hot. A U.S. Forest Service sign at the top of the

serpentine trail stated: "VILLAGE OF SUPAI, 8 Miles. CAMP-
GROUND, 10 Miles. No Water Until River, 6 Miles."

A young Indian man, packing a mule with salt blocks for the
trip down, paid no attention to us. A half-dozen scrawny, listless horses
were tied alongside a small tin-roofed shed amidst an unsightly litter
of tin cans and other rubbish. These were the noble steeds that had
been offered us as transportation to and from the village—at $28 rental
fee for each animal, $140 total for the round trip. We'd already decided
to hike in, but now I realized that we'd be walking out as well, for with
such horses we'd be on foot leading them most of the way anyhow. Two
plump young missionaries—man and wife—panting, with heavy knapsacks
on their backs, climbed from the trail as we started down it over the
cliff edge.

Our embarkation was less than felicitous. I started off cranky and
got progressively worse. I'm not the ideal outdoors type, and I'm especially allergic to hiking, having been exposed to too many traumatic,
blistering 14-mile hikes when a Boy Scout—never got beyond Tenderfoot and proud of it. My frame of mind got everyone on edge, especially
Whiskers. She bridled, got up a good Irish dander, and pushed resolutely
ahead, taking on the role of Great White Mother Nature Guide. That
riled me even more. It was a bad scene.

The zigzag descent was about 2,000 feet into Lee Canyon in less
than half a mile, the pale gray limestone and buff sandstone walls
getting higher as we got deeper. Sounds were muffled; shadows grew
longer. We dropped quickly to a spine alongside a swale, followed it
to the sandy floor of the deep-set canyon, and walked along a stream
bed. Walked and walked and walked. Vertical red rock walls got
higher. We met nobody. Sunshine, asters, sand verbena, greasewood,
birds, stones. Boulders had fallen from the cliffs to the stream bed and
could be matched with cavities above us. Cliffsides were marked by
shallow caves—like small bandshells—worn by floodwaters. Water had
washed around large stones and left them standing as tables. The bases
of the canyon walls had been undercut by rushing water. We passed
a stinking dead horse. The trail was so rough—traversing such huge
sharp rocks—that we wondered how saddle horses could possibly carry
people over it.

"You'd have to get off and lead your horse three-fourths of the
time," said Whiskers.

A live stallion, sorry with saddle sores, joined us for a while. Lulu gave him a tomato from our lunch pack. He didn't like it. Whiskers tried to soothe the wounds with sunburn lotion. When we stopped in shade he ambled on, but then came back to whinny at us. The trail dropped away in a series of huge boulders. There were stagnant emerald-green and turquoise pools, stone held, alive with polywogs. We were looking for the path when our horse buddy called out, his voice echoing between the walls. We couldn't find him at first, then saw him ahead and below us and followed his lead. More trees, but the canyon deepened, narrowed. Thunder rumbled far off, ominously; the sky darkened.

"Oh, lordy," said Whiskers, "pray we don't get caught *here* in a thundershower. We'd have to climb the walls."

Finally, a cross canyon came in sight. Willows, tall cottonwoods and a narrow, tree-shaded rushing creek, the water splashing clear, like rhinestones over the rocks. We drank from it, then stripped down and tumbled into it, letting the force of the water carry us along. After we'd cooled, we dressed and squatted on the muddy shore to eat our peanut butter and jam sandwiches. Tim found a ditch full of beautiful watercress and we gathered some to munch on.

Barefoot, we forded the stream, crossed back, then took a footbridge (slats on a log) across again and became hopelessly lost.

We passed horses, mules, donkeys, and a cow grazing, but saw no buildings. Finally, we came upon some Indian women and children bathing and washing their hair in the stream—like a Gauguin painting. We asked which way to the village. The women giggled, but, not wishing to offend us by recognizing our stupidity, one, pointing through the trees, said softly, "Maybe *that* way? *Maybe* there is the village. Post office is there in that white building."

So we crawled ignominiously through a barbed-wire fence and walked edgily through someone's backyard, past a sweat lodge, assorted debris, a brass bedstead with mattress (evidently for sleeping outdoors), a rickety outhouse, and down a bank onto a sort of road that soon met a wider path, ankle-deep in rich red dirt fluffed by horses' hooves. And that was Main Street, Supai—a long straightaway lined with tall cottonwoods (fence posts, I learned later, that fortuitously grew). A sign said: "Visitors Register At Third House on Right," and there we arranged rooms for the night at the lodge operated by the tribe.

The side canyon in which the village is located is only about a quarter mile wide. On the 18-acre reservation, Supai is the only village. We were charged admission to it—50¢ a head.

En route to the lodge, we stopped at the village store and bought tinned goods for dinner (no restaurant). There was no bread, and the Indian proprietor told Whiskers the soda was all sold out. "Is all your fault," he said bluntly. "Too many people come, want soda. Can't keep enough." Then he handed Whiskers a mayonnaise jar in which there was a live scorpion, thinking, I suppose, to get a female screech out of her. She disappointed him by merely smiling and saying, ladylike, "Very pretty." Shucks, what's a little scorpion to the pet tarantula Whiskers' Uncle Ron keeps at his beach house, or to our circus friend Percilla, the Monkey Girl? As we left the store, a couple of Indian boys emerged, happily gurgling 7-Up.

All the government buildings in Supai are built of materials brought in by helicopter. No land vehicle has yet made its way into the village. Mail is delivered on horseback. From 200 to 300 people live here, the People of the Blue-green Water, which is the meaning of Havasupai, the tribe's name.

The one-story lodge, built of native rock, is at the very end of the village, past the two-grade elementary school, the mission church (run by the United Indian Missions, Inc.–Protestant interdenominational), and the missionary's home, guarded by a fierce gray Weimaraner. Our rooms each had a shower; there were two other rooms (ten beds in all) and a communal kitchen.

After dinner I called on Lee Marshall, the tribal chief and chairman of the seven-man governing board (four tribal councilmen and three hereditary chiefs). I was walked to his home by a white employee of the tribe, Ted Schaffer, whose father had worked for the Bureau of Indian Affairs. Most of the government-built houses we passed en route were shabby, low-slung affairs and had the glass broken out of all the windows.

Chief Marshall's small place was in somewhat better condition, built of native red stone with green tar-paper roof. I didn't get to see inside it. We met in the dirt backyard strewn with empty tin cans— fashionable, proving to peers that the homemaker is affluent. There were some picnic tables, a ground-level cookstove—a primitive arrangement of rocks and a stovepipe. Under one of two large cottonwood trees was a low wooden bedstead painted sky-blue, its soiled mattress covered by old torn blankets and rags. Over it, tied by the neck to a tree limb, dangled a large baby doll, naked and pink. I was told that three grandchildren sleep in this outdoors bed.

The chief's shoes were paint-spotted and he wore a dingy white T-shirt, which was unable to hold in his relaxed ample belly. He had a hairline mustache. Many Havasupai Indian men have hair on their faces—unlike most Indians—and there is a strong Eskimo caste to their features.

When the chief was told that I was a writer, he said, "Why don't you go to work? Do something with your hands?" I was touchy and tired and took his remark as a slur on my profession. I felt like striking back. ("Look, chiefy, why don't *you*? You can start by picking up this rubbish we're standing in.") Instead, I decided to cool it. A kid and a young man, both on horseback, came into the yard. They were not introduced. The adult Indians bummed cigarettes from Ted. The three men talked together for a long while, ignoring me and the kid. Finally the conference ended. Ted and I left unceremoniously. The chief didn't bid me good-bye or even glance in my direction. In the dusk tiny bats flipped about.

On our way back along the quiet dusty road, Ted told me a little about the peculiar Indians of this remote place. They are one of the four plateau Rancheria tribes (the others: Hualapai (or Walapai), Yavapai, and Paiute) and are culturally related to the southern Rancheria peoples (Pima and Papago). The plateau Rancherias are characterized by extreme simplicity of social structure and, except for the Havasupai, are traditionally nonagricultural. These canyon Indians were introduced to peach growing and taught to farm (truck, figs, apricots, apples, pomegranates, and pecans are now grown) by John D. Lee, a Mormon pioneer who'd hidden out down here for three years after he'd been accused of taking a leading part in a massacre in an isolated section of Utah Territory known as Mountain Meadows, where 115 members of a Missouri-and-Arkansas emigrant train had been killed in 1857. (Lee finally was convicted and executed in 1877.)

The Havasupai are intensely individualistic and have clung to the lack of formal organization of their ancient days. Ted explained that these Indians have only the dimmest idea of the outside world, although hordes of visitors come here each year, about one-fifth of them in the ten-day period over the Easter holiday. It is difficult for the Havasupai to communicate with strangers. Family self-sufficiency is so powerful that it hampers cooperative community effort. In that regard, Ted told of mission people who wanted to bring in dentists to give all the villagers free dental care. The project fell through when the village packers declined to furnish free horse transportation to the dentistry team of 15—it was either pay or walk—on the basis that some families would be benefiting without expenditure of effort. The tribal council couldn't, or didn't want to, work out any plan to distribute the responsibility equitably, so everybody's teeth continue to rot.

The kids of Supai don't get much of a break in any case. They attend only the first two grades in the village school and then are sent off to an Indian boarding school run by the government at Fort Apache, which also is for Indian delinquents.

With an annual federal grant of only $1,000 with which to conduct tribal affairs, the Havasupai are very poor. They have resisted advances of outside civilization. They've no wish to be "modern." Proposals for stimulation of tourist business by linking Supai with the top of the canyon by motor road, chair lift, or helicopter have all been flatly turned down.

Just before reaching the lodge, we met a young college girl who'd been in the village for some time studying and recording the language, customs, and songs of the Havasupai. Ted asked her about a "sing" scheduled for that evening.

"They called it off," she said. "Between the threatening weather and the liquor, nobody wanted to be blamed for starting a fight."

Most of Supai's visitors go on beyond the village two miles to a tribal campground containing lovely Navajo Falls, a 50-foot-high, broad curtain drop framed by travertine fans covered with maidenhair fern and other greenery flourishing in the veil of white spray. The pool below is a milky blue-green. A half mile farther, Cataract Creek passes over handsome Havasu Falls, about 100 feet high—three near-perfect streams dropping into a turquoise pool, a favorite swimming hole of young Havasupai, who swing over it on grapevines. In another mile is Mooney Falls, a 220-foot drop into a wide pool (60 feet higher than Niagara Falls). Mooney is named for a prospector who dropped to his death on the rocks while being lowered by Indians on a rope to set up mining operations in the area below the falls. A footpath worries down through caves and tunnels to the foot of the falls. From there a resolute hiker can go on to Beaver Falls, three miles on down the creek, a series of cascades roaring through a tight gorge of vivid red sandstone. Anyone who doesn't mind wading—sometimes knee-deep—about 40 times through the creek can go on to the Colorado River itself.

The storm hit about midnight with great rolls and claps of thunder and vivid blue flashes of lightning silhouetting the cliffs around us. Rain clattered on our roof and streamed down the windows. The barks of disturbed village dogs echoed off the high rock walls. At 4:00 A.M. the roosters all began to crow, each clarion call setting up two or three echoes until there seemed to be hundreds of crowing cocks. They began again at five, and then we got up and were glad of it, for the dawn striking the tips of the cliffs softly with rose was a grand sight.

Whiskers' and Lulu's moccasins had been worn through on the trail so they were given innersoles cut from the cornflakes box. Tia bound her feet in bandages torn from her underpanties. A few hungry dogs came sniffing around the gate, and we fed them the remains of our breakfast. We were glad not to be riding out, for the trail, after the storm, would be even more difficult for horses.

When I paid our bill (five entrance fees and $15 for the two rooms) I asked the clerk what the chief did for a living.

"Nothing," he said. "He's the *chief*."

We meandered out of town, past shacky houses where people sat outside on rumpled beds eating breakfast. Lulu wondered how the chief's grandchildren had fared during the storm. A little black-and-white dog—one of the cornflake eaters—walked with us despite our discouragements.

We found the right path; it, too, went through someone's backyard. The log bridge was washed out, so we waded barefoot through the creek. The sand of the trail had been washed smooth. Had it not been for a mule packtrain that had gone ahead of us, the way would have been difficult to find. Our gentle, clear-water swimming hole had been turned into a dirty brown torrent; the watercress patch was overwashed. We kept trying to send the dog back, but he'd have none of it. The power of cornflakes! As we turned into Lee's Canyon, a young Indian rode by, followed by a mule loaded with household goods; the man's wife, baby, and water container followed on another horse. I guess he'd had it.

What had been a dry wash now was a little running stream. Tiny pink frogs with green circles and green frogs with tiny pink circles jumped about. A young lady anthropologist and her party passed us on horseback, nodding polite greeting, not seeing the frogs. Because of the early morning hour, we met many hikers and riders coming into the canyon. The little dog led us on, stopping once to pick up a leg of the dead horse and to carry it as far as he was able.

It was cool and lovely after the heavy rain. When we got to the turn that started up to the ridge, leading to the rim climb, a few drops of rain began to fall. A packtrain of horses came scrambling down the rough rocky trail and passed us. The switchback climb was arduous. In the hot sun it must be almost unendurable. Luckily, there was a light drizzle. Still, we sweated and were huffing and puffing by the time we reached the top.

I emerged from the Canyon feeling that I'd added something to my soul by getting close to the earth, by dealing in realities rather than symbols—such as an accountant, banker, or public relations man does. Yet I hadn't been so carried away as was the Welsh-born author Colin Fletcher, when he journeyed from Hualpai Hilltop all the way through the Canyon to Point Imperial on the North Rim. He undertook that hazardous 60-day trip, he said (in his book, *The Man Who Walked Through Time*) to "get close to the web of life" and to "come as close as we can at present to moving back and down through the smooth and apparently impenetrable face of time." I hope he made it.

Neither had I undertaken the hike to prove my masculinity as a certain long-distance runner must have done when he made it all the way down to Supai and beyond to the Colorado River and back in one day—a distance of 38 miles. To me, it had just been a torturous long walk that told me I'm still in good shape and have a remarkable partner and three kids who are good sports, unspoiled.

At Hilltop, a neat church-organist-type man was starting down alone on a mule. I thought immediately of the Reverend Doctor Davidson of Somerset Maugham's *Rain*. He was hatless, draped in a black nylon raincoat, wore black dress shoes, and carried an attaché case. He was followed by a mule bearing a little squarish leather trunk, and behind were a couple of Indian packers with other things.

"Why must she be so reluctant?" the man asked us in passing. "Usually a horse or mule is eager to go toward home and the barn. I can't understand it." *We* could.

From the rim we watched him disappear down the zigzag trail until he was only a tiny moving spot on the rocks. How much more would he be among those obdurate Indians?

Back at the camper, we wolfed cold canned spaghetti, meatballs, and cheese chunks. We swilled water, stale cold coffee, and warm soda pop. We fed and watered the dog, but we had to leave him. He belonged to the Havasupai, whether he liked it or not. Some Indian kid would miss him. He couldn't believe it. It was awful. Another betrayal by white man. I had to speed away, the dog pathetically running after the camper, barking and yipping fiercely. From the back I could hear the kids wailing. "Daddy! *Daddy!* Stop, Daddy, *stop!*" Finally the dog too became just a dot. Whiskers wept. And I felt awful.

■II■II■II■II■II■II■II■II■II■II■II■II■II■II■II■II■II■II■II■II■II■II■II■II■

The Big Ditch

■II■II■II■II■II■II■II■II■II■II■II■II■II■II■II■II■II■II■II■II■II■II■II■

South Rim

In my distraction over the mutt from Supai, I almost missed the 33-mile primitive shortcut that took us to a point only 13 miles south of Grand Canyon's South Rim. The road saved us from driving about 200 miles— back the way we'd come, east to Williams, and then back north again.

The Canyon came as a surprise, for the pine trees are thick until one is almost upon the awesome broad gorge—four to 14 miles between the main rims, not just some ordinary old narrow slit in the earth.

I am terribly impressed each time I see Grand Canyon. It is always so much broader than I'd remembered it—a great misty-blue, pinkish-violet, gray spread that seems to stretch forever, studded with carved and color-banded buttes which fancifully suggest oriental temples and do in fact bear the names of Shiva, Buddha, Brahma, Zoroaster, and Confucious. Nothing moves; the Canyon stands so quiet that it is almost terrifying. It's better than any photos of it you've ever seen, but even more unbelievable. The color is so flamboyant, the mists, prisms, tints, and filters so outlandish and abundant that Grand Canyon might best be viewed in a condition described as stoned.

We arrived there just before sunset—a good time, for then the

191

crowds of sightseers have thinned out, allowing the essential loneliness of this classic example of erosion to be best appreciated. The wearing away of the land is something a man should be allowed to contemplate pretty much by himself.

We stopped first at Mather Point, then went on to Hopi, Mohave, and Pima points—all offering superb panoramic views of the big ditch. At one of those places, where tourists can walk out on a narrow thrust of rock, separated from space only by ironpipe railings (which I don't trust) there was a small family drinking in the wonders. Mother to littlest boy, "You're hurting my hand." Father to same, "You came all this way to see it, and now you're afraid to come out to the edge." The kid swallowed hard, said nothing and still hung back, terrified. His big brother said, "I want to throw some rocks." "Aren't any," said Daddy. "Grandma has two," said the boy. Grandma gave him one, which he heaved. She threw the other. "It's stupidifying," said the boy. His grandma agreed.

An overweight, middle-aged couple walked up to the rim. "Ain't this a *sight!*" exclaimed the man. "It sure *is* a sight," agreed his wife.

I never know what to say when looking out over Grand Canyon. It *is* overwhelming. I feel somewhat like our little white cat at home, who likes to stand on her hind legs and hang her head over the bathroom toilet seat looking at the water flushing in the bowl—with utter fascination, but completely puzzled.

Grand Canyon is the world's greatest earth sculpture. From the Canyon's rim only the most obvious statements of this natural treatise on geology can be read. To learn more, the student must descend to the Canyon floor, 5,000 feet below. Hundreds of people, many well past middle-age, make the trip each summer on muleback, safely over a wide switchback trail. ("Never lost a mule yet," say the guides.) In terms of climate, those who go down into the Canyon travel through something like 3,000 miles of latitude at sea level. Within the Canyon are six of the northern hemisphere's seven botanical life zones. While cool at the rim, it may be hellish hot at the bottom. Sparse vegetation, as well as the character of the rock, changes as the descent is made.

The river capable of such carving gets its name from its reddish color, made by an overload of silt. Rivermen claim the Colorado is too thick to drink, too thin to plow—just about our muddiest river. On warm days, say old-time river rats, you have to break the crust with your oar. These boatmen of the Colorado tell passengers, "In case of rain jump in the river and you'll only get half wet because it's half silt."

At flood time, the load of suspended solids and dissolved material carried by the Colorado is as much as 27.6 million tons a day; the average daily load is 500,000 tons. Someone figured out if that amount were put into five-ton dump trucks it would take 100,000 of them—bumper to bumper—about 24 hours to pass a given point. The river also moves an aggregate of pebbles and boulders equal in weight to the suspended solids.

Looking over this vast expanse of eroded rock, I find it hard to understand the clamor raised by naturalists and conservationists over various proposals to create dams in the Grand Canyon. Every time a dam on the Colorado is mentioned, its defenders claim the river will be despoiled and the natural balance of nature upset by taming the ancient wilderness. How insignificant such man-made affairs would be in the immensity of the whole Canyon! Actually, the river can be seen from only a very few points on either the North or South rim. How possibly could one or two little concrete plugs spoil all this grandeur? There seems to be more than enough for everyone who ever wants to look at it or wander into it for a thousand years to come.

River dams aren't necessarily "technological arrogance toward our landscape," as their more militant opponents claim. Dams can be a means of spreading the pleasures of nature more equitably, less snobbishly; thus they can bring about a wider appreciation of the wilds. Not everyone can afford wilderness expeditions or indulge in the luxury of taking a few dozen friends for a week of white-water boating.

I side with Floyd Dominy, the dam-loving Commissioner of the Bureau of Reclamation, who once said, "We're gonna turn that mean, dirty, maverick Colorado into a beautiful blue trout stream."

From the parking lot of the El Tovar Hotel, while Whiskers prepared dinner, the kids and I wandered over to Bright Angel Lodge. In the lounge were some of the brave, elderly souls who'd ventured down into the Canyon that day on the mules. Bundled in blankets and heavy coats against the chill evening, they didn't look so good—all sprawled out behind the plate-glass windows staring across the great expanse, glassy-eyed, pale and puffing, blood pressures no doubt soaring. Alas, they'd waited too long to be adventurers.

After dinner I took the kids to the Kolb Studio at the Canyon's edge for the evening showing of Grand Canyon movies and slides dating back to 1911, when the Kolb brothers, Ellsworth and Emory, went down the river in wooden boats and took the first motion pictures in the Canyon. Some of the movie shots of running the river were historically interesting and showed the great courage and insouciance of the two men, but on the whole the show was a crashing bore.

We took the East Rim Drive out of the Canyon. Because there was a full moon, we stopped at every viewpoint. By moonlight, Grand Canyon is eerie, like a landscape imagined on another planet. From one point could be seen the twinkling lights of Phantom Ranch on the Canyon floor near the river, base of the saddle-mule trail trips from both South and North rims. Our last view of the Canyon was from Navajo Point, elevation 7,450 feet. Then we had a winding, thrilling drop along the Little Colorado River to the crossroads of Cameron, at 4,201 feet, a distance of 32 miles. From there we headed straight north through the silvery moonlight about 85 miles to Page. Wearily, we crossed Glen Canyon Dam and, in our tired bare feet, checked in at the Wahweap Lodge.

Dammed Big Playground

Lord of the Wahweap Lodge is an old-timer river rat named Art Greene, a pioneer along the Colorado. He's run the tongues of its most savage rapids, bucked oars against the muddy ruffian's wildest plunges, built many a campfire on its sandbars, and watched stars trip over the canyon rims. On its own terms, Art has met the Colorado. He knows it well, loves it dearly.

Art Greene is short and heavyset, with a ruddy, round, Irish face. His eyes squint and twinkle; his wide mouth cracks into a grin; he becomes a mischievous gamin. You warm to him immediately. Art long ago discarded appearance for comfort and threw away his dental plates, saying people would have to take him as he was.

The Colorado has been good to Art. Now past 70, happy and active, Art is president of Canyon Tours, Inc., a family-owned corporation providing lodging, food, and boating concessions in the Glen Canyon Recreation Area through a recreation lease with the National Park Service.

The facilities, operated with son "Bill" (Art Greene, Jr.) and wife, and two daughters and their mates, include a marina with a fleet of 46 powerboats, ranging from single outboard jobs to large excursion cruisers, and an aquatic service station 50 miles up the lake, three miles from famed Rainbow Bridge. In the corporation's employ are ten pilots licensed by the U.S. Coast Guard.

Art is in his glory. He'd always wanted to work with powerboats—to hell with those rubber hippos, the neoprene rafts that old-time rivermen call garbage scows; farewell to rowboats. His favorite craft, one which he designed, is a flat-bottomed adaptation of the catamaran, powered by twin 50-horsepower outboards. Art calls this type of boat, acknowledged to be the best on the lake, *Tseh Na-ni-ah-go Atin,* or "Rock That Crosses Over." A Navajo Indian, watching one of these twin-hulled boats coming to dock, once said, "Closest deadheat race I ever see."

A good many Navajos are employed at the Greene family's motel and lodge. Art speaks only a few words of their native tongue. "If I knew how to talk it too well," he explains, "them fellas would bring all their troubles to me and cry on my shoulder, and I'd feel so sorry for them, I'd give in, no matter what they wanted."

Art has been a High Westerner all his life, born in Telluride, Colorado, on the western slope of the Continental Divide near Mount Wilson, over 14,000 feet high. He worked first as a sheepman, then a cowpoke, until, as he puts it, "the government started knowing more about raising cows than I did." Art's first venture as a commercial riverman was in 1915, when for five dollars he ferried a sheepherder by rowboat from Blanco, New Mexico, down the San Juan to Farmington. Now known far and wide as "the Baron of Northern Arizona," he pretends to be insulted by the sobriquet. "I know what a barren cow is," he says. "You can figger how I feel." Art is known for such atrocious witticisms. When he was guiding trips upriver to Rainbow Bridge (the first boatman to do so), his favorite gag was to tell a tourist he could bring along an electric razor because there was plenty of current in the river.

Just because the money is rolling in, Art Greene isn't taking it easy. He works harder now than ever. On our first day at Wahweap, I got up early—about seven—but Art had already been on the job for half an hour. When I went to the lobby for a newspaper I found him in his office expecting me. Over coffee, I learned how he happened to latch onto such a lucrative, enjoyable proposition.

"I was up against some pretty big people," he said, chuckling. "Fred Harvey, the Union Pacific, and Bing Crosby. I couldn't outbid them, but I found out five years before the contract had been signed to start the dam that the Park Service would rather have someone handling the service facilities in the dam's recreation area who was already on the spot. So I put up eight cabins over near Lee's Ferry—that's fourteen miles below here." (From 1872 to when the Navajo Bridge was built over Marble Canyon in 1929, the ferry was the only possible way to cross the Colorado until you got to the mule-and-foot suspension bridge on the Kaibab Trail in the Grand Canyon.)

"I had a little store, too. If you wanted a haircut you could get it—*I'd* do it. If you wanted a can of tomatoes or a box of crackers you might be able to get it. If you needed a boat we sure had it. Then I built a landing strip and connected it up to the end of the road the movie people had built out from Kanab. First I went as far as I could with a jeep. When it bogged down, I got a six-by-six—a command car—and when it couldn't go no further I got a half-track up from Phoenix, and finally we had a road—not a superhighway, but passable. Now the dam workers—I mean the workers on the dam—could drive out from Kanab where they mostly was staying and then take an airplane across the canyon to the work site. There was no town of Page yet, no bridge, nothing over there but a few tents and a couple trailers for the construction bosses. Or they could put up at my cabins, and a lot of them did. In the morning, and at quitting time, the contractors' planes, each with three workmen, would take off about one every few minutes. So when time came to give out the contracts for the concessions I was well established on the spot."

Art saw to it that we got a look that morning into the mysteries of Glen Canyon Dam—seven years in building at a cost of $300 million, including the creation of the town of Page on a remote barren mesa alongside the dam, and the erection over the canyon of the world's highest single-arch bridge (river elevation at this point, 3,142 feet; bridge roadbed, 700 feet higher).

I'd much rather go through a wallpaper, cornflakes, or glue factory than the innards of a great river dam, so I will report only that Glen Canyon's works out-Brobdingnag the most Brobdingnagian. There are gargantuan turbines and astounding banks of monitoring gauges and recorders watched over assiduously by Orwellians in enormous, absolutely spotless, glassed-in, soundproofed rooms. The main generator room is a city block long, five stories high, and contains eight huge generators, each with 112,500 kilowatts capacity. The total capacity of the power plant is 900,000 kilowatts, or enough, we were told, to meet the electrical needs of a city having 1.5 million population. Don't ask how they know this—they just do.

Despite its impressiveness, Art considers the big dam a mere side attraction to the main show—Lake Powell, named for Major John Wesley Powell, the one-armed Civil War veteran who in 1869 planned and captained the first successful descent through Grand Canyon. Lake Powell enthusiasts are sure it is the coming sportsmen's aquatic paradise of all America, with plently of room for everyone. When filled, the lake will extend 186 miles up the Colorado River, 71 miles up the San Juan, and have a surface area of 162,700 acres, an indented shoreline of 1,900 miles, and a capacity of 28,040,000 acre-feet of water (an acre-foot is 43,560 cubic feet of water, or enough to cover one acre to the depth of one foot). Normal reservoir elevation then will be 3,700 feet above sea level.

The creation of Lake Powell was strongly objected to by those who knew and loved Glen Canyon. Its passing was widely mourned. Despite salvage efforts, important archaeological sites were lost by creation of the lake. Masonry ruins dating from A.D. 900, priceless petroglyphs, exquisite canyons, and favorite rock formations have been inundated.

The Colorado, twisting and many-branched, ran the Glen Canyon for 200 miles, making stone cuts 800 to 1,200 feet deep. It was not for those who wished to be impressed by overwhelming grandeur, but more for quiet enjoyment. The camping on sandbars was superlative, under cliffs that whispered with willow and tamarisk. The river accommodated pleasure seekers by flowing swiftly, calmly, without major rapids. A boat trip through the canyon was suitable for old ladies and kids with braces on their teeth. Even a one-armed, cockeyed boatman with a sprained wrist could negotiate Glen Canyon.

Those who lament its passing say that what was flooded had the potential of a marvelous national park. They moon over pleasant little side canyons, gardens of fern and redbud, ponds banked solid with watercress, grottoes with quaint names—but mostly they remember the gentle stillness, the total absence of civilization's decibels.

Yet, relatively few made the boat trip down Glen Canyon—hundreds, compared to the hundreds of thousands now able to enjoy the beauties afforded by Lake Powell. Many attractive places, impossible to reach from the river, have been made accessible by the flooding.

Everyone hopes for a permanently stabilized lake at about the level it was when we saw it—still about 150 feet below its planned level of 3,700 feet. If the water is raised much higher a lot of the landscape's present beauty will be lost. Some proponents of the wild advocate throwing a boom across the mouth of the Escalante River so that its canyon could be restricted to rowboats and canoes. In the name of scenery, silence, and sanity, they say, why not keep one limited tributary free of powerboats? An excellent idea.

Of the Glen Canyon Dam, the Navajos say, "White man put a lock on the water and charge people for it."

Art Greene told us of the visit to Lake Powell of England's Princess Margaret and her husband, Lord Snowdon. Art was official greeter.

"Howdy, Ma'am," he'd said, ignoring the prepared speech furnished by State Department minions. "Welcome to Lake Powell." Art hadn't thought it necessary to put in his teeth even for a princess. She smiled graciously and Lord Snowdon winked.

Of the accommodations furnished the royal couple at Art's highway motel, Princess Margaret said, "It's the biggest room we've had so far." Lord Snowdon added, "It's bigger than the one she gives me at the palace."

Upon embarking on one of Art's 40-passenger excursion cruisers, Princess Margaret's husband had a Bloody Mary, and, according to Art, one more every fifteen minutes throughout the cruise. ("But he walked off sober as anything.")

Lord Snowdon had asked how far the ship-to-shore telephone could reach.

"How far do you want?" asked Art, who was piloting the boat.

"New York."

"Go ahead, you can get it."

Art could hear the other end of the conversation.

"Where are you?"

"In the middle of Lake Powell," said Lord Snowdon.

"Drunk again," said New York.

We spent the rest of the day swimming, resting, and writing picture postcards, and next day, up early, Whiskers fixed pancakes for us in the camper. At ten we went to the marina to begin a powerboat trip to Rainbow Bridge.

After leaving Wahweap Bay, we entered the Narrows, a riverlike channel where rock walls are steep, close together, and horizontally striped by the limestone deposit of high-water level.

As we pushed on, our pilot, Art's son-in-law Earl Johnson, pointed out a rock formation that he thought resembled Danny Thomas. The kids promptly found one that looked like Pooh Bear. I discovered

Khrushchev, De Gaulle, Eisenhower, Martha Raye, Dean Rusk, H. Rapp Brown, the Smothers Brothers, Bette Davis, and Sammy Davis, Jr., and hoped I'd put an end to *that* silliness.

Soon the lake broadened. Then we rounded Dominguez Rock, a promontory that marks "The Crossing of the Fathers," where men used to wade across the Colorado, a historic ford that for centuries was part of an aboriginal highway used by Indians. In 1776, Father Silvestre Velez Escalante, first white man to enter Glen Canyon, crossed here on his way to Sante Fe. The stone steps chiseled by the Father and his associates to get their mules and horses down to the ford now are deep under the water.

Old-time white-water river runners, when boating on Lake Powell, at first followed the landmarks of the old river channel, but gradually they are adopting those of new young pilots who have never run the river nor seen the canyon that the lake has erased.

The scale of the region is immense. Gigantic russet-colored buttes stand back on their peneplains of slickrock. Against them, even big boats are tiny chips on the water. The combination of deep water with cliffs, towering rock cathedrals, and domes is wonderfully satisfying.

The water itself changes color because of the walls overhanging it or the amount of light hitting it from the sky. It becomes vivid green, black, Prussian blue, and turquoise—with flecks of murky gold, pearly gray, and diamond sparkle. There are pinks and purples in wild combination. As the light strikes the water it bounces up to send crystalline patterns of light flickering on overhangs of vast rock amphitheaters. Passing boats send the reflections scampering into new patterns.

Textures of the rocks vary greatly. Each stretch of cliff face, each rock temple offers something different. There are marvelous stripes of brown, gray, black, white, red, blue, and violet caused by weathering and water painting. Ferns, columbine, monkey flowers, moss, and lichen make bright patches of green. Russian thistles grow in the sand.

Whiskers said, "You could swim for a week up here and never find a place where you could climb out." I hoped Earl had remembered to pack life vests.

Each of the lake's finger gorges, creeping in among the rocks, has its own air of enchantment, each intriguingly beckons to a secret inner region where there is extraordinary tranquillity and isolation. In one off-shoot was an appealing little rock island, a mere nubbin sticking saucily out of the water. In Cascade Canyon, Earl said we should yell, "Board of Health." When the kids did, the echo came back, "Go to hell." I supposed that when Princess Margaret tried it the echo came back, "Go to hell, your Highness." The laughter didn't cause any waves, but I got a dry chuckle from Earl.

We finally came to the Rainbow Bridge Marina, a long, skinny, floating-dock complex of gas station, snack bar, restrooms, and small living quarters for attendants, at the base of simply enormous and stunning purple-gray rocks.

"This," said Earl, "is where everyone wants to live—for about a week."

We gassed up and then went on a bit farther to the Rainbow Bridge landing. From there it was less than a mile and a half hike, through a beautiful canyon with purplish stone floor, into the bridge itself, star attraction of Lake Powell—a salmon pink sandstone span between red, buff, brown, and gray walls of the canyon carved by Bridge Canyon Creek, a tributary of the Colorado.

The world's largest natural stone arch has a span of 278 feet; its vertex is 42 feet thick, and it is 306 feet high—more than twice the height of bridges that clear oceangoing ships. Unlike most natural bridges, this one is not flat on top; both its arch and crest lines are curved and symmetrical.

Navajo Indians long ago knew this rock formation as *Nonnezosheboko* (great arch) and Paiutes called it *Barahoini* (the rainbow). The first white men saw it in 1909, guided there by a Paiute Indian, Nashjabegay. By 1936, only about 2,000 signatures were in the registry book at the bridge. Until 1963, only 22,000 names had been inscribed. Many were repeats, so that in roughly half a century perhaps no more than 10,000 people had made the strenuous trail trip of four days minimum to view this natural wonder, which that superlative describer of natural wonders, Teddy Roosevelt, once called "the world's greatest natural wonder." I still think he should have gotten rid of those pop-bottle glasses, for while Rainbow Bridge is a massive and curious hunk of stone, a freak of nature, I wouldn't hike four days to see it even if it looked like Doris Day in the nude.

Earl told us that before the dam was built Art had taken only about 200 people a year by boat-and-hike combination to the bridge.

"Art used to have a time jollying the hikers," said Earl. "It was the hardest part of his job, because it was rough getting in here—what I mean *rough*. He always tells about one especially grumpy old lady. Art sensed she needed something to cheer her up, so he puts his arms around her and says, 'Why don't you pour the blood out of your shoes, ma'am, and let's you and me set down over here on a rock and have a beer together.' "

Back then, visitors to Rainbow Bridge were glad to lay out $250 each for the privilege. Now you can go by boat to the bridge and back in a one-day excursion for $25 a head. The new popularity of the bridge is indicated by a carpet of hundreds of overlapping footprints made in the soft reddish-brown earth under the arch. In season, at least 100 people a week come here.

We stopped to look at the latest entries in the register: "Rake the buffalo chips" . . . "Don't fill the goddam canyon with water" . . . "Leave the canyon like it is" . . . "Put in elevators" . . . "Gorgeous!" . . . "Pave the trail" . . . "Put in drinking fountains" . . . "Move the bridge closer to Wahweap."

Evidently the ranks of dedicated lovers of nature are being infiltrated by those who can take it or leave it alone, who are easily bored by scenic grandeur. How soon will these register inscribers give vent to their feelings by scratching graffiti on the arch itself? When will the littering begin? Already thoughtless people are throwing trash into Lake Powell from their boats. There's no doubt in my mind that the onslaught of tourist visitors is going to have an adverse effect on the pristine beauty of Rainbow Bridge. It may never become as corrupt an attraction as Niagara Falls or as commercialized as Grand Canyon, but the great stone arch is bound to be cheapened.

"You got to remember," said Earl, "that for some people this little stroll in here is the most they ever walked in their whole lives. Some get carried out with sprained ankles, and every once in a while we get one that has a heart attack from the combination of fatigue, heat, and the elevation. You're not too high here—only about 3,200 feet—but that sun can be damned hot."

On the way back, Earl took us into special favorite channels. We passed again the many stately temple upthrusts, more beautiful now in late afternoon light. We got to the marina sunbaked and fairly exhausted. Took the family to dinner at the lodge. Slept. Didn't even dream. None of us did.

North Rim

While the two rims of Grand Canyon are about 15 miles apart by trail through the Canyon, it is almost 235 miles by motor road from one to the other. From Wahweap Lodge on Lake Powell, the distance is about 125 miles. The kids felt that, since we'd had so little daylight at the South Rim, they deserved a visit to the North Rim.

"Let's do it," said Whiskers. "We'll never be this close again."

The last time she'd said that was when we were in Arequipa, Peru, with Tia newborn, Bridget and Toby at one and two years. Then, we were just over the montaña from the Amazon River, and Whiskers urged that we go home that way by paddle-wheel steamer—which we did (eight days on the river from Iquitos to Manáos, by plane to Belém, and 13 hours by air from there to New York). My wife has a blithe conception of distances, but an instinct for doing what is exactly right at the moment.

So we embarked for the North Rim, crossing the Colorado over the Navajo Bridge at Marble Canyon, which until the Glen Canyon span was built was the canyon's only highway bridge for approximately 1,000 miles—from Moab, Utah, to Boulder Dam. From the bridge we went west, possibly 20 miles, along the Vermillion Cliffs—perpendicular rock rises over 1,000 feet high, their sanguine reds, casually smeared with burnt sienna, tawny orange, and ocher, ablaze in late morning sun.

We moved through a seemingly boundless land of poignant emptiness, where cedar and sage struggle against sand, high grass, and dry wind. Forlorn of people, this high northwest strip of Arizona—7,000 square miles—is cut off from the state's main body by Grand Canyon. It is lonely up here. The area's towns are mere rude settlements. Every six square miles averages one person. Folks, while standing on Arizona soil, speak wistfully of "going down to Arizona."

In sweeping switchbacks we approached House Rock Valley, where only seven families live. One of the residents is the cowboy who looks after about 200 head of wild buffalo roaming over a refuge of more than 51,000 acres—79 sections of 640 acres each, off the paved road about 25 miles. It is not a place where seldom is heard a discouraging word. I'd visited it once and found there the world's loneliest cowboy, a 26-year-old Swede born in Brooklyn, New York, and he was full of discouraging words. "This country can sour a man pretty quick," he'd told me.

The buffalo, however, were sleek, their beautiful black and seal-brown coats glistening in the sun, and their shoulder wool nice and thick. The buffalo keeper was especially discouraged by the buffalo kill, held every other year to thin out the herd, when hunters licensed by the state come in, each to bag a buffalo for his $40 fee and also to get the hide, one quarter, the privilege of buying the other three, and the head to mount and hang on the wall to show everybody what a brave hunter he'd been.

Cowboys round up those buffalo to be killed, and they are turned out three at a time into a big corral, while the hunters stand inside as close to the fence as they honorably can and try for the only possible fatal shot—right under the horn behind one ear.

We'd climbed steadily since leaving Navajo Bridge, and when we reached Jacob Lake we'd come up to 7,921 feet. We turned there and, still pushing into the sky, went south through the Kaibab National Forest's northern section, which has dense stands of spruce, fir, and pine as well as sizable groves of quaking aspen. In ponderosas high above the ground were bushel-basket-size houses of the nonhibernating Kaibab squirrel, a hefty, churring, gray creature with skunklike stripe of rusty red, long tasseled ears, black chest, and feathery white-plumed tail. We also sighted Rocky Mountain mule deer, part of the Kaibab herd.

Just inside the Grand Canyon National Park entrance station we jogged west by primitive road to Point Sublime, overlooking the Canyon at the end of a ten-mile promontory rising between basins 3,000 feet deep. From its tip is the ultimate Grand Canyon vista—a 150-mile east-west stretch unmatched at any other point on either the North or South rim. Here the circusy excesses of the travel brochures come true. There truly is a "Crimson Blushing, Golden Muted Purple" and a "Misty Blue Concept of Sublimity and Awesome Immensity, the Divine Abyss, Unequalled on Either Side of Paradise." Well, almost—but dizzying altitudes of rhetoric do seem justified here. Even those who scorn the carnations of Mother's Day, who prefer crepes suzette and Yves Saint Laurent to pancakes and Sears Roebuck, do not knock the Grand Canyon from this viewing point.

The North Rim is closer to all the stone monuments and is 1,285 feet higher than the South Rim. From Point Imperial, highest point of both rims (8,801 feet) can be seen Navajo Mountain, 100 miles distant, at 10,416 feet one of the area's best-known landmarks.

We also stopped off at Cape Royal, at the end of Walhalla Plateau. Along the way there were mountain and field flowers, and near the plateau's end pine forest turned to piñons; locust hedges sent out a wisterialike fragrance. At this viewpoint the chasm is widest (18 miles), and there is a glimpse of the Colorado, curving between sandbars more than a mile below. The colossal stone mound, Wotan's Throne, is very close here—separated from the rim by a deep gorge—and just below Cape Royal is Vishnu Temple, a graceful, white-topped butte. Many smaller buttes surround it; below them long graceful arms of red limestone reach toward the river. Along the south horizon are the San Francisco Peaks and Hendricks, Sitgreaves, and Bill Williams mountains.

The only place you can get a good clear look straight down at the raging Colorado is at Toroweap Point, in Grand Canyon National Monument, which adjoins the park at its western boundary. Recent lava flows also are visible from Toroweap, including one that flowed over the canyon rim and into the river. The gorge here is only about half a mile wide, and there is a huge cinder cone called Vulcan's Throne. But to reach that unusual viewpoint of the Grand Canyon requires a 96-mile drive—62 of it on rudimentary road. We didn't attempt it.

Our bed-down for the night was at the North Rim Inn in two stone-and-log cabins. After settling in and lighting a log blaze in each—aided by kerosene-soaked sawdust—we drove out to scary Bright Angel Point for still another canyon view. This one was slightly rained-on, misty, and adorned with a modest rainbow that enthralled the ubiquitous photo snatchers.

We'd wanted to have dinner at Grand Canyon Lodge in its magnificent rustic-beamed dining room, but it had closed on Labor Day, so we had to be content with a meal rustled up in the camper. After tucking the kids in, Whiskers and I toasted in the dark by our fire and watched the clouds scud dreamily by the cabin window and the moon slide out and set off across the Canyon.

More Indians

Navajo Heritage

Upon leaving Grand Canyon National Park at Desert View we'd entered the Navajo Reservation, but traveling in the dark we'd been unaware of it. Now, however, by daylight, there could be no question that we were in the land of *Dineh,* the people, which is what these Indians call themselves. The pace had slackened without our realizing it. People here moved more gracefully, were quieter, more self-contained, and dignified. The very atmosphere slowed to a crawl. Time and distance stretched lazily, limitlessly.

Indian lands make up one-fourth of Arizona, and the Navajo Reservation is largest of the state's 14. It has 24,000 square miles (15 million acres) and encloses joint Hopi-Navajo holdings of 4,000 square miles, inside which is the Hopi Reservation. The elevation of the entire area is from 3,000 to 10,416 feet. There are more than 95,000 Navajos, and they are increasing at a rate three times faster than that of the rest of the United States' population.

Navajos are more attractive than most reservation Indians. Few live in tar-papered shacks held together by spit and the grace of God, although many are addicted to front-yard clutters of defunct autos and

205

the company of nondescript dogs. (Dogs are supposed to ward off evil spirits.)

The women wear long-sleeved, high-necked, velveteen blouses of wild warm colors—turquoise, deep pink, purple, vermillion, and seal brown—trimmed with strings of sewn-on dimes and quarters—and long, full, pleated, satin skirts similarly colored; the cut of the costume is from the dress of army officers' wives in Kit Carson's time. Navajo females wear much handwrought silver and turquoise jewelry, and fix their jet-black hair neatly.

The men dress conservatively—Western-style, in Levis and plaid cowboy shirts. Some older men bind their long hair with cloth strips into a thick tail. Most males affect heavy silver bracelets called "bow-guards" (originally to protect the wrist from snap of the bowstring).

Navajo kids are as clean as they can be without running water. Everyone seems reasonably content and free from undue tension.

Navajos are an ethnological enigma—a medieval people in the atomic age. Not only have they retained their cultural uniqueness, but Navajos constantly strengthen it by appropriating whatever Anglo customs they find useful, while rejecting those deemed distasteful.

To a Navajo it is sinful not to live harmoniously with nature. That is the main lesson contained in the parable of the tribe's creation, which reads like science fiction as the Navajo Adam and Eve materialize from the bowels of the earth.

Despite the legends, Navajos are a mixture of many Indian tribal groups. Their melting-pot origin no doubt is responsible for the tribe's remarkable endurance. Less than 500 years ago there were no Indians named Navajo, or *Dineh*. These people then were only scattered groups of half-naked hunters beginning to penetrate the Southwest—savages drifted south from the Athapaskan tribes in what now is Alaska and northwest Canada. These Navajos-to-be integrated with Pueblo farmers, warlike Utes, and various desert nomads skilled in food-finding and basketry. Each host's culture was dipped into to form what we know today as Navajos.

These Indians have kept their native tongue intact while many other Indian languages have been lost by deterioration or deliberate abandonment. Other tribes have deserted tepee and longhouse, but Navajos stick stubbornly to the hogan—a windowless, mud-covered, cedar-log, usually octagonal construction with earthen floor, rooftop smoke hole, and single door that always faces the rising sun, worshiped as the cradle of life. Always some part of the door is painted turquoise blue.

Navajo society is untainted and communal, such as Jesus advocated; each person is judged strictly by his behavior, rather than by worldly possessions. There is a tone of democracy, with no class or racial distinction. Half-breed is as good as full blood; rich and poor are treated alike. No man is master of another.

Navajos don't hold grudges. It is a sin for them to lose their tempers. There are no Navajo cusswords. The worst thing you can call anyone in Navajo is "coyote"—not even *dirty* coyote or son-of-a-coyote. No Navajo has ever shot or stabbed another in anger or because of passion— not even over poker, the favorite gambling game. It makes little difference to the Navajo whether he wins or loses at cards, but a cunning gambler is revered by his clan. Navajos always deal from the bottom of the deck. Cheating at cards is regarded as being clever. If the trickster is caught he simply loses the pot.

While such chicanery is condoned, Navajos are puritanical regarding sex. They have little, if any, interest in erotica, sexual deviation, or concupiscent orgies. Nudity is taboo. Young Navajo boys are told they'll go blind if they so much as glance at their sisters in nakedness. Ordinarily, Navajo women never expose more of their hide than faces, hands, and a few inches of leg at boot top when mounting a horse. Even when husband and wife take a sweat-bath together—a Navajo sauna in dwarf dirt igloo—they cover their genitals, but this could be less for modesty than for protection against infiltration of dry sand used in lieu of a towel.

One key to the puzzle of the Navajos is the splendid isolation of their land. It is not touched by great rivers, railroads, or transcontinental highways. Until recently, only true travel connoisseurs knew much about the Navajo reservation's interior. The dirt roads—crater-pocked, offering such hazards as deep sand, sucking mud, and slickrock—discouraged all but the most determined travelers. The only recommended vehicles were a small airplane, a four-wheel-drive, or a healthy horse. Today, new blacktop highways have made this wild place available to anyone with a driver's license.

The first sizeable community we came to was Tuba City, metropolis of the reservation's western half. It has a large, modern community center, used for everything from committee meetings, sewing circles, and medical clinics to dances, movies, and such stellar attractions as Fred Waring's

Pennsylvanians and the Harlem Globetrotters. At the edge of Tuba City we had hamburgers and milk shakes at a Dairy Queen next to a Laudromat where ladies in velveteen jackets and long full skirts waited with piles of clean laudry to be picked up by their men. Nearby, a family was packing supplies in a low-slung covered wagon.

So that Whiskers could look at "old pawn" (handmade jewelry that has been in hock a long time), we went into the trading post, a large, one-room country store—very oldfangled—with canned goods stacked up the walls and bolts of yard goods held high on its rough-hewn log pillars. An absence of good pawn indicated the reservation's current prosperity; the finest jewelry was being worn by women waiting their turns at the counters, standing alongside the meat freezers and soda pop vending machine. Among the beautiful soft Navajo rugs for sale to tourists were gaudy, aniline-dyed Mexican sarapes that the Navajos themselves buy to use as shawls and saddle blankets.

On the way to Monument Valley is one of the Southwest's loveliest Indian ruins, Betatakin—Navajo for "houses in the rock shelves." It is one of three such sites of the Navajo National Monument (the others: Keet Seel and Inscription House). Of all the easily accessible ancient cliff dwellings of the High West, Betatakin is the least known and least visited. At the height of the summer tourist season only about 20 persons a day come to enjoy this breathtaking sight. The 14-mile journey in from the paved highway used to be over a bone-shaker dirt road, but now it has been blacktopped and is less gruesome.

From the tiny museum a "Sandal Trail" leads to a point from which the ruins can be viewed at a distance. In order to protect them, a ranger guide must accompany visitors who want to trudge down to the canyon floor for a close-up look. There are two tours: one at 8:30 A.M., the other at 1:30 P.M. We missed the afternoon one, but because the ranger had read one of my books, he let us go down alone.

Betatakin is an entrancing place, well worth the hike to it of a mile and a half, after a sharp 700-foot descent. The major part of this ruin stands on steps hacked into the sloping floor of a huge recess in a delightfully deep-pink sandstone cliff, which forms the 500-foot north wall of the picturesque and beautiful Segi branch of the Laguna Canyon.

Few sections of this 700-year-old hillside apartment house, which is 150 feet in depth, are higher than two stories, although the different levels of their foundations give a terraced effect to the whole. Once there were about 150 rooms, of which more than 50 were residential, 30 for storage, six for ceremonial kivas, and two used as grinding rooms. Thirteen open courts were interspersed. The cave roof projects far out over the community. The structures are rectangular and made of stones set in adobe or of adobe plaster interwoven with willow rods. Roofing beams found here were cut as early as A.D. 1242. Especially impressive is the shadow carving in some of the wooden window frames and stone lintels—a decorative touch seldom found in prehistoric ruins.

Fronting Betatakin are tall, slender, quaking aspen. Clear water flows from a rock at the entrance to the buildings. Box elder, Douglas fir, and piñon deck the talus slopes. Juniper and piñon cap the bordering cliffs.

After we'd sent the kids off into the canyon to fetch some prickly pears, Whiskers and I sat in the stillness of the ancient dwellings, wondering what it was like to be man and woman, half-naked and completely dependent upon nature, in those long-ago times. Was life utterly serene then, a heaven on earth, or were there pressures, problems, and frustrations just as today? The kids weren't gone nearly long enough. Upon their return we all sat together in the sun, rubbed the spines off the prickly pears, and relished the sweet purple fruits. They couldn't have tasted any better to any Indian.

Away from It All

Continuing northward on the main road, we passed absurd Owl Butte, an odd stone creature glowering across a plateau at sinister Agathla, a sooty-black volcanic neck whose craggy pointed spire rises 1,255 feet above the sloping base and marks the southern boundary of Monument Valley, which extends north to the San Juan River. The valley is a handsome, flat, lowland bowl studded with outcrops of red sandstone, many of them as high as skyscrapers. The monoliths have been eroded into pillars and spires or into huge rectangular blocks with grooved sides that suggest columns. Talus slopes extend outward at their bases in terraces and resemble steps, so from a distance these rose-colored, blue-shadowed chunks of stone appear to be ruins of immense Greek temples.

We were heading into Navajoland not only to absorb its dramatic, sculptured sandstone landscape and visit archaeological sites of this mysterious civilization, but to allow our minds to brush against the distinctive

Navajo culture, and we wanted to relax again at Goulding's Trading Post, a remote tourist lodge that stands unobtrusively against an 800-foot-long, V-shaped redstone mesa, *Tsay-kizzi*, next to a rock monument known as Old Baldy.

Harry Goulding has been in these parts since 1921, as a rangy sheepherder out of Durango, Colorado. In 1924, he got lucky and was able to buy a square mile of this spectacular real estate for $320—50 cents an acre—before the plot was taken off the homesteading market by the United States government and restored to its original status as reservation land. For three years Harry and his wife lived on their purchase in a 12 x 14 tent, trading with visiting Navajos and operating a modest sheep, cattle, and horse-swapping business.

Today, a lineup of air-conditioned units, housing 50 guests, faces across a gorgeous expanse of Monument Valley. Through an arrangement made by Harry with Knox College at Galesburg, Illinois, all profits of the lodge, after operating expenses and a small retirement income for himself, go toward college scholarships for young Navajos.

We got to Goulding's not too long before the black-iron mealtime bell on the high front porch clanged its supper call. The heady view across the valley hadn't changed one bit—still the same stretch of reddish flatlands studded with huge stone monuments, reaching to the valley's craggy rim and hazy blue mountains beyond. The sun was slipping away, sliding shadows of the monuments, long and skinny, for miles across the flatness and changing the rocks' colors from warm tan to orange to hellfire red and rosy violet. Eventually, a somber purple shrouded what Goulding calls his front-yard fence—a string of seven red rock formations rising abruptly from the valley floor, seemingly within strolling distance, but actually eight miles away. The air—sharp, dry, and clear—gave us, and the other guests, good appetites. Stacks of steaks and heaping side dishes were quickly leveled at the ranch-style long tables, with each diner accommodated on a padded wooden stool.

After dinner, with the kids gone to bed, in cobalt blue darkness Whiskers and I perched on the trading post's rail fence and watched a thunderstorm crawl over the rim of the valley and sweep majestically across it, tickling the rocky mesas with spider webs of lightning, impudently spearing the monuments' stone faces and topknots with sharp dazzling thrusts, flashing them into brilliant silhouette.

Finally, droopy-eyed, we slouched off to bed, leaving open the curtain of our bedroom's window wall that faced the valley. The storm passed. The fresh wet smell was grand. Myriad twinkling stars tumbled into the sky. I counted only 87 before I dropped off.

I'd just made it by pitons, hacked-out steps, and climbing rope up the Grand Teton and stood chest-out triumphant, surveying the neon sprinkle of Las Vegas at my feet, and sniffing a glass of brandy brought me by a mountain goat bearing a cask around its neck labeled "Aspen Humanistic Institute" and wearing Teddy Roosevelt's glasses. "Bully!" I said to him. "Billy, Bully Whiskers!"—just as my wife poked me awake.

"Look," she whispered, "over on that mesa."

On the biggest stone monument facing us there appeared to be a fire. My first thought was to arouse Maurice Knee, the lodge manager, so he could call the rangers. Then I realized there couldn't be a forest fire on solid stone. Maybe it was a camping party. But who could climb those sheer walls? Suddenly the fire took off straight up into the sky and hovered there.

"It's a UFO!" I exclaimed.

"I think it must be," said my wife, all atremble.

We both were dumbstruck. Our alarm clock said one-thirty. The thing hovered for a minute or so, then took off across the sky with sparking, glowing tail looking sort of like an old-fashioned skyrocket. It made a long neat arc—stopped still—and all at once it was gone. We watched the sky for a long time, but nothing more happened. Finally, we slept.

At five I was awakened by a light fingernail tapping at our room door. It was Harry Goulding.

"Thought you folks might want to view the sunup," he said shyly. "I never miss a one myself. A Navajo had better not by golly be still in bed when the day's first sun hits his hogan door."

Our hogan had plate glass facing the sun, so we didn't have to stir from bed to enjoy the wildly satisfying sunrise spectacle.

At our breakfast table was a trio of French professional cinematographers who were junketing around the High West recording it on film for the Gallic public. They'd been on the road since May.

"American tourists," said one of the men, "are flash-bulb mad. At the Yosemite Park we photograph the firefall at night. In the pitch black they shovel hot coals off a high cliff in a cascade. *Splendid!* From cliff top we look down on it and as soon the fire begin to drop into the valley, a thousand feet below in the dark was *pop! pop! pops!* from flash cameras. *Incredible!* Like artillery attack." He shook his head in disbelief.

"Many times," said the young lady of the party, "we see people taking pictures of sunset with flash cameras—shooting *POOFT!* right into the blazing sun."

"Ah," interjected the second man, "but at Grand Canyon was best. One little old lady, she have a little eight-millimeter movie camera. She wind it up so, put it to her eye and start it off. *Bzzz-z-z-z-z. Bzzz-z-z-z-z.* Like a bee. She move it fast—up, down, across, and back, up and down again, back, forth. *Bzzz-z-z-z-z, bzzz-z-z-z-z.* Then when the winding run down, she says, 'Well, I got it all—the whole Grand Canyon.' She put the camera away, walk to her car, and drive off. She spend only five minute at one of America's *magnifique* wonders. But she is very happy. She take the whole Grand Canyon home in her little black box to Tolendo, *Hi*-oway, or Inde-apple-plus, Mitchigan." He laughed heartily.

"Once in a desert at sunset," said the first cinematographer, "there is this trailer parked. I think, *how* very nice! they have come to admire sublime nature. Then I see a wire running from the trailer to electric generator and I look closer and inside is a couple sitting in front of a television set."

When I asked these Frenchmen what was the oddest thing they'd seen in America thus far, they agreed on the sight of three bird's-eye diapers drying on a sage bush outside a mud-roofed hogan in Monument Valley.

The big attraction at Harry Goulding's place is the sight-seeing in four-wheel-drive vehicles that can negotiate the deep sand and afford close-up looks at the mastodonic monoliths of the valley that Navajos call *Tse-bizi* (valley deep inside rocks). To them, the monuments are *Tseh-yahn-delja* (rocks that stick straight up). Viewed from the valley floor, they give a sobering glimpse of nature's power.

After breakfast, we found Harry Goulding outside the trading post greeting some Navajo young men who'd come to take road tests for automobile driver's licenses. He went quietly among them, greeting each with the traditional single gentle handclasp that marks the passing of trust between two people. The length of time the hands are held depends upon how long it's been since the people have seen each other.

There is no Navajo equivalent of our own "Good morning"; the closest phrase is *"Ya-at-eeh-abini?"* or "Are you well at sunup?" The nicest reply is *"Ye-te-hay,"* or "fine." Another greeting of the Navajos: "I am thankful I have the eyes to see you with when I meet you."

I knew that I could not be introduced to any of the Navajos by their real names for these Indian ones are never spoken to a Navajo's face. It is permissible to voice only their Anglicized names.

"Did you see the guided missile go over last night?" Goulding asked us. "They send them off regular from the base up at Blanding. Usually they're so accurate—they been knocking derby hats off with them over in New Mexico—but the radio this morning said that one last night got away and ended up in old Mexico. The Mexicans are mighty upset about it."

"I'd be too," I said. "Those things are no play toys."

"You and your UFO," said Whiskers. "Waking me up in the middle of the night."

I don't think it was a missile. Since when do missiles park on rock mountains, take off straight up into the air, arc off, stop, and then disappear? I prefer to think it was a Navajo god.

You feel the mysterious power of Monument Valley the moment you reach the bottom of the twisting 400-foot drop into it from Navajo Tribal Park headquarters. A sighing silence settles over everything. The time of now shuts off as though a curtain had descended.

Goulding's trips into the valley feature prearranged stops at various hogans and scenic spots where Navajos in their best clothes await to pose for photos (small gratuities accepted gracefully).

We began at a sheep-watering hole. The next stop always is at a hogan where women sit on the earth before a crude homemade loom working on a coarse rug, while boy kids are preoccupied with bubble gum and the girls demonstrate how to card wool and spin it into strands on a wooden spin stick, how to comb and brush their hair with a sheaf of stiff-stemmed brush grass called *baijo*. Jesse Black, our young Navajo driver and guide, brought us bark of a plant which these Indians call the cliff rose or baby brush (*aweitzad*), because this very soft, extremely absorbent natural material makes the mattresses of their babies' cradleboards—onto which they are bound for nap times—and also is used as swaddling, the first disposable diapers.

On schedule, old John Cly was posed on his horse atop a great slab of rock, too big to fit into the Astrodome. At another picturesque point a mother and two daughters showed up on horseback with a colt only a day old. All that morning we pushed through the sands of this land of room enough and time enough, meeting Navajos as if by chance, as we threaded an unmarked way among overpowering mesas, slender spires, arches, bridges, and huge balanced boulders.

All this prearranged posing seemed artificial and, to us, was an unsatisfying way of meeting Navajos, yet how else can tourist groups be easily accommodated? I especially disliked one particular aspect: tour members are specifically instructed to bring plenty of quarters to dole out as gratuities. It was a bit like buying a ticket to the theater (these tours are not cheap) and being asked by the management to pay the actors; I was told that the Indians get no other compensation for their posing for photographs. And I also thought it rather irresponsible for tour leaders to pass out to Navajo kids so much soda pop and so many lollipops, considering the effect those sweets have on young teeth already battling against poor nutrition and sand in the food.

Jesse knew the names of all the monuments—the Navajo names, that is, which are quite different from those Anglos have bestowed on them. "Rooster Rock," for instance, is known to Navajos as "Mother Leading Her Child."

We lunched in the shade of a simply stupendous rock mass, and directly after visited the Big Hogan. While we were in this huge stone chamber a sudden downpour sent a cascading torrent of rainwater through a hole in the roof 150 feet above the ground. Following the shower we drove to The Eye of the Sun, a large opening in a high stone wall, with lashes caused by water stains, and to The Ear of the Wind, a great eroded-stone arch easily 200 feet high.

"Where Navajos come to talk to the wind," said Jesse. "It tells them when to plant, when it will rain, when a bad winter is coming."

These arches are but two of dozens, so gracefully contoured that anywhere else each would be a leading scenic attraction. In Monument Valley, they're lost in a wilderness of beauty where the spectacular is commonplace.

In late afternoon we came to Yei-bi-chai Mesa, where stands the incredibly tall, thin spire called The Totem. At this place there occurred the supreme Navajo happening of the day—the driving, by girls on horseback, of a herd of sheep down a steep windswept dune of apricot-colored sand. Sheep bleated, camera shutters clicked, and scads of quarters were passed to the sheepherder women by a large gathering of onlookers—not only from Goulding's but from several other guide outfits.

Driving out of the valley we passed the stout, lame woman who'd been in and out of the cast of snapshot characters ever since she'd been the star of the rug-weaving tableau that morning. As she hobbled along across the sand, she sent Jesse a big goodbye wave. I hoped she'd latched onto plenty of the coin of the realm.

That these trips of Goulding's are so well coordinated with Navajos is due largely to Harry's longtime associate, Maurice Knee, who came to Navajoland from Colorado at the age of 17. He's been around Navajos so long he thinks like one. That evening in the lodge Maurice showed assembled guests some of his color slides of the valley, accompanied by informative and jocular remarks.

Afterward, Whiskers and I were invited to the Knees' living room, casually decorated with museum-caliber Navajo art and crafts—rare pieces of ancient pottery, medicine-man amulets, and gorgeous rugs, including one made by Hopis that has a snake winding back and forth among cryptic symbols, much like Peruvian designs we'd seen. Maurice told Whiskers that the shell-slice bracelet that I gave her when Lulu was born in Sarasota is an example of *ho-ho-kam*—shell etched by cactus juice, a method used by ancient Indians of about A.D. 300, who went to the Gulf Coast to gather seashells for wampum. She was delighted to think she might own an item of such historical significance.

From Maurice, we learned something of the Navajo language, so little understood beyond the reservation that it was used as code in the Pacific during World War II.

"Maurice can sing some of the chants," said his wife, Rosemary, "and he knows all the long words like the one for double horse blanket, *ah-ka-da-hot-nilthe.*" I wrote it down phonetically.

"That 'l' should have a diagonal line through it," Maurice advised over my shoulder. "No, the other direction. Here, let me do it. That's for a kind of phlegmy sound—like clearing your throat."

Spoken Navajo sounds like Chinese—singsong and hesitant, graceful and easygoing, with a lot of slurs and dropped syllables. Some of the words no doubt have Iberian roots. Bread, for instance, is *bah,* which could be a mispronounciation of the Spanish word *pan* (pronounced "pah-n"). The Navajo word for death, *yoss,* could be a lazy way of saying *adios,* "to God." *Beel,* for an old-style, double-paneled, shoulder-hung women's garment, could trace to *huipil,* the Mexican word for it. Navajo babies are not called "papooses," but *awais,* pronounced softly, losing the last two letters. The word is similar to the Peruvian term for baby, *wah-wah*—from the sound of crying.

As in German, Navajo words sometimes are built from the function of the designated object. Train is *koo-nas-passey,* a fire which turns around. Soda pop is water that bubbles, *to-toh-del-chosi.* Auto is *chidi* and airplane is *chidi-natai,* flying auto. Ship is wooden duck, *tsin-na-ethle;* an ocean liner is *peshna-na-ethle,* iron duck. The ocean is *toh-ena-enkale,* water wide. Candy is called *as-kaz-gizzy,* which means something twisted (the first candies seen on the reservation were old-fashioned licorice and peppermint twist sticks). The Navajo word for tourist is the same as that for Spaniard, *nakai*—to these Indians, the men from Spain were travelers and traders. The word Navajo is not in the language. It comes from a Tewa phrase, *Apachus de Nabahu,* meaning "strangers to the cultivated fields."

The next day, Maurice took us to Navajo homes off the beaten tourist path. Some were hogans, others one-room wooden shacks, neat enough but with no frills—bare floors and not even window drapes or curtains. No radio, no TV. In fact, no electricity. No running water. Metal shower-room lockers often were used as wardrobes; in one hogan a discarded electric refrigerator held some of the family's clothes. Usually, however, they hung on pole racks placed around the walls. Between a pair of ladies' panty-hose and a white leatherette jacket hung two medium-sized pieces of mutton jerky—shade drying. Several hogans had piles of U.S. government surplus beef and cornmeal in bags.

In one rude house a woman was weaving a stunning large Navajo rug. Alongside sat a grandmother restringing her wampum—said she'd danced so hard it broke. In another household, the wife and mother was suffering an absent drunken husband. Her children were friendly and beautiful. On one wall was a big, gaudy tapestry of some Appaloosa horses grazing in a forest. The alcoholic's wife said her man had brought it from Kooskia, Idaho, a river resort in west-central Idaho. I remembered seeing a nightmare of these plush Syrian creations hanging from the ceiling of a souvenir shop there. We encountered few men; they mostly were at work in towns off the reservation, Maurice said.

We spent the most time at the homestead of John Kaytso. That he was a cut above the average Navajo was apparent from the layout. Compared to the other abodes we'd seen this was a magnificent country estate: main hogan; a smaller one; a summer house (*chouho*) of logs and brush roof; two conventional, small boxy wooden houses; a house trailer that had attached to it a cedar shade with a floor of railroad ties; and a separate shade. The accessories were an outdoor drying pole and clothesline, a couple of incinerators, two outhouse toilets, and a brush corral—

all very neat and spread about a big flat of swept brown earth. Two tightly hobbled mules were in the brush; twin puppies and three other friendly mongrel dogs frolicked about.

The principal hogan, octagonal, was large enough to have around its walls five double beds, including two pallets on the floor, and still allowed ample space around the center stove. Over a calendar hung on the wall of cedar logs were pasted four colored pictures cut from magazines. The caption under the one of Frank Sinatra: "Hollywood's Most Shocking Story. How Mia Got Frank's Kids To Betray Their Mother." The youngest member of the family was a three-month-old son of Jenny Kaytso, named Emerson Whitney, who was being swaddled and bound by thongs onto a cradleboard. (A squirrel's tail on it is supposed to prevent the baby from falling.)

While Whiskers and the kids visited with mother and grandmother, who spoke only Navajo, Maurice took me out past the family's spring to meet John Kaytso. We found him squatting in his cornfield, smoking. He told Maurice he was "watching the stalks grow." A stocky blond young German pulled up in a jeep and was introduced to me as Oswald "Ozzie" Werner, from Northwestern University, living on the reservation while compiling an anatomical and physiological atlas in the Navajo language, financed by a grant of $30,000 a year from the National Institute of Mental Health. (Jenny Kaytso was typing his manuscript.) He was on his second year of work. "I keep finding synonyms," he said.

He told us that the body functions of a Navajo are all explained in legends and that winter was the best time for getting information about them, as it is sacrilegious to tell the legends in summertime. I mentioned to Mr. Werner that a California anthropologist had drawn parallels between the Navajo language and that of the Mongolian Tibetans. He looked on me as if I were a retarded cockroach and said emphatically, "That would be methodologically inadmissible."

The back of his jeep was fitted with filing cabinets and drawers, and Mr. Werner showed us the method of preparing his gathered information for feeding into a computer to be sorted into easily available form. On the long lists of anatomical terms I found the word for nerve center, *ha-lohk'e'nimazi*. *Biohni-zhdil-chi* means "the part you can't reach," the middle of the back (three synonyms). *Asdzani-ji hati'ehgi bil haz'aanii* refers to the female sex organs, i.e., "things that occupy space in the general area of the crotch in women's manner." There didn't seem to be any four-letter words.

When Maurice, Papa Kaytso, and I got back to the hogan, a dozen other members of the family had gathered—a teen-aged brother, two other sisters (the older one, Bessie, in from goat herding, was busy chasing the goats back over the hill) and a married brother, his wife, and children. We all went to a picnic in the rocks by a clump of cedars, where Bessie made Navajo fry-bread of hand-mixed batter heavy on the baking powder (by the handfuls), fried in deep fat over an open piñon-wood fire. We traded our box lunches for chunks of it, and everybody had superstrong coffee poured from a black iron pot, chilled strawberry pop and melon. After eating their melon, the Kaytsos carefully hung the rinds on juniper trees—for the birds and animals, I surmised, or maybe for some god with epicurean taste. The married son sat apart from the family. Maurice explained this was customary, for he now belonged to his wife's family, although once married, a man never looks at nor speaks to his mother-in-law in the belief that if he does so they both may go blind.

"It's just a way of helping kids mature," said Maurice, "by learning social responsibility. They keep their daddy from going blind, and also their grandma, by keeping them both occupied in little social ways. When the time comes for them to move into the adult world they're ready for it."

Navajo divorce is easy. The woman merely sets her husband's saddle and other gear outside the hogan door; a man divorces his wife by riding off without looking back. If a husband is made cuckold, he doesn't shoot the interloper, but accepts trespass payment from him of a sheep or two and some cash. The errant wife may not be beaten or otherwise physically chastised, but it is permissible to strip her naked in public. Since most Navajo women are strong as bulls, this seldom is attempted. Navajos have no single word for prostitute. Such a freewheeler is known as "she who stands by the side of the house." No stigma attaches to illegitimacy; plenty of Navajo spinsters happily rear bastards. Rape and incest are considered the most serious sex crimes. In olden days, along with grave robbing, they were regarded as witchcraft, punishable by death.

Back at the lodge we found Harry Goulding involved in a discussion with two well-preserved, silver-haired guests. We came up just in time to hear one of the men sputter, "The niggers are going to take over this country, because they've got smart guys running them."

"Maybe they'd be better'n we are," drawled Harry, "at pouring money down ratholes. Right now we have some pretty bum things to look at for the people we're trying to influence. If you want folks to buy your product, you've got to have something pretty nice in your show window. We've got to straighten out right here at home before we go trying to reform the whole world."

He seemed relieved that we'd come along to extricate him from what might have developed into an unpleasant situation.

"Did you see in yesterday's paper," he asked us, "where a young feller from Harvard University, out here doing legal-aid work for the Navajos, got lost for four days while hiking in to Rainbow Bridge on the old trail, and had to be rescued by helicopter? He ate acorns and cactus pears, and stuck his worn-out shoes together with piñon sap. There's still some real men left in this country."

Before dinner we went with Harry to the Seventh Day Adventist Hospital, established on a piece of high land adjacent to the lodge and set aside by Goulding on long-term lease. The hospital has 36 beds and a five-chair dental clinic. About 100 outpatients can be accommodated per day, plus from 40 to 150 dental patients. On file are outpatient records of 5,200 Navajo families (8 to 10 in each). Treatment is free, though donations are accepted. (A recent gift: a fully equipped fire engine—the donor, a doctor of Long Beach, California.) The hospital was built by Navajo labor at one-third the cost of such a building.

"If ever a chunk of heaven fell," said Harry, "it sure struck right here. That hospital has taken the pinch off of living out here in this valley. Our Navajos used to have to go a hundred miles to find a doctor other than one of their own medicine men. That's some walking in this country, or even on horseback, or in a spring wagon or pickup truck, if you're under the weather or pregnant or have a broken arm or whatnot."

Harry turned down a number of other religious orders before settling on the Adventists.

"I talked to each one and told them it had to be seventy-five percent medicine, twenty-five religion. That's the only way I'd give the land. 'What are you,' one bunch said to me, 'anti-Christ?' They made me mad. 'You sons of bitches,' I said, 'you're not gonna convert a guy before you cure him. Get off my land!' And they got. I never seen people like these Adventists. I didn't dream there was people among us who'd bend so far for their fellowman."

While the Navajos now rely greatly on the white man's hospital, they still put faith in their own medicine men, the *Hala-alii,* or singers. Alas,

Navajo singers are becoming fewer and fewer. The old ones are dying. Young bucks, having been exposed to the outside world—beginning with participation in World War II—decline to invest half a lifetime preparing to be a medicine man. It takes five years to learn only two or three ceremonials. Complete understanding of just one ceremonial has been likened to learning a complete Wagnerian opera by heart: words, music, and stage business of all the characters; all details of lighting, staging, costuming, and scenic design and painting—not merely in a general way, but well enough to perform any and all functions perfectly, all without help of a single written note or prompting. Scores of ancient legends must be assimilated as well.

Ideally, a medicine man begins his studies when five years old. The medicine kit, each singer's prized and guarded possession, is difficult to assemble. The leather pouch that contains it must be of tanned hide from a deer killed by hand—smothered by cornmeal so there will be no blood. This means that the prospective medicine man must run down his deer on foot—several days' tracking and pursuing. Birds also must be captured bloodlessly, by hand, to obtain feathers and bones which become part of the healing paraphernalia.

One factor in a Navajo's cure by a singer is the considerable investment made for the ceremonial. A sing costs from $5 to $500, depending upon the time involved. Navajos have strong faith in anything that costs money, time, and thought—in that order. These Indians dislike to concede that something in which they've invested has been a failure. On the average, a Navajo family spends 20 percent of its income on religion.

Anglos are inclined to ridicule the practices of Navajo medicine men as witch-doctoring nonsense, yet do our doctors do as well in alleviating uneasiness and fear; do our professional medicine men smooth the difficulties of personalities as expertly? Is the inner man always treated with the same care and understanding as the outward manifestation of disease?

A principal message of the Navajo medicine man is reassurance. Before the singer arrives, the patient is told he will be cured; when the ceremonial begins, the rituals and songs reiterate that theme in rhythm. Only pleasant topics are permitted in the talk of sing participants—and only positive thinking. The crowd that attends a sing is not casually gathered, but handpicked to be composed of all the persons who have been, or are now, important in the patient's life—all his human guideposts. Their very presence implies that powerful curative forces are at work.

No doubt the yucca-root bath, sweat sessions, and emetics prescribed by a singer soothe a patient's nervous system, for medicinal herbs have pharmacological properties. But mainly the singer exerts a very definite psychotherapeutic influence by bringing a metaphysical presence that is missing from the antiseptic corridors and chambers of a hospital. The solemn communal ceremonials contribute to a patient's sense of security and build his morale by recognizing the Indian's place, not only in his community, but in the entire universe. This sort of faith-building enables these Indians to survive despite the burdens on them by a harsh environment and the pressures of a surrounding hostile white culture.

On the Green Table

Just after sunup, fortified by a staggering amount of thick-sliced ham, scrambled eggs, French toast, orange juice, and coffee, we set off down the hill from Goulding's Lodge and turned north.

Mexican Hat, Bluff, Montezuma Creek . . . Navajo oil fields, and Aneth . . . then out of Utah, into the southwestern corner of Colorado . . . through the Ute Mountain Indian Reservation . . . and to the lofty city of Cortez. From it, only ten more miles to the entrance of Mesa Verde National Park. And there, enough prehistoric ruins to more than satisfy any amateur archaeologist.

The name is Spanish for "green table" and that's what it is—a plateau of 120 square miles (8 by 15), rising abruptly 1,500 feet above the Mancos Valley to an elevation of almost 8,000 feet, and made green by a thick mixed cover of piñon and juniper. The mesa is reached by a snaking switchback paved highway from which can be seen the peaks of the La Plata Mountains.

Park Point, on this road, is the finest lookout. On clear days, parts of four states can be seen by those who care for that sort of thing. The lake-dotted Montezuma Valley lies below, and to the north rise the Rico Mountains. Westward are Utah's Blues and La Sals; southwest, 115 miles distant, is Arizona's Black Mesa. Park Point offers a fine view of Shiprock, 40 miles away in New Mexico, a hulk of igneous rock rising abruptly from a vast plain of the Navajo Reservation. When seen head-on, this rock mass is supposed to look like a ship under full sail. It doesn't. Beyond

Shiprock to the west are the Lukachukai Mountains, the Navajo Alps—also called the Chuska and Tunitcha mountains.

For those who respond to Indian ruins, Mesa Verde is a paradise. There are five accessible major ruins and ten surface sites where are remnants of pit houses and pueblos. Twenty-eight canyons, containing hundreds of other ruins, splay down from the mesa.

Indians occupied Mesa Verde in pre-Columbian times, beginning at about A.D. 1, and they settled in for 13 centuries, only to disappear; no one knows why. Our calendar will have to show 2792 before the white man can claim this continent for as long. The United States hasn't yet celebrated its *second* centennial. We're social adolescents, savages-come-lately.

Some archaeologists think perhaps these people were driven away by a great drought that occurred between 1276 and 1299. Others believe that they died out due to gastric disorders and rheumatism caused by bad teeth. (Much sand was introduced into the food from the soft sandstone grinding tools, causing teeth to wear down to the gums—as evidenced in most skeletons discovered.) Scientists have deduced that cliff dwellers, after the age of 30, suffered constant ill health. There is a theory that these early settlers were destroyed by warlike Indians or absorbed by them as captives. Some anthropologists believe that Navajos are descendants of these prehistoric victorious belligerents. There may be significance in the fact that today pueblo Hopis are completely surrounded by Navajos, who call ancient Hopi relics *anasazi*, or "remains of the enemy."

When the Mesa Verde ruins were first discovered in the 1870s there was irresponsible plundering that caused much of the architecture to suffer greatly. One ruin was almost totally destroyed by avaricious diggers, some of whom used dynamite to get at the buried relics. In 1906, a portion of the mesa was set aside as a national park and the period of commercial exploitation came to an end.

We arrived at Mesa Verde and suddenly were very tired and wanted only to relax in the late afternoon sun hitting the small terrace outside our motel rooms. I was feeling sneezy, coming down with a cold, so we all rested until dinner time. At the tourist center we were served by amiable middle-aged waitresses, the first blacks we'd seen since Cheyenne. We bedded down early to be primed for the tight schedule that Whiskers, the ruins enthusiast, had plotted for the morrow.

We got up at 6:30, breakfasted at 7:00, then drove to the museum as soon as it opened at 8:00, and stayed there until 9:15 (or was it 9:17?).

There I learned that Basket Maker Indians cooked food by dropping hot rocks into it, dried meat the same way Mrs. Kaytso's daughter did, made yarn from dog hair—facts that I could have done without. We saw ancient beads of pink hornstone, black lignite, and elegantly polished juniper berries—all strung on human hair. Whiskers fell in love with one necklace nine feet long, made of 119 strands of white beads 1,500 years old and still in mint condition.

The curator of this museum seems obsessed with counting things: 5,735 stone and shell beads in a necklace; 2,969 pendants and inlay pieces found in a pottery jar; 31 pounds, four ounces of corn, measuring 22 quarts, the largest amount found in the region (how many grains, curator?). I noted that the greatest contribution of children to museums is grubby fingerprints on showcases. I counted 267 on one case which enclosed a mummy.

From the museum we hurried to the viewpoint 200 feet above Cliff Palace and waited there with about 50 impatient tourists for the ranger to show for the morning's guided tour. Enclosed metal stairs down over the cliffside joined a dirt path leading to the ruin, where the ranger gave a pseudo-erudite talk in an intolerable nasal drone, which I finally shut out by inserting earplugs. He also answered questions from the audience. A typical one: "Were these a family-type people?"

Here more than 200 rooms and 23 kivas were built under an enormous overhang of apricot-colored rock, the houses rising in some sections to four stories. Once 400 people lived in this cave, 300 feet long by 100 high. There are six distinct floor levels, the structures built on terraces, due to the natural sloping cavern floor. There are many storage rooms with bins made by thin rock slabs and with chinks mortared against rodents. A feature of the ruin is its round tapering stone tower near the cave center —the rounded stones placed with exacting care. We were permitted, one by one, to thrust our heads through the small window on another four-story tower to see bright red cliff-dweller paintings on the white inside walls. We left the Cliff Palace by climbing crude but sturdy ladders, beside which were ancient hand and toe holds cut into the sheer rock. There were some tight squeezes for the more wide-hipped sightseers.

My cold was gaining on me, but we raced on to the next scheduled guided tour, of Balcony House. The young ranger there was a better showman and a master psychologist, not telling the mob of tourists— largely middle-aged, paunchy, and flabby-muscled—what lay ahead, but leading them blithely down a wide sloping dirt trail to the ruins. It was easy getting there, but climbing out was a cat of another stripe. A short rock tunnel had to be negotiated on all fours, and then, from a ledge at the edge of a 700-foot dropoff into Soda Canyon, there was a climb of 40 feet up a double-width, almost vertical ladder of heavy pine poles. To the tourists' credit, not one balked—to see those rear ends, both fat and bony, bobbing two-by-two in a long line up the cliffside was enough to gladden anyone's day. A happening! I didn't think the stuffy old National Park Service had it in them.

Balcony House is beautiful, with little shelves under some of the second-story windows (hence the name), a spring in a back room, and rock overhangs blackened by cooking fires. There are about 40 rooms and a broad terrace front, divided in twain; a retaining wall is built dam-like into the cliff face, topped by a stone parapet about three feet high. All the rooms were artistically made, and I'm sure it was an inspiring place in which to live.

After a motel-shower and camper-lunch pause we hiked into Spruce Tree House, best preserved and third largest cliff dwelling. It is built in a natural cave 216 feet long, 89 deep, and 35 high. Some of the small door-ways are T-shaped, allowing handholds to boost a person through the opening. Interior wall decorations were made by plastering on colored clay. The proportions of everything, the spacing of architectural details, were so just right, I couldn't help but think of the abstractions of Georgia O'Keeffe.

Shortly before A.D. 1300 this compound contained 114 rooms, some in triple rows. The dark, poorly ventilated back ones probably were used for storage, though I prefer to think they were for confining people who go berserk looking at ruins. By midafternoon, I was a likely candidate for tenancy, but Whiskers had still more on her list: Square Tower House, the Sun Temple, Fire Temple, Oak Tree House, and New Fire House Ruin. Some were seen only from the rim of Fewkes Canyon (named for J. Walter Fewkes, of the Smithsonian Institution, who excavated Spruce Tree House in 1908). Others, we were able to get close to. Then we had to visit all the mesa-top ruins—pueblos and pit houses. In my nonarchaeological opinion, you see one pit house you've seen them all.

By nightfall, my eyes felt like a couple of old adobe bricks. I had a feedback headache, and my nose wouldn't stop running. I felt that if I never saw another Indian ruin it would be too soon. Whiskers was happy as a coot. She'd had a delightful day. I was glad for that, because soon she'd be leaving for back east. We were on our last High West days together.

The Hopis

It was now well into September, and the kids were a week overdue at school. But for what they'd learned in the last seven days, I was willing to go to the mat with the most bellicose truant officer. I wanted Tia, Tim, and Lulu to see something of the Hopis, and so gave the kids a short stay of execution.

Our route south took us through Four Corners, the only place in the nation where four state lines meet. There a man can get down on all fours, face west and put one hand in Utah, the other in Arizona, one knee in Colorado, the other in New Mexico—and look like a silly jackass.

We went through the Navajo settlement of Teec Nos Pos, just north of the Carrizo Mountains, and turned south along the Toh'atin Mesa to Rock Point. At the trading post, where we gassed up and Whiskers went looking at wampum, there was a placard advertising a dance, with music by "The Transistor Bananas."

Thirty miles more was Chinle, a Navajo agency post and educational center at the entrance to Canyon de Chelly (pronounced "shay") National Monument. De Chelly is a Spanish corruption of the Navajo word *tsegi*, which means roughly "rock canyon." The place is an 83,840-acre maze of sheer rock walls and twisting canyons in which are the remnants of three successive Indian civilizations. (Dear God! *Not* more ruins! But Whiskers was adamant.)

Canyon de Chelly is rich in history. Here, in 1863/4, Kit Carson proudly conducted his infamous Navajo roundup and sent its survivors on the cruel "Long Walk" to Bosque Redondo, a concentration camp in New Mexico. Carson's biographers call this "his greatest feat." The most vicious, heartless acts of militarists often are whitewashed into heroism. Some light is thrown on Kit Carson's morality by a letter which he wrote at the time to his superior, Colonel James H. Carleton, regarding sanction to allow Utes—in Carson's service as spies and guides—to keep women and children they captured "for their own use and benefit." Carson said:

". . . I make this request the more readily as I am satisfied that the future of the captives disposed of in this manner would be much better than if sent even to the Bosque Redondo. As a general thing, the Utes dispose of their captives to Mexican families, where they are fed and taken care of, and thus cease to require any further attention on the part of the government. Besides this, their being distributed as servants through the Territory causes them to lose that collectiveness of interest as a tribe which they will retain if kept together at any one place. Will you please let me know your views on this matter as soon as possible, that I may govern my conduct accordingly? . . ." The request was denied.

Before setting out on the 27-mile rim drive around the canyon, we had ginger-ale ice cream sodas at the coffee shop of the Thunderbird Guest Ranch, a cozy oasis of log and stone in a shady cottonwood grove. The store here has been "trading out" with Indians for about 60 years. Its welter of merchandise includes horse collars, harness hames, pajamas, the gaudiest oilcloth this side of Singapore, and a great variety of perfumes and cosmetics. Among modern Indian women, flower scents are beginning to nudge out the aromas of cedar chips, piñon smoke, and bacon grease. Women, it seems, are more attractive lovers when they don't stink like sheep. There is increasing demand for bras, but girdles have not yet attained popularity; some of the bravest braves now wear underwear. When I'd visited here about five years back the Indian homemade jewelry left in hock was kept in a formidable vault behind the refrigerated meat counter. Now, next to the store, a gift shop had materialized, an elegant establishment out of character with its homely surroundings.

Canyon de Chelly and its branches, Canyon del Muerto and Monument Canyon, contain more than 300 prehistoric sites and 138 major ruins, most of them too high on the cliffs to be accessible. (Hooray! Hooray!) Close-up looks of the others are afforded only to those afoot, on horseback, or in four-wheel-drive vehicles. The White House is the largest, best preserved of the ruins, occupied between A.D. 1060 and A.D. 1275, according to tree-ring dating. Some think the abandonment of this site coincided with the arrival of the Navajos, who for years regarded the canyon as their stronghold.

The rim drive was under construction—torn by deep sandy ruts and barely negotiable—but we made it around. From it, red sandstone walls drop downward 700 feet, practically perpendicular. On the canyon's floor, billiard-table smooth, Navajos maintain summer hogans and cultivate peaches and corn. We had a look at Spider Rock, an 800-foot obelisk—

only eight feet less in height than the 59-story PanAm building in New York City. According to Navajo legend, ill-mannered children are carried to it by a monstrous tarantula. My kids just hee-hawed at that. "A *helicopter* tarantula," said Tim.

And that's about all we could manage without embarking on extensive hiking tours, for which Whiskers had the inclination, but none of us the time or energy. She especially wanted to go into Canyon del Muerto to see Antelope House ruins, noted for brown-and-white painted pictographs of antelope.

We drove through Beautiful Valley, so named because of its gaudily colored rock strata and petrified forest. At the intersection with Arizona Route 264, the east-west reservation highway, we turned west and headed for Hopi country, past Steamboat Rock Butte, which looks more like an aircraft carrier than a riverboat.

While my fellow travelers were resting in the camper, I picked up a Hopi hitchhiker. On a reservation this is a frustrating business. You rarely find a talkative companion. An old man keeps his lips tightly buttoned. You will learn nothing from him. You pull up, open the car door, he scampers in without hesitation or comment. He settles down, sits solemnly for 5 miles, perhaps 20 or 40—nary a word—then signals for a stop. At roadside, he nods his thanks—maybe smiles—and then heads off into the sandy distance, no sign of human habitation, but obviously he knows where he is and where he's going. A young hitchhiker, when prodded, will answer questions—especially if he has a purloined family heirloom he wants to sell—but if he is a Navajo don't count on the answers being correct. Navajo tradition decrees that a man may lie three times with impunity—falsehood harms a liar only after that limit of prevarication is reached. Three lies usually are enough to worm out of any embarrassing situation. Often youthful Indian hitchhikers have been up all night at a "sing" and will fall slack-jawed asleep the moment they hit the cushions—particularly if your car is air-conditioned—not to blink awake until they sense instinctively they've arrived at their village or jumping-off point.

My Hopi hitchhiker, nattily dressed in city clothes, was not typical. He was returning to First Mesa from a visit to Gallup. We chatted and he became friendly enough to invite us to see his village. We went to the mesa top via a viciously tilted, rough and narrow, rock-studded dirt road hacked from cliffside, with no guardrail—the saints preserve anyone driving up here after a heavy rain.

A sign crudely painted on a roadside rock said: "NO PICTURES ARE TO BE TAKEN OF THE VILLAGE OR ANY DANCES SO PLEASE DO NOT ASK PERMISSION TO DO SO. LEAVE YOUR CAMERAS AND RECORDERS IN YOUR CARS. BY CHIEF."

We were headed for Walpi, most spectacularly situated of the Hopi's 11 villages (all but one on mesa tops). Walpi is a tiny concentration of primitively constructed adobe-and-rock homes perched precariously on the precipitous, extremely narrow promontory of a high rocky mesa. The small two- and three-story buildings are casually terraced like those of Betatakin, built with not an inch to spare and merging so imperceptibly with the chalky stone that the village suggests a castle in the sky.

Before reaching Walpi, we skirted the Tewa-speaking hamlet that the Hopis call Hano. It adjoins the village of Sichomovi.

For more than 200 years the Hopis of Walpi and Sichomovi lived as neighbors to the Tewa villagers of Hano with no social integration whatsoever. Intermarriage was forbidden, and in all that time only a single Hopi term crept into the Tewa language, the expression for "thank you"—and even so, Tewa women continued to use the Tewa term.

The schism had been brought about, according to legend, because the Hopi had reneged on promises made to the Tewa of rewards for coming to the mesa to act as the Hopi's protectors. The Tewa had fled Sante Fe, where they'd been enslaved by the Spanish. Tewa response to Hopi treachery was to put a curse on them. A pit was dug between the two villages. The Tewa made the Hopi spit into it, then spat upon the Hopi spittle and filled the pit with earth, thus sealing forever Tewa culture from appropriation by the Hopi. The Hopi accepted this symbolic humiliation and tolerated the Tewa as mercenaries willing to perform useful functions as protectors and intermediaries with other tribes and white authorities.

This state of arm's-length separation might have continued indefinitely had not the white man's culture begun creeping over the reservation toward the end of the last century. The Tewa, being more aggressive, self-reliant, and flexible, cooperated with the white settlers and prospered. The Hopi of Walpi and Sichomovi eventually noted this and began to take steps to erase the old enmities. Today, hostility between the villages has virtually disappeared. Only the old men try to keep alive the ancient Hopi injustices; the young Tewas laugh them off and scoff at the curse.

Social scientists make a great deal over that Hopi-Tewa *rapprochement,* but really all it proves is that money talks to those who are listening.

I don't believe that the Hopis were especially noble to make peace. They did so because the Tewa were getting the drop on them economically.

To left, right, and ahead, from the sky-high village of Walpi the valley spread in magnificent panorama. The location is stunning. Our grateful hitchhiker bade us climb to an earthen rooftop overlooking Walpi's ceremonial court, a small, well-stomped clearing flanked by two underground kivas—its sentinel, a heroic rock phallus. Here are held the most-publicized of the Hopi snake dance ceremonials, to bring rain.

To these people, rain is the prime requisite for life; water, the universal blessing. Crops are grown by the Hopi—in desertland, at the foot of their mesas—with no other moisture than rain, no mean agricultural achievement. Besides being excellent dry farmers, the Hopis are sheepherders and cattlemen, masons, mechanics, carpenters, machine operators, and the most skillful of Arizona's forest fire fighters. In crafts they excel in basketry and woven plaques. They are famous for their kachina dolls, carved from cottonwood, and are becoming known for overlay silver jewelry. The Hopi tribe is the only one in which men do the weaving. It is traditional that a man weaves the wedding and ceremonial robes for his bride and also makes her a pair of buckskin moccasins for the marriage.

Hopi society is matrilineal. The houses are owned by women, the land by clans. Men own sheep, horses, cattle, wagons, cars, and trucks, and they hold all the important village offices. When a man marries, he goes to live in his wife's house and works in the fields of her clan.

Home to a Hopi is always the house where he was born. A Hopi will say, "I live in Shipolovi, but stay with my wife in Mishongnovi." He goes home for all important ceremonies and is taken there to die.

The Hopi are the only pueblo Indians in Arizona. Hopi villages are autonomous. Each has its own lands, its own social and ceremonial organizations, distinctly separate from those of other villages. In solidarity the villages are akin to the Greek city-states. All speak the same language and have similar customs, but there is no feeling of unity among Hopi villages.

The government of each is the same as it was in pre-Columbian times. The order of command is: hereditary House Chief or Town Chief; council of elders; town criers, who make announcements; and warriors, who attend to policing. The council meets once a year, in mid-December, at the Soyal Ceremony to plan the tribe's business and its ceremonials. The dates of winter ceremonies are established from the setting sun's position; in summer, ceremonies are fixed by sunrise position. Snake dances are held at Hotevilla, Shipolovi, and Shungopovi in even-numbered years; in odd ones at Mishongnovi and Walpi.

Of all the pueblo Indians, only the Hopi have been able to keep their annual cycle of ceremonies untouched by white man's beliefs. The dominant theme of Hopi religion is reliance on the mystical forces believed to control weather and natural environment. The Hopi believe that if rites and ceremonies are performed regularly, properly, and with "good heart," there always will be enough to eat and good health for everyone. They depend upon magical powers to provide for the needs of the tribe; they appeal to deities to deflect or immobilize enemies so that they need not be attacked by force.

The Hopi deities are a group of vaguely conceived ancestral gods known as *kachina,* or *katchina,* represented by the grotesque, hand-carved dolls familiar to Arizonans and by dancer-impersonators in Spring. In July kachinas depart for their home on San Francisco Peaks, but they return in August as thunderheads, ponderous and moisture-laden, to bring rain to the parched land. Hopi mothers, pointing to the great clouds, tell their children, "Look! Your grandfathers are coming!"

The Hopi, more so than any other tribe, have an enormous preoccupation with religion. It pervades every facet of their daily life. Casual conversations in the villages center around rituals; gossip often concerns the implications of a misstep in a ceremonial dance. The Hopi dance more frequently than most tribes. In the prayer-songs, the priests say to the gods, "We shall be one person." The priests are not permitted to experience anger, lest such strong emotion detract from concentration on the sublime. Participants fast before a ceremony and, directly after, the dancers purify themselves with an emetic and vomit at the mesa edge before resuming their regular lives.

The average Hopi lives in harmony with his neighbors, and is dignified, affable, generous, and nonaggressive. Gentleness and temperance are greatly admired. The Hopi is taught not to display arrogance, not to retaliate against injustice. Sin is unfamiliar to a Hopi, and guilt never gnaws at him. Sex is regarded as a basic, natural part of life, not to be tainted by vulgar innuendo. To insure fertility, girls run ceremonial races; boys shoot arrows—representing lightning, the male symbol—into bundles of cornhusks (female symbol, as corn is the sacred mother of all). The power of reproduction of all living things is in the gentle hands of a two-horned god called Alosaka, who lives aloof from people in the Underground.

Some of this Hopi lore we knew and told to our children as we stood above the ceremonial court. The rest came from our volunteer Hopi guide, the hitchhiker. He was most proud of the school in the village of Polacca, far below. The shortcut to it, used by the pupils of Walpi, is a steep cliffside trail that only the most confident mountain goat could negotiate.

After we'd clambered clumsily from our vantage point, the Indian boy graciously invited us into one of the pueblo homes, where relatives of his were making *piki:* large charcoal-gray, paper-thin wafers consisting of ground blue cornmeal and wood ash. One of the women mixed and pummeled the batter; a second thinned and stirred it; a third deftly spread by hand a very thin coating on a hot flat rock under which a fire blazed. Politely, we were refused a sample, as the piki was being prepared for a sacred rite.

No TV aerials sprouted from Walpi's rooftops, but through windows and open front doors of the ancient adobe houses we caught glimpses of other modern amenities such as butane refrigerators and ranges, and chrome-and-plastic furniture on linoleum floors. In one window was a forlorn red-white-and-blue political placard, faded and fly-specked: "Steve Shadeg for U.S. Senator." At the head of the school path, Lulu picked up a mimeographed copy of the *Hopi School News,* not much different from the elementary school creations back home in Rockland County, New York. In the rock underfoot were fossil deer footprints, and at the very end of the mesa were many square, oval, and oblong washbasins worn into the rock. Whiskers decided the little round hollows alongside were made by scrubbing out stubborn spots.

It was strange in this prehistoric-looking village (some of the beams had been cut with pre-Spanish stone axes, and the stick-and-adobe construction paralleled that of Betatakin) to see dogs with metal license tags dangling from their collars and a girl with fishing rod practicing flycasting off the cliff edge. Overhanging it were sturdy outhouse toilets with free-fall plumbing. Boys raced past, recklessly pushing a baby buggy —the occupant completely calm, although the wobbly wheels were less than a foot from the drop-off.

As we got back into our camper, parked at the edge of the village, a dusty Hopi kid approached and said forthrightly, "I want to see your icebox." We invited him in. "Old fashion," was his comment. "It has to got ice." But he liked the intercom, the radio, and the copy of *Playboy* I gave him.

After descending from First Mesa, we stopped at Shongopovi, noted for its albino Indians: pink-skinned, blue-eyed, and blond. None were abroad, but three tourists asked me to pose for a picture. One offered me a quarter. I took it.

Less than ten miles west, atop Third Mesa (elevation 6,497 feet) is the deteriorating village of Old Oraibi, which some say is the oldest continuously inhabited community of our land (since about 1100, and visited by Padre Garces in 1776). We found the ancient place partially deserted, dreary, and unkempt, much less beautifully situated than Walpi. Old Oraibi is a town of scattered rocks and dung-yellow earth with dried deer legs and corncobs littering the dusty streets. Many adobe houses were neglected and falling to pieces. At the edge of town is an ugly tin-can dump. The people we encountered were glum, unsmiling, and withdrawn.

"When the last residents leave Old Oraibi," Maurice Knee had told us, "its excavation will prove to be an outstanding anthropological revelation." Meanwhile, it decays.

Only the children of Old Oraibi seemed optimistic. A few toddlers ran alongside our politely creeping camper, hanging to it, smiling up at us, chattering, begging bubble gum, touching the vehicle's smooth surfaces. From the endgate of his truck a benevolent white trader was passing out watermelon slices and paper cones of strawberry ice to a scramble of kids, some of them armed with plastic bows and arrows.

Capital of Navajoland

We went back the way we'd come, and continuing past the turnoff north to Canyon de Chelly, arrived at Ganado. There a national historic shrine has been made of an establishment that looms large in Navajo history, the Hubbell Trading Post, founded in 1876. Its monarch was Juan Lorenzo Hubbell, son of a Connecticut Yankee and a Spanish aristocrat, whose parents owned the Pajarito land grant. Congress set aside $925,000 for the 150-acre site, 11 buildings of the original compound, all the fixtures and historic mementos contained in the Hubbell home, and its eventual complete restoration.

The National Park Service continues to operate the place as a trading post to the Navajos, rather than confining it to an impersonal museum. Most early trading posts were tents, lean-tos, or crude shacks, but Don Lorenzo's was built like a hacienda, the buildings handsomely constructed of red sandstone to form a large patio. They are thick-walled with iron-barred windows and have high, beamed ceilings.

The store is much as it was in the old days, except that coffee no longer is 25 cents a pound nor calico 10 cents a yard, and there is no center of trading activity called "the bull pen," the smoky room where friends gathered around a potbellied stove. There, saddles, harnesses, bridles, and blankets hung from the ceiling; the walls were lined with sacks of sugar, flour, coffee, and pinto beans. On towering shelves were stacked groceries, dry goods, tools, and cooking utensils. In the dimness of the bullpen, Indians would squat on the floor or lean against the walls—smoking, chatting quietly, enjoying the sight of each other, inhaling the delightful perfume of burning piñon, acrid leather, tobacco, and sheep dung. Always on the counter was an open can of tobacco—free for the taking—and when travelers came in off the road, Don Lorenzo would open for them cans of peaches, tomatoes, or sardines to dispel the fatigue of traveling.

He did a great deal of trading in handwoven blankets and rugs, but the post prospered most from the sale of Indian wool and hides. I asked the Park Service guide showing us through—an Indian—if perhaps Don Lorenzo's hyperactivity in that direction hadn't been the cause of the overgrazing that had depleted the range by the early twentieth century.

"You're the first person that ever asked that question," he replied.

The Navajos were tremendously influenced by the traders. They brought the first new way of life since the Navajo changeover to sedentary living 300 years before. Now, almost a century beyond the era of benevolent exploitation by traders, the Navajos not only are doing their own trading on a large scale, but managing their own government.

From Hubbell's it is only 29 miles east to Window Rock, the Washington, D.C., of the Navajo nation, near the New Mexico border. It is named for a sandstone cliff pierced by a huge hole that *could* have been poked by a god's finger, as the Navajos say, but actually was formed by wind, water, and sand over millions of years.

Among Window Rock's smooth, raspberry-colored sandstone hills (called "haystacks") are federal and tribal buildings and an enormous octagonal, hogan-like tribal council chamber, with a ceiling of interlocking logs and native murals depicting Navajo history; 74 elected legislators, representing 11 reservation geographical regions, assemble here to discuss solemnly Navajo problems and projects. Traditionalists buck against modernists. Two opposing cultures meet head on—sometimes mingling quietly, at other times clashing harshly.

The old pastoral way of life is changing. The Navajos' ruling body, realizing that the arid land is becoming more and more limited for sheep and goat herding—long the principal source of Navajo income —has begun developing policies of diversification, which are steadily broadening the tribe's economic base. Income has been invested in such tribal enterprises as irrigation projects, coal and uranium mining, oil drilling, the manufacture of forest products, and wider distribution of arts and crafts. Private corporations have been encouraged to establish plants on reservation lands.

A new era in Navajo housing has begun with construction of low-cost housing units; new, planned towns are slated for the future. (One such, Navajo, New Mexico, is already in existence, designed by a San Francisco planning firm and erected from scratch near a new lumber mill.)

Tourist facilities are being established. Travelers have been wandering this high mesa land for decades, but since pavement has pushed across the reservation the Navajos' remote and beautiful land is being swamped by look-and-run tourists. Although in some ways the invasion is distasteful to these shy people, the Navajos would like their visitors to stay longer. For all the commercialization and attendant clutter, the influx of tourists has been beneficial, and will be more so. It has sparked a social and economic revolution on the reservation.

The Navajos' journey toward the twentieth century still is a slow crawl, but eventually they'll get there. Already there is a Miss Navajo beauty contest; television sets have appeared in some trading posts; the young have abandoned the traditional dress of their elders. It won't be long. At Window Rock, movies are shown twice weekly in the community center; Hollywood and Broadway performers sometimes appear there. I'm sure it will be some time before the screen there will be illuminated by anything like *Bonnie and Clyde* or a supersexy Swedish or Italian film, for a sign inside the door says: "No Females in Slacks, Toreador Pants or Levis PLEASE." The notice was hardly meant for the girls who work in the government offices, as they do not dress casually. Although they may live in dirt-floored hogans without electricity or running water, they all are as clipped and polished as any stenog or secretary in our national capital.

The Navajo's health has improved since the Public Health Service took over responsibility for it in 1955. There is less infant mortality, and there are fewer cases of tuberculosis, trachoma, and respiratory and intestinal diseases caused by squalor.

Diffidence toward schooling has long been a stumbling block to the Navajos. Chee Dodge, the Navajos' first council chairman, once said, "My children, education is the ladder. Tell our people to take it." Ladders still are in short supply, but there has been an astonishing rise in the percentage of school-age children attending classes—from barely 50 percent to over 90 percent within ten years. There are hardly enough boarding and day schools and traveling trailer teaching units to accommodate the almost 30,000 school-age population.

Some say it will be 40 years before the Navajos conquer their educational problems. In 1886, when the tribe—totaling then about 8,000—was returned from exile in New Mexico, in a procession strung out for ten miles, the United States government promised one schoolhouse for every 30 children "who could be induced or compelled to attend." In those days, children actually had to be kidnapped to be put in school. The first school, started at Fort Defiance in 1869, still had only 11 pupils ten years later. In 1903, with an adult population of 23,000, only 300 children were in school. But the government was lax as well. As late as 1947, only 6,000 of 22,000 children ready for education could find space in classrooms. Nor is the tribe blameless. The more thoughtful Navajos feel that some of the tribe's oil, timber, and uranium earnings should be applied alongside federal and state expenditures for Navajo education.

With enough education, the Navajos could throw off their medieval yoke and make strides in the modern world, but the old tribal ways are hard to shake.

A disgruntled Bureau of Indian Affairs official—a white man—with whom I struck up a conversation in the lodge restaurant at Window Rock had this to say about Navajos: "They're somehow out of gear, like all Indians. They're Navajos first, Indians second, and American citizens third. And there's too many willing to blame everyone but themselves for everything that goes wrong in their lives."

Town & City

Pueblo People

Adiós, Navajos. *Buenos Días,* New Mexico.

Also *adiós* to *los niños* and Whiskers, for school beckoned. Time had run out for Tia, Tim, and Lulu. They'd get but a glimpse of our nation's only bilingual state, the fifth largest—almost three times the size of New York State with one-eighteenth as many people—just over one million.

New Mexico has the nation's highest concentration of scientific talent —one Ph.D. for every 350 adults. Research and technical projects of the armed forces, the Atomic Energy Commission, and the National Aeronautics and Space Administration employ 6,000 engineers and scientists supported by a labor force of 90,000, with an annual payroll of $450 million.

Only Arizona and Oklahoma have more Indians than New Mexico, with more than 56,000 living in 19 pueblos—Zuñis being the most numerous (almost 5,000) and their reservation the third largest of the total 1,827,950 acres.

We found Zuñi Pueblo, a communal village, drab and unprepossessing, but its young people laughing and lively. Some putted about on shiny Yamaha motorbikes. Many of the women were doing their weekly washing, boiling the clothes in the baked-clay ovens (*hornos*) that are in every backyard. The Speed Queen Zuñi Launderette, near tribal head-quarters, was doing no business at all. The ovens look like igloos for midgets, and most are in close proximity to the wooden outhouses. The kids thought that amusing, until I pointed out that the cooking facility and toilet of our camper were no better separated.

At the time of our visit, the Old Mission Church, antedating the pueblo by 63 years, was being restored. Its four-foot-thick walls were raised in 1629, and the present settlement was built in 1692 when the Zuñis returned to this area for the first time after the bloody pueblo rebellion of 1680, the most successful Indian revolt in history. It marked the end of 82 years of domination by the Spanish—cruel masters whose favorite punitive measure was to sever hands, feet, arms, and legs of troublesome Indians. (Perhaps that's why the girl at Pine Ridge Reservation believed the priest-librarian would tear off her leg and beat her with its bloody stump if she didn't return a book.)

Since the uprising, Zuñis haven't bothered much with *padres*. The religious rites of these Indians have not been much influenced by Christian ways, and are the most ancient and most dependent on the supernatural.

As an ex-clown, I've long been fascinated by the Zuñis' *Koyemshi*, the queer-looking "mudhead" buffoons of the Shalako Dance, the tribe's most important religious ceremonial, a house-blessing ritual held in late November or early December. By dramatizing gossip, these bulb-headed dancers, feigning imbecility, act as a control of the villagers' moral behavior, and also are credited with the power to bring about fecundity. In spurring sexual interest their actions are likely to be not only extremely vulgar, but obscene. There are ten different types of these comics, each with distinctive name and duty.

We were told that the recent mission diggings had turned up the headless skeleton of a Spanish Franciscan martyr, Pedro de Avila y Ayela. According to church records, his head was beaten to a pulp by a church bell while he clung to a cross during a Navajo raid in 1672 on the Zuñi village of Hawikuh. Coronado, who called it Granada, had expected it to be one of the legendary Seven Cities of Cibola, with walls made of gold, but found instead only a huddle of ordinary adobe shelters.

The ruins of Hawikuh, about 15 miles southwest of Zuni over a miserable dirt road, are a hilly tumble of stones and earth, strewn with potsherds, some beautifully colored and bearing parts of what must have been striking designs. Sadly, nothing has been done to excavate or restore this historic place.

Ahead of us, en route from Zuñi to Albuquerque, lay half a dozen Indian reservations: Zuñi, Ramah-Navajo, Acoma, Laguna, Cañoncito, and Isleta.

As a going-away present to Whiskers, we climbed a trail to the mesa-top Acoma Pueblo. There the Indians first revolted against the Spanish invaders, murdering a nephew of Governor Juan de Oñate, first colonizer, and all of his company of 18 soldiers save four, who died by suicidal leaps off the rock cliffs.

Acoma Rock rises abruptly 357 feet from the windswept plains and covers 70 acres. On its fairly level sandstone top is the pueblo, called the Sky City by promoters of tourism—altitude, 7,000 feet. The ancient dwellings of stone and adobe, 1,000 feet long and 40 in height, are built in three parallel lines—each structure three stories high. Ladders lead from ground to second story, but top story and roof are reached by steep narrow steps against walls dividing the various residences. Some of the oldest apartments have windows made of selenite, a sort of mica mined in the vicinity.

The pueblo's most remarkable structure is the San Esteban Rey Mission (Saint Stephen the King), claimed by some historians to have been built in 1629. An exceptionally fine example of old pueblo missions, its walls are ten feet thick, and the heavy roof beams, 40 feet long, were cut in the Cebollata (tender onion) Mountains 30 miles distant and carried on men's backs to the mesa top. The adjacent burying ground is a 200-square-foot area of earth fill held in place by a ten-foot-high retaining wall. To make this *campo santo,* every bit of the dirt was carried to the high rock in sacks from the plains below by women of the pueblo.

We ate in Albuquerque, off the beaten path in Old Town, the original townsite of 1706, a comfortable cluster of pueblo-style establishments built around a tree-shaded plaza that has the flavor of Old Mexico. On one side is a church where mass has been celebrated since before George Washington's grandmother became pregnant.

The graceful and tranquil *alameda,* lined with charming shops, stores, and restaurants—all doing a brisk business—proves that a shopping center need not be an ugly, untidy marketplace crassly thrown up at the edge of a blacktop parking-lot wasteland. We dined Spanish-style at La Placita, a loving restoration of an old residence—our table alongside the shaggy trunk of a tree 100 years old, grown up through the dining room roof.

No place could have been further away from the oppressive militaristic and nuclear research atmosphere that pervades Albuquerque, which is home for the Defense Atomic Support Agency and the U.S. Air Force Special Weapons Center, as well as Kirtland Air Force Base and Sandia Army Base, and a branch of the Atomic Energy Commission. More than 165 firms here are directly concerned with space contracts. In addition, there are 114 agencies and divisions of the federal government in Albuquerque. The city's newest skyscraper is the 13-story, $6.9 million Federal Building.

In the morning, we all tried to make it seem like any other day— made jokes at breakfast, read aloud odd items from the local newspaper, remembered funny things that had happened. But the time of parting finally came. I lingered long at the airport gate, after everyone had gone from the departure lounge, watched the plane get buttoned up, taxi out, and then stay earthbound interminably waiting for clearance, watched until it was airborne, and then until I could see only the streak of its jets across the eastern sky. She was gone.

The Royal City

In the shock of aloneness I wanted to wander quietly from Albuquerque to Santa Fe. Instead of shooting directly north on the superspeed Pan American Central Highway, which follows the route of the early Spaniards, I went through the low-shouldered San Pedro and Ortiz mountains to the sleepy towns of Madrid and Cerillos, both once prosperous coal-mining centers, now little better than dilapidated ghost towns.

About ten miles beyond them I came onto the state penitentiary, set well back from the road. Thinking to have a close-up look, I turned into a long tree-bordered entranceway and arrived at a broad turnaround. Immediately an amplified aggressive bellow from a loudspeaker in its center ordered me to state my business.

I said I was a harmless sightseer and was ordered away gruffly. The guard's apprehension was understandable. The camper was a perfect hideout for a gang of machine-gunners all set to pull off a jailbreak. I fancied that I looked like Jimmy Cagney in an armored car. I'll bet they even had a bead on me with a telescopic sight. I felt much better. I was *dangerous*. By the time I had to get back onto the superhighway leading to Sante Fe, I was almost my normal cocky self again.

This last stretch of El Camino Real, the Royal Road, is a nightmare of brash billboards, glaring gas stations, motels and cafes with nervous-tic neonitis, and the beautiful sky marred by telephone and power lines. As I headed north, big trucks rumbled alongside and also roared at me. But in compensation for all the nerve jangling, the majestic Sangre de Cristos—the Blood of Christ Mountains—rose ahead aloof and serene, the most youthful of the Rockies, strong and ready for anything. Yet, in the light of white man's written history, the Sangre de Cristos are our oldest mountains, for Spanish adventurers were in these foothills before the Pilgrims set foot on Plymouth Rock. At the end or beginning of day these mountains, ranged almost due north and south, catch the sun broadside in full benediction and take on the marvelous rosy glow that gives them their unusual name.

While dusk is the best time for viewing the mountains, it is not the ideal hour to arrive at La Fonda ·del Sol, a remarkable, moderately priced Fred Harvey hotel that stands on the site of the old adobe inn that marks the end of the Sante Fe Trail. This larger, more modern establishment was built in 1923 as much in the style of an adobe pueblo as is possible in the heart of a city. It is managed by Bill Harvey, 28-year-old great-grandson of the original Fred Harvey, who did more than any other entrepreneur to bring southwestern Indians to the attention of the traveling public.

At the end of day here, the normally supercilious room clerk becomes even more up tight. His carefully spiked mustache fairly bristles with superiority, even though his boutonniere has wilted. The Mexican bellboys set aside their usual smiling good humor. What Whiskers calls "furniture music" drones over the P.A. system, competing with a vulgar blare of piano accordion coming from the Fiesta Room cocktail lounge. Elderly tourists, tuckered out from sight-seeing, sprawl in the gloomily lighted lobby's leather chairs. Pale, wrinkled, and gray, the senior citizens stare blankly ahead.

I was permitted to register and was taken aloft in an elevator enameled cherry red and lined with smoky, antiqued mirrors embellished with large cutout aluminum stars. I'm in a magician's cabinet! was my first thought. Thurston is going to make me disappear or stick swords in me. I'll be turned into a pigeon!

My room was beautifully furnished with Spanish antiques—what matter if the blankets were threadbare and mended and the view from my window a rooftop of ventilators that squeaked like chirping birds? Luckily, I had earplugs.

In the morning, I was awakened at 8:30 by Whiskers phoning from New York. They'd got home okay. The kids had gone off to school okay. She was tired. Hadn't slept at all. Weather was nice. The dogs had been glad to see them. The cats paid no notice. Everything back east, since they'd set down at Kennedy, seemed such a dirty mess. Hate the East, she said. The car was knocking; the brakes were making scratchy noises. She said she loved me and I said I loved her and then we hung up. I felt so sorry for myself that in the shower I sang that old Irving Berlin number, "All Alone by the Telephone" and so forth. From now on, I'd be talking to myself on the intercom.

I went out to the camper in the parking lot, turned on all four gas burners to take off the October chill and boiled myself two of the last three eggs, which I ate standing up, with a piece of stale unbuttered bread and an orange that was beginning to go. We'd run out of ice. Then, in the La Fonda's Cantinita, I had a cup of hot *café con leche*.

Sante Fe began its existence in 1609, bearing the florid title, *La Villa Real de la Sante Fé de San Francisco* (The Royal City of the Holy Faith of Saint Francis). It has been a capital continuously for more than 300 years—the oldest seat of government in the United States—and over it have flown the flags of Spain, Mexico, the Confederacy, and the United States. The city nestles in the little valley of the Rio de Sante Fe where it emerges from the foothills of the Sangre de Cristos.

Surrounded by mountains that are snowcapped until June, Sante Fe is a delightful place of ancient, narrow, tree-arched streets, modern, unpretentious business buildings (no skyscrapers), and light tan adobe houses having patios dappled by the shadow of cottonwoods and brightened by nodding hollyhocks. There is an impressive, somber cathedral built of sandstone and volcanic rock, quaint old Spanish churches of adobe, and more modern ones built in the old mission style. There are heavy wooden doors and gateways, crumbling walls, and the smell of piñon smoke is always in the air. It's a lot like a city of Old Mexico. There is about it the same feeling of mañana.

The major industry is the vacation trade, and the main attractions, the museums. There are six major ones—three of them on the tree-shaded central plaza, a haven of serenity just right for loafers and lovers.

At the Hall of Ethnology I was amused to learn that Indians shot craps before anyone ever thought of Las Vegas. For dice, they used halves of nutshells, the numbers inlaid with semiprecious stones. I don't imagine the term "snake eyes" was any problem, but what did the Indians call "boxcars"?

The Palace of Governors next door is the oldest surviving public building in the United States, built in 1610. There, early Spanish life is well portrayed in many large display rooms. In the Fine Arts Museum next to the palace are examples of pottery made by all of the state's Indian pueblos—each adhering to a distinctive design and technique. In the art galleries, when I visited, was an exhibition of stunning Japanese prints and the New Mexico Fiesta Biennial, showing the work of local painters and sculptors. (In this town there are almost as many artists as Indians.) Some of the modern painters represented in the show had borrowed freely and wisely from the ancients. The work equalled, and in some cases was better than, that which spills into New York's Madison Avenue and 57th Street galleries—and it was a lot less expensive.

Many local artists and craftsmen maintain studios and shops along Canyon Road, a narrow meander that skirts along the Santa Fe River's south bank and climbs above town. The Museum of Navaho Ceremonial Art, Inc., and the International Folk Art Museum are both up that way on Old Pecos Road. The first was founded in 1937 by a wealthy woman "for the purpose of preserving for posterity the full range and meaning of Navaho ceremonialism"—to quote the brochure. This museum is built in the style of an enormous hogan, and the atmosphere is sanctimonious. Visitors must ring a doorbell to be admitted by buzzer response, a la speakeasy. On each of the octagonal room's inside walls is an enormous oil-painted, faithful reproduction of a particular Navajo sand painting, and lying flat under glass is an actual one. The whole thing struck me as being ostentatious and sacrilegious. How much better to have invested the money in Navajo scholarships or in a hospital for those benighted Indians. I secretly hoped that some outraged Navajo god would send a bolt of lightning crashing down, if only to short-circuit the front doorbell and buzzer and maybe in passing knock the sky-blue door off the pay toilet in the men's room. I don't believe it even faces east.

The Folk Art Museum had an exhibition called "Magic and Medicine"—including such amulets as a beaded Arapaho turtle from the Great

Plains, an Ethiopian tiger claw (like an Elk's Lodge elk-tooth emblem) and an ostrich egg fetish for the home (from Tanganyika)—something that Whiskers might like to have around during my absence, but I hardly knew where to look for one. The primitive implements of petition on display all concerned fertility, rain, hunting, gifts and treasures, or longevity—the things every man and woman look for, civilized or savage.

The museum's main exhibit at that time was of the art of weaving all over the world. With examples from our southern highlands in the Appalachian Mountains was a photo and statement of one Mrs. Sadie Grindstaff regarding her chosen craft: "I figgered anything anybody could do a lot of I could do a little of mebby." An admirable philosophy.

Of Sante Fe's other touted attractions, I passed up the "Oldest House" because access to it was through a souvenir store. I avoided a "Historic Point of Interest, the Miraculous Staircase" at Our Lady of Light Chapel. But I did drop around to the Chapel of San Miguel, built about 1636 for the use of Indian slaves of Spanish officials and nearly destroyed in the Pueblo Revolt of 1680, but restored in 1710. The old paintings all are still richly colored. One has two arrow holes made by hostile Indians while it was being carried in procession. A section of the original adobe floor can be seen through a trapdoor in the modern wooden floor before the altar. I left this holy place when one of the Christian Brothers slipped out of the sacristy and flipped on a tape recording that I felt sure was leading to a financial appeal. I react badly to tape-recorded exhortations.

One morning I called on famed architect-designer and folk-art collector Alexander Girard in his studio and workshop adjoining his home high on the south side of town. He was in the midst of assembling a 40-unit exhibition of folk art, "Magic of a People," for the San Antonio, Texas, Hemisfair.

In storage bins and boxes were literally thousands of Latin-American papier-mâché, carved-wood, and pottery figurines in great variety. There were fig-leafed Adams and Eves by the score, brides and grooms, commoners and merchant princes, cowboys and rancheros, horses, lions and elephants, acrobats, skeletons, and devils—more devils than anything else ("Every culture has its devils," said Mr. Girard, "for every man has devils inside him"). There were also lots of clowns, but then they too are devil characters. (The clown's big red nose derives from Charon, boatman on the River Styx, who had a large smeller for finding the dying and dead.) There were hordes of dolls from Peru, Spain, Portugal, Puerto Rico, Brazil, Argentina, Chile, Ecuador—from every Latin country. I couldn't imagine what Mr. Girard was going to do with them all. Where would he find the time and the patience to arrange this horde of colorful toys and religious objects into meaningful tableaus?

"It will be an entire building," explained this elfish, slight, graying man. "A whole building full of little folk-art figures in settings that we have designed, each covering a different activity of everyday life."

Mr. Girard deplored the fact that the pueblo Indians now are making things only for sale to tourists—sometimes better than the old ones, but mostly worse.

"The indigenous use of handmade objects among the pueblo Indians is finished absolutely," he said. "What they make now is both marvelous and horrible at once."

I gathered that Mr. Girard referred to wonderful technique and craftsmanship too often accompanied by atrocious taste.

In one of the workrooms, painted high on a wall, was: *Entre los hombres, infinitas son las expresiones de la belleza y del amor; al abrirse a ellas los ojos, los oidos y los corazones se uniran los pueblos del mundo.* Translated: "Infinite are man's expressions of beauty and love. Open your eyes, your ears and your heart to them and you will unite the peoples of the world."

"What Spanish philosopher said that?" I asked.

"I wrote that myself," said Mr. Girard. "Do you like it?"

I did. I do. *Me gusto mucho.*

As I prepared to leave, he suddenly announced there was someone I must meet—Georgia O'Keeffe.

"I cannot give you her phone number, because I have promised, but I will call at once and arrange an appointment." He left the room to do so.

Georgia O'Keeffe! Since I was a kid I'd been crazy about her work. Steiglitz, The American Place, and all that. A pioneer of modern American art. How I'd admired those handsomely stark abstracts, her inimitable portraits of skulls and bleached pelvis bones with light-blue skies seen through the holes, her magnificent magnified flowers. Landscapes of the intellect, her work has been called.

Mr. Girard came back and said, "Georgia will see you tomorrow at eleven-fifteen, and I don't know for how long. She seldom sees anybody, so I just don't know." Then his wife gave me detailed directions to Miss O'Keeffe's desert ranch.

Whiskers will never forgive me, I thought. Ever since Mesa Verde she'd been raving about the proportions of the façades there, how they were like the paintings of Georgia O'Keeffe. What would I say to such a genius? What *could* I say? How long would she suffer a clown? How old must she be, anyway? Would she still be beautiful?

Old Bones & Flowers

A Visit with a Lady

Georgia O'Keeffe's ranch hideout is 65 miles north of Sante Fe and about 15 miles beyond Abiquiu (pronounced Ab-ee-cue), where she has had a town house since 1946—her permanent home. En route are places with names that roll wonderfully off the tongue: Tesuque, Pojoaque, Española, Hernandez, and Mendanales.

Abiquiu is an eighteenth-century hilltop Spanish village—mud-brown, quiet, and dusty, with flowers potted in coffee cans in many windows of the flesh-colored houses. Probably 150 families at most live here. Miss O'Keeffe's house, largest in town, is hidden behind a long, high, adobe wall. There are no stores—only a small frowzy bar presided over by a melancholy Spaniard with a withered arm. The few streets are dirt, narrow, and winding. There are gauzy tamarisk trees and views of far-away mountains. The small Roman Catholic church is simple; inside, a Christus, three-quarters life-size, wears a lace skirt, Mexican-style. At the time of my visit, a big black dog was asleep on the altar. We didn't disturb each other.

The village is known as a last stronghold of the Penitentes, a flagellant lay sect of the church stemming from the Spanish Inquisition. Each year, during Holy Week, these religious fanatics whip their bare backs until gory and reenact Christ's crucifixion by lashing one of their members to a cross; they used to spike him in position. I drove up the hill to see one of the two Penitentes' meetinghouses, called *moradas.* It was a stark, one-story building of cracked adobe, doors locked, windows securely shuttered—completely undistinguished but for a small cross in the courtyard.

I drove on out of town and reached Miss O'Keeffe's ranch just about on time. As I parked my camper, she came from her sprawling one-story adobe house to greet me and introduce her smoke-toned Chow dog, Oso (for bone). Head on he looks like a small Chinese temple lion. The great lady was dressed in a simple soft black wraparound—long, flowingly cut, belted, and unadorned except for a white scarf at the neck. She was smaller than I'd expected her to be. From her paintings I'd envisioned a tall, lanky, and rawboned woman. Not at all. She was petite, trim, and dainty, and moved with the assurance of a dancer, with no feeling of fragility, although she then was going on 81.

We sat outside near the house, at a small round table on a slight slope, tilted just enough to keep me subtly sliding in my chair. I wondered if Miss O'Keeffe had ever heard of that old trick of restaurants that need a fast turnover: to slant the seats slightly so that the customers won't linger too long. Then, too, the sun kept coming around to hit me in the eyes, forcing me to move my chair several times. I think that I was being sized up. I felt that I was walking a tightwire.

Then we got to talking about the circus and I asked Miss O'Keeffe, in relation to her large flower abstractions, if she'd ever considered painting an elephant. She thought that an amusing idea. I realize now that it was an awful thing to say to her, but it did seem to make us better acquainted. We went on to a discussion of some children on a teeter-totter she'd seen at a carnival in Korea and then on to rattlesnakes.

"Of course, I kill them," she said. "I never used to, but since I got my dogs, I do. I have to protect the dogs. They say they don't rattle in August when they shed, but they do."

I learned that Miss O'Keeffe likes the early morning hours best. She rises just before dawn, makes tea and a fire and then sits in bed to watch the sun come up. She likes it then because there are no people around.

There were fewer inhabitants when Georgia O'Keeffe first came to New Mexico in 1929. She wasn't a youngster—already past 40. Immediately, she fell in love with the countryside, but it was some time before she found the desert mountains among which she now lives. She'd gone first to Taos, simply, as she says, "because Mabel Dodge Luhan had my trunk sent up there." She'd had a look at the badlands. ("Grasshoppers ate the paint off cars. And I asked why are there no leaves on the trees.") Finally, she'd found this ranch.

"I came onto these high plains one night when the moon was full. I said, '*This* is my land!' and I've stayed on it. There always is a time when you must recognize what is exactly right for you and stick with it."

She explained that the ranch is really home to her, though she'd done less renovating here than at Abiquiu. The ranch is where her inspirations are; here is where the important ceremonials of transforming nature into paintings are performed. It was here that her love of the West was born.

"It took me ten years to get that house in Abiquiu," Miss O'Keeffe said. "The church, which owned it, could think of more reasons why they wanted to hold onto it. Then I had a brainstorm. I asked my lawyer if I could donate tax-free to the church and he said yes, I could. So I sent three thousand, five hundred dollars as a gift and an additional sum to buy the place and I got it. I hated to have to do it that way, but I'd waited long enough. I don't care much for charities—never give to the Red Cross. I didn't like what they did to those boys in the war, our Western boys. They rode the range and didn't know what war was about really, and nobody took the time to tell them. Even a few weeks would have been something before they were sent over to be killed."

The place at Abiquiu then was filthy as a pigpen. The roof was caved in. Doors hung awry; windows were broken. The grounds were overgrown. Walls needed pointing and plastering.

"But the view was so beautiful," said Miss O'Keeffe. "I so wanted to make it *my* house, but the dirt resisted me. To make the earth your own is hard. It never occurred to me then that I could use the vacuum cleaner on dirt floors. I'd have had more dirt floors had I known that. You just use more bags, that's all."

She said that although life at the ranch was harsher she likes the place because nothing can grow there, therefore she is not distracted by gardening and can use all her time for painting and exploring the landscape. She loves to pick up rocks and has many favorites, including one she carried in her purse halfway around the world—found outside her hotel room in Phnom Penh, the capital of Cambodia.

"When I first came here," she said. "I had to go seventy miles for supplies. Sometimes no one would drive by on our little road in weeks."

When the sun got directly overhead, Miss O'Keeffe suggested that I stay to lunch. Her hired girl was off in the city for the day, but perhaps between the two of us we could rustle up something edible from the icebox. We went inside. I was given cold roast beef to slice while she made a green salad. I sliced the home-baked, whole wheat bread, fetched yogurt, and poured milk. Miss O'Keeffe insisted that I set aside two or three monster homegrown tomatoes to take along in my camper. She grows vegetables at Abiquiu—everything from rutabagas to endive, grinds her own flour, makes her own yogurt and baked goods.

It was a delightful luncheon. We talked about parties ("I do not enjoy parties at all") and jewelry ("I never wear anything around my neck except sometimes some old ivory that I have") and of one of her contemporaries, Frank Lloyd Wright ("He never would admit that his roofs leaked and the fireplaces smoked"). She adored Mr. Wright's controversial Guggenheim Museum in New York City. She'd been to it before it opened to the public. "I just turned the knob and the door opened and I was inside all alone for hours. It was marvelous."

After lunch, we went to the patio and sat in the shade. Many bleached skulls and other bones lay about. One handsome cow's skull hung against the warm-colored adobe wall behind us. When Miss O'Keeffe started painting bones, critics and art fanciers judged them to be symbols. They were, but not of what everyone said—Miss O'Keeffe intended them only as symbols of her beloved desert, nothing more.

"They stand for everything that is alive out there, where there is no kindness. I haven't sense enough to think of any other kind of symbolism. I like bones. They're beautiful—not dead, but living."

We sat on faded canvas chairs that had begun to go stringy. We spoke of young people and of the pressures under which they must live in these brutal, bloody times. Miss O'Keeffe is fond of all youngsters, but admires most those with get-up-and-go. As an example, she mentioned the son of James Sweeney, curator of New York's Museum of Modern Art.

"He traveled all over the world on his own just to learn languages. He'd take just any old kind of job. Once he had only one hour to get ready to go on a fishing boat to the Faeroes. Another time, to learn Basque, he spent months herding sheep. I think that's wonderful, don't you?" Miss O'Keeffe paused and added, wistfully, "I've always wanted to paint sheep—those big soft mounds."

From sheep somehow, we got onto photography. Miss O'Keeffe told me that Philippe Halsman had taken some beautiful pictures of her (I trust not his famous jump ones, though I'll bet she still can get pretty high off the ground) and that she'd given him a vertebra, which he'd asked her to autograph.

"Eisenstadt made a wonderful photo of me and I wanted it to be used in the article in *Harper's Bazaar* about famous women, but they wouldn't pay for it. I didn't care at all for the one they used."

Everyone remembers the marvelous pictures taken of Georgia O'Keeffe by her husband of 22 years, Alfred Steiglitz, one of the world's most sensitive photographers. I wanted to photograph Miss O'Keeffe but was hardly qualified to join the illustrious company of Steiglitz, Halsman and Eisenstadt. Nevertheless, toward the end of the afternoon, I got up enough nerve to ask anyway. What could I lose? Miss O'Keeffe graciously consented.

She posed uncompromisingly without smiling. "Americans open their mouths too much," she said. "Why do all photographers like to take my face?" she added, as if she didn't know. It is inspiring. Not even a poor photographer could make a bad picture of it, and a good one can come up with a masterpiece. Though Georgia O'Keeffe certainly must be Irish, she looks a great deal like my Scottish grandmother. I asked Miss O'Keeffe about her ancestry.

"There was one ancestor," she said, "who was either a Hungarian or an Italian revolutionary, although he didn't look at all like one. But I guess you can't really tell. The quietest ones are sometimes the fiercest."

After I'd taken a number of head shots, she suggested that we go up on the roof and get some with mountains in the background. "I'm very fond of my Indian ladder," she said, as ahead of me, she nimbly ascended the crude peeled-pole affair. I was amazed at her agility. "I like it up here," she said, posing against the chimney and the cloudless blue sky. "The only trouble is, a snake can get on the roof by climbing up that bush. You have to be careful."

Before I left, we strolled about, admiring the harshness of the hills that stretch behind the ranch house—those Georgia O'Keeffe so loves to paint—and the mountains that push up beyond. I could understand why only two years ago she'd attempted to put the sweep of clouds and sky on the largest canvas of her career—24 feet long. Now she thinks she might try a seven-foot-high painting of the nearby cliffs.

"But it must wait," she said, "I'm painting badly these days. I know when it's bad or not."

We went inside the studio, where Miss O'Keeffe had strung up bleached vertebrae on strings to look, I thought, like bomber squadrons in flight.

"They are just my birds," she said. "Not airplanes."

We looked at some old Indian pottery she'd come upon, glinting in the setting sun on a creek bank during one of her late afternoon walks, and finally I was allowed to see some of her latest paintings, which I thought as good as any of hers I'd ever seen, despite her own disparagement of them. Amazingly, at 80, her powers of creativity apparently had not diminished one iota. I was especially struck by a painting dated 1963, *Sky Above Clouds*—a sea of small white clouds, like paving stones on a light blue street, stretching back to a slightly rosy horizon.

"I like big paintings," she said. "I began to paint big flowers for one of those good-for-nothing reasons. I thought if I make them big people will take notice. And they did. The big flowers got a lot of attention. Charles Demuth and I were always going to do a big flower picture together. I was to do the tall ones up high and he'd do the little things down below. But we never did it. And now it's too late."

She looked across the hills, and I thought of a quotation of hers that I'd read somewhere: "I used to think I would be cremated, but now I think I'll just be put in a box and stuck in some old arroyo out there."

As I was preparing to leave, Miss O'Keeffe said there was an old Spanish adobe house nearby—the oldest one in the state, built in 1612— that I must take time to see.

"It's the only really old two-story adobe house around," she said. "The downstairs wall must be well over five feet thick."

She'd put the present owner onto it—Charles Collier, a son of John Collier, who was head of the Bureau of Indian Affairs longer than any other man and a man highly respected for staunch championing of pueblo Indians that greatly improved their welfare. I was given explicit directions to the house that didn't seem too clear to me—but then, I guess I was tired.

"It's on the old San Juan Road that goes to Taos," Miss O'Keeffe said, "at Los Luceros, but you won't find that on your road map. Too small. Between Velarde and Alcalde. The house is on the Rio Grande, way back off the main road. You'll see the clumps of trees before you're very far in on the dirt road. It's a big place—ninety irrigated acres and lots of desert. You cut over off eighty-four—that's the road you get on out here—just before you get to Hernandez and go to San Juan Pueblo. Don't go into the village, but stay straight on the dirt road. You watch for a high sign that says, 'Swan Lake' and there's a couple of bridges and a tall white tank on the right. It's right where people stop so they don't meet each other on the bridge. You can't miss it."

I said I'd give it a whirl, but I *could* miss it.

"Of course you won't," said Miss O'Keeffe emphatically. "Anyone who's been on a circus can find his way anywhere."

Legendary Taos

A Traveler's Welcome

The old adobe hacienda was worth the effort of finding it. Beautiful. Just like it must have been for a weary traveler to have come onto it in Spanish colonial times. I arrived at the mansion just at dusk. When I told Charles Collier that Georgia O'Keeffe had sent me, he made me welcome immediately. We had a drink in the narrow upstairs front room, all of 60 feet long, with a rough-beamed ceiling and overflowing with Spanish colonial paintings, which the Colliers collect. The invitation soon was extended to dinner, and since both wife and housekeeper were absent, Mr. Collier prepared the meal—the mainstay a couple of deep-freeze steaks.

My host was an affable companion. After dinner, he thought it too late for me to go on to Taos, my next stop, and offered me a bed in one of the small downstairs guest rooms. He then retired upstairs. In an enormous tub that practically filled a narrow bathroom off the entry hallway, I bathed, then lay back in the water to let the peace and quiet, the long historic past of this handsome old house settle around me. I felt good.

Finally now, I had time for reading one of the books I'd brought along. Not having a robe, in my nothings I slipped out the front door and in the starlight dark went to the camper, which was parked on the graveled road in front, and got the Charlie Chaplin biography. The night was a mite chilly. I scampered back, rinsed the soles of my feet and then warmed my hide before the bell-shaped fireplace in my room—a *fagon de campaña*. I snugged under the covers to read until my eyes began to cross. Slept well.

Breakfast, built around scrambled eggs and homemade sausage, was elegantly served. Mr. Collier, who is an architect, and I discussed a number of topics in the cautiously polite manner used by persons who've just met or don't know each other well. I was told that, in its heyday, the hacienda kept Navajo Indian slaves, had its own courthouse and jail. ("Any service you wanted, they could give it to you.") We touched on America's involvement in Vietnam and its relation to civic riots. We probed the frustrations of trying to help reservation Indians, on whom Mr. Collier's father had expended so much devoted effort. There wasn't time to get deeply into any topic, though I learned that Mr. Collier preferred what he called "work fare" in preference to welfare, and that he was firmly against automation because he felt it was putting unskilled men out of work and dumping them onto governmental-aid rolls, thus causing taxes to increase. He also believed that the manufacturers of machinery were profiting most from mechanization. ("We had eighteen hundred acres of farmland in Maryland and I calculated once that with horses it could have been worked just as profitably as with farm machinery.") Mr. Collier, incensed by littering tourists, wanted them apprehended and punished. ("There are tin cans in every lake in the Rockies and fingerprints on every can. Why don't the rangers haul them out and get the people responsible for such vandalism?")

I left for Taos relaxed and heartened by such a show of High West hospitality. I seriously doubt that anyone back east would have done the same for an utter stranger.

Mr. Collier suggested that I take the less used, more picturesque road to Taos, winding around from Chimayo through Truchas, Trampas, Penasco, and Ranchos de Taos. The old adobe churches along that route were unbelievably beautiful, he said, and at this season many of the homes would have long strings of red peppers, *ristras,* hanging down their front walls. I was promised plenty of shade. He sold me.

This is very high country. Chimayo, at 6,872 feet, is noted for blankets woven in a manner handed down from the time of the conquistadors. The work largely is in the hands of the Ortega family, now in its fifth generation as weavers, but nearly everyone in Chimayo weaves. Antique-church aficionados concede that here is the most charming of all southwestern shrines, that of Santo Niño de Atocha, otherwise known as *El Sanctuario,* which has a self-replenishing mudhole to which miraculous healings are accredited.

From this town, the road climbs along the crest of a hogback dividing two comely valleys, goes past Cordova, where wood carving is a fine art, on through huge, humped mountainous shoulders, and comes to Truchas, a decrepit old village of adobe, rough-log, and timber buildings, with only very few more conventional homes. Farming at almost 8,000 feet is poor and winters are rough. The superb view must be what keeps people here. It sweeps from the Las Platas 150 miles away in southern Colorado to Mount Taylor, the same distance southwest, and on around over the Jemez to the Sandias and the Pedernal Hills down Albuquerque way. Behind the village rise the Truchas Peaks, at over 13,000 feet; below, the Sangre de Cristos fall away in magnificent rock buttresses and long sinuous ridges, with canyons and valleys galore, reaching finally the valley of the Rio Grande.

Ahead is Las Trampas, a stronghold of the Penitentes, with a gem of a small church embellished by excellent wood carvings that warn unrepentant sinners what is in store for them; and beyond is Penasco, descendant of a Spanish colonial town built in 1796.

This high mountain region, little touched by time, clings to its colonial ways. Its vital people stubbornly claw and poke at the insensitive soil, keep horses and cattle in rickety corrals alongside propped-up, pathetically shabby little barns, and industriously pile up firewood against the dread winter. *That's* life?

With great expectations, I approached Taos. It rests on a 7,000-foot-high mesa in the foothills of the Sangre de Cristos, but far enough back from the heights to give it a wide panorama, one which prompted D. H. Lawrence on his first visit to write, "I think the skyline of Taos the most beautiful of all I have ever seen in my travels around the world."

Taos actually is a combination of three settlements: Ranchos de Taos, the old Indian farming center; the Spanish-American town, properly called Don Fernando de Taos; and the Indian pueblo, San Gerónimo de Taos, which is two and a half miles north and is the oldest part.

I'd heard much about this enchanted place of pueblo Indians—that "high, halcyon tableland in a region of magic," as Mabel Dodge Luhan, the community's most noted social arbiter, once put it. I'd read about the titillating peccadillos of that triumvirate of lovers: D. H. Lawrence; Frieda, his wife; and Lady Brett, the deaf painter who so adored him. I'd often wished I could join the town's horde of artists, craftsmen, and authors for a few pecs of my own, and to bask in the "dusk of soft-spoken Spanish, the blanketed bronze of the Indian" and all that high-flown twaddle.

Lawrence of Erotica

Alas, I came too late to Taos. Its glands have changed. I found the romance all but strangled by commercialism. Even that late in the season —well after Labor Day—the place had about it an air of dowdiness and middle-aged avarice. What must it be like in midsummer, overrun by a herd of tourists attracted by travel brochures and the siren songs of the Chamber of Commerce?

"Northern New Mexico's Most Unique Vacationland" . . . "a retreat from the monotonous humdrum of today's world of speed, confusion and stress" . . . "unmatched temperate climate and awe-inspiring scenic luxuriance" . . . "you will not want for comfort and convenience" . . . "the past is ever present" . . . "time loses its meaning" . . . "a refreshing example of human cultural relations at their most harmonious."

The small plaza, which in the old days must have been a cozy haven, slumbering undisturbed in the sun, was glutted by a jam of autos and trucks parked flank-to-flank, headed into the curbing. Facing their staring glass eyes were cheap-looking and garish stores and shops, lacking in charm and grace, stocked with souvenir rubbish and overpriced Indian artifacts and jewelry of the fanciest sort. I saw more young Indian girls in white lipstick and miniskirts than picturesque old ones in blankets and with pots on their heads.

On this south side of the square, my eye caught a sign in the doorway of the La Fonda de Taos Hotel: *D. H. Lawrence, Author of 'Lady Chat-*

terley's Lover'. This is the only Showing of D. H. Lawrence's Controversial Paintings Since His Exhibition was Permanently Banned by Scotland Yard When His Show Opened at The Warren Galleries, London, in 1929.

I dropped in for a look, feeling somewhat sheepish—like an over-age fallen-Presbyterian voyeur taking in a 42nd Street nudie movie. I wondered if viewing erotic art is considered tax-deductible, and how many tourists think they're going to see Lawrence of Arabia having at a sheik or a camel, or in bed with a small Bedouin? At the hotel desk I paid a short, swarthy man one buck admission to a little locked cubicle off to the right. Now I really felt wicked. Without a word, he admitted me. It seemed to be the hotel office—a cluttered desk, file cabinets, three or four heavy straight chairs, four pairs of shined black shoes on trees lined up against one wall.

"Begin in this corner," said the man, "and come around to the right." I hate to be told how to look at dirty pictures. After he'd gone, I began in the other corner and came around to the left. The little windowless cubicle was terribly confining, but if there was smut in Taos I was determined not to let it slip by just because of a little claustrophobia. The paintings were hung frame against frame on two walls. Below them were framed 8 x 10 photos: Winston Churchill; Angelino Ravagli (Frieda Lawrence's second husband); David Garnett (a literary contemporary of Lawrence); several of Rudolph Valentino, the sultry, sexy, silent-movie star; Phil McGraw, who either was a boxer or someone in dirty underwear shorts; and Mextaxas, noted Greek statesman. (The hotel's owner, Saki Darvas, is Greek.) On a third wall was a lineup of large colored lithos of Greek heroes and more photos.

The paintings not only were awfully large but largely awful. Lawrence began to paint at 40, and these examples certainly show it. He couldn't even paint teats very well—not even male ones, which are easier. Each painting had its price affixed. *Summer Dawn* at $15,000, No. 7, was first in line—or last, depending on which end you start from. It depicts two nude torsoes—both female, I judged, though I could be sure only of the one facing head on; the other *could* have been a predatory faun or a bearded lady. Under this portrait of buttocks and pudendum was a framed photo of Tyrone Power and what appeared to be a bride. Alongside it was a note signed by Albert Einstein thanking Saki Darvas for the translation of a Greek poem.

Painting No. 1, *Flight to Paradise,* was seventh in the lineup of eight paintings. Number 9 was painted by Lawrence in collaboration with Frieda and Lady Brett. The most horrible one was a close-up of a kiss, looking like something done for therapy in a mental hospital. I was puzzled by *The Rape of the Sabine Women,* which includes 26 nudes (I think—I'm not sure I untangled them correctly), a snarling dog, three horses, seven small Indians, plus Lawrence, Frieda, and Lady Brett, fully clothed—a bargain at $15,000.

On one wall were some press reviews of the period. "Indecent pictures of the most distasteful character," said the *London Sunday Times,* July 17, 1929.

"Even readers of his novels couldn't have expected anything like some of the pictures on the wall. Disgusting and rather silly." The first statement is merely amusing. With the second, I agree.

Not one stiff peccadillo in the whole lot. I felt cheated. To get my money's worth, I went around again. If the proprietor was watching through a peephole and tried to charge me again, I'd just say the paintings were so powerful that I didn't dare open more than one eye each time around.

Lawrence, of the skimpy flaming beard and blazing social life, first lived in Taos when he was 37. He spent periods of about six months each here between 1922 and 1925. He came at the insistence of Mabel Dodge Luhan, the town's most lavish art patron. She hoped he could interpret "this mysterious and complicated land." He used very little Taos material directly, being a regional writer only in the broad sense, as his paintings indicate. But his philosophy crystallized here and his Taos experience is woven into *The Plumed Serpent* (1926) and other of his works. He was the leading light of writers working in New Mexico during that period.

Returning to the plaza, I felt that somehow I'd violated the privacy of a nicely uninhibited, properly erotic British gentleman.

There is such a pervading reverence in Taos for D. H. Lawrence that you almost expect the Union Jack to be flying from the flagpole in the plaza instead of Old Glory, which flaps up there night and day, every day, year-round, because Kit Carson is credited with having kept it flying under gunpoint during the Civil War after Confederates had ripped it down a few times. Taos residents make a big thing over this flag deal, some going so far as to say their town is the only place so honored. Not so. Our flag flies 24 hours a day at 19 other places—sanctioned by special laws, proclamations, or long-established custom. Among the spots are the U.S. Capitol; Fort McHenry, where Francis Scott Key was inspired to write our national anthem; Key's grave; that of Betsy Ross and also of Captain William Driver, who bestowed the name "Old Glory"; the burial place of Jennie Wade, only civilian killed in the Battle of Gettysburg; Lafayette's Tomb, Paris; the Castle of Death Valley Scotty (ah, come on, fellas); and in the cemetery at Deadwood, South Dakota.

On one of the narrow streets stemming off the plaza I stumbled onto the Kit Carson Home and Museum, run by a local Masonic order. Carson was married to Maria Josefa Jaramillo, member of a prominent Taos Spanish family. A brochure advertising the museum claims that the Kit Carson family lived in this thick-walled adobe building for 25 years and that seven of the Carsons' eight children were born there. Carson is on record as having used the place for headquarters, office, and commissary for eight years, from 1858 to 1866, while he lived in rooms at the back of the patio.

I paid the small admission fee, hoping that the exhibits inside would shed some light on that nasty Indian-baiter. Instead, I found history being commercially exploited in the most brash way—little on display about Kit Carson that is authentic, but instead, a clutter of old attic rubbish not worth looking at. I hardly felt like wasting time viewing old coins, saddles, buttons, the small arms of warfare, Donald Duck made of dried marshmallows, a nun doll with a marshmallow head, or a "Typical Bedroom of the Kit Carson Period, which we believe is what Kit and Josefa would have had in their home." I learned nothing, except to be wary of private museums that charge admission.

Greenback Redskins

One thing cannot be denied Taos—its pure and rarefied atmosphere, which provides wonderful clarity of light and gives colors extra luminosity that delights painters. This is nowhere more apparent than at Taos Pueblo. In the sunshine the adobe buildings there have an especially golden glint that would have driven Coronado mad.

The pueblo is a working village occupied by more than 1,400 Indians, whose ancestors have lived here for about 800 years. The old mission, reduced to walled ruins with graveyard behind, was erected in 1704. The present small adobe mission was built in 1848. It faces the pueblo's plaza and stands on the site of the original church put up by Fray Pedro Miranda in 1617 and destroyed in the Pueblo Revolt of 1680.

The pueblo is composed mainly of two moderate high-rise terraced apartment buildings—the south one of four stories and five in the north one, across the clearwater creek, bridged by heavy logs laid lengthwise. Scattered around these two masterpieces of Indian architecture are smaller buildings, corrals, and pole-supported platforms (*tapestes*) used for storage of grains and other produce. Tall protruding ladder ends indicate underground kivas. Alongside some of the houses are typical beehive-shaped ovens.

Taos Pueblo has no television aerials poking up, no electric or telephone wires. A tall water tank off to one side is not close enough to intrude in photographs. The pueblo has great sculptural dignity. Its architecture completely expresses the needs of the Indian, making the best use of materials at hand earth, trees, straw, the sun's warmth. The adobe structures are elementally simple, with enough variety in detail to avoid monotony.

The Taos people, antiassimilationist, want to stay unchanged. They cling tenaciously to ancient tribal ways, are extremely secretive about rituals, and do their damnedest to keep from revealing anything of the distinctive Tiwa tongue. Some Taos Indians even try to conceal their own names. One ethnologist gave up in despair when he found 58 different ways of saying "I."

A Taos folk tale says that if the people ever leave their pueblo, then the world will end. The elders do everything possible to keep the community together and unspoiled by progress. Taos Indians concentrate so much on time gone by that they seem to have gotten stuck in it. Some scholars of Indian life claim that Taos Indians' pride seems to be all in the past, with little respect shown for the present and only slight belief in what the future promises. However, they have quite a healthy respect for present-day dollars. Taos Indians, fiercely independent, don't much care whether you visit their pueblo or not, but when you do, bring money. At times the only sound in the home grounds of these extremely quiet people must be the swish of dollar bills and the clink of silver coins being counted. A rigid system of tourist fees has been established at the pueblo: for admission to the village; for carrying cameras; for posing for pictures; for painting and sketching; and for tour buses, including a per capita fee for their passengers. Lo, the rich Indian.

Taos commercialism seems to carry over into their dancing. No one can say that the dances of this pueblo aren't worth watching, for they are exceptionally beautiful and noted for precision. Yet they do not have the earthy dedication, the thrilling intensity of passion found elsewhere in Indian country. The Taos Indians have become blasé and cater to their audiences. Here it is more show business than devout religion.

R.I.P.

Mabel Dodge Luhan gave D. H. Lawrence a ranch 20 miles north of Taos near San Cristobal. It is at 8,000 feet, on a mountain slope called The Lobo, part of the Sangre de Cristos. Frieda later paid for the ranch by giving Mabel the manuscript of Lawrence's novel *Sons and Lovers*, written in 1913 when he was 28 years old. After his death, Frieda, as a memorial to her husband, turned Kiowa Ranch over to the University of New Mexico to be used as a summer retreat for faculty and students. A pair of large modern buildings have been erected for a summer school, and cabins in the woods are used by visiting scholars and faculty members. The cabin in which the Lawrences lived is made available in summertime to the poet who annually is awarded the university's D. H. Lawrence Fellowship.

I was directed to the ranch by a large sign, which brought Lawrence's tubercular demise to mind—very thin, pale blue lettering on a great expanse of white. It was late in the day. The headquarters cabin was closed, so I climbed the hill behind it, along a serpentine path that led up a wide swath—bound on both sides by evergreens—to the shrine erected to Lawrence by Frieda, a simple stone building painted pale cream and facing the setting sun. To the left of the chapel entrance Frieda is buried. She died in Taos in 1965. An oval photograph of her is set like a cameo in her headstone. On the rectangular grave cover were some cut evergreens—long dead—and a large bunch of plastic flowers. There is no door on the small building—just an opening—and cartwheels are inset high in front and rear walls, allowing light to enter through the spokes. The room is divided by a low stone railing with two carved wooden swinging doors; behind is a burial chest of concrete imbedded with seashells. It contains Lawrence's ashes, his typewriter, and some of his clothing, including a battered hat. On the wall behind the chest is painted a large sunflower, and a carved stone bird occupies a niche.

Displayed above the registry desk are framed certificates relating to the interment, among them a copy of the death certificate, signed by the *Directeur des Pompes Funebres* of Maire de Vence, where Lawrence died, and a certificate of *Proces-verbal d'incineration.*

No doubt about it, his flesh is gone. But Lawrence lives on. For those still storming through life, someone should engrave on the tomb's walls these words of his: "To be alive, to be a man alive, to be whole alive: that is the point."

From the open doorway the coppery high desert, streaked by the cool blue of sagebrush, stretched out to meet the crisp fall sky. The only sound was the persistent buzzing of a few large horseflies hanging onto summer's end by living in the tomb, sheltered against the cold night, their shiny bodies catching the sun's last rays.

Firebrand

Courthouse Raid

From Kiowa Ranch I backtracked and turned west over the new (1965) Rio Grande Gorge Bridge, a $2 million high-flyer 650 feet above the river. Through the San Juan Mountains, I headed north along the eastern edge of Carson National Forest, within sight of San Antonio Peak. After about 30 miles, the road nipped over into Colorado, turned west, then back south through La Manga Pass and returned to New Mexico via Cumbres Pass—Chama Peak off to the west, its jagged crest well frosted.

The highway was under construction—all chewed up and with wide long stretches of rolled gravel. As darkness came, I met no other travelers. I was alone in this extremely beautiful high country and wished that I'd come in daylight. That night I camped in a state park miles off the high-way—in the morning, a glaze of ice was on the camper's roof. I decided against a bath in the nearby lake and went on to Tierra Amarilla.

No one outside New Mexico ever heard of this mountain hamlet until one day in June 1967, when a modern Pancho Villa named Reies Lopez Tijerina (Tee-hair-*ee*-nah) and a ragged mob of 16 cohorts armed with rifles, pistols, carbines, and a dynamite bomb, staged an old-time frontier raid on the town's Rio Arriba County courthouse, which includes the sheriff's headquarters and county jail. The raiders held the village for an hour and a half, after allegedly freeing one of their members from the basement cellblock and seizing two hostages: a deputy sheriff and a United Press International reporter. In the melee a policeman and the jailer were wounded. The raid left two state police cars riddled by bullets, a scatter of bullet holes inside the courthouse and through its plate-glass front doors, a telephone ripped from its booth, the county's radio transmitter smashed and scattered, the hallway littered with spent cartridges, and pools of blood on the front steps and inside stairway.

The story of this anachronistic Wild West ruckus hit the wire services and television, and thereby the whole nation learned of Tijerina's fantastic Robin Hood plan to restore to poor Spanish-Americans, through his newly formed *Alianza Federal de Mercedes* (Federal Alliance of Mercy), all the New Mexico land he believes was stolen from them by the government.

Tijerina's strategy was to force authorities into a confrontation in a federal court of law, and specifically to place on the United States government the burden of proving its rights to former land grants—totaling more than 1,000—which he believes are based on authority of the Spanish crown as far back as April 17, 1493, when the "Kingdom of the Indies" was instituted under the leadership of Don Barne Quinto Cesar, "King of the Indies." Tijerina feels that Mexico had no right to cede the grants land to the U.S.A. when our Senate ratified the Treaty of Guadalupe Hidalgo in 1848, ending the Mexican War and taking from that defeated nation the territories of New Mexico and Northern California.

In 1879 the railroad pushed into this territory and opened things up for cattle and wool merchandising. In a single generation of frantic range-grabbing and land speculation, the Spanish-Americans of New Mexico lost what their forefathers had held since the sixteenth century. By the 1900s, of the original 33 million acres in Spanish grants, all but 1.9 million had vanished into national forests or into public domain—and from there, by land frauds, into the hands of cattle companies and individual Anglo ranchers. Virtually every Spanish-American family in New Mexico has a folkloric legend of how their lands were ruthlessly, often violently, appropriated.

The principal land grant in contention, the Tierra Amarilla, is an area of rich green valleys and sage mesas in the north-central part of Rio Arriba County, which is about the size of Vermont and has one sixth that state's population, or 23,000. The county's southern boundary comes close to the Atomic Energy Commission reservation at Los Alamos, and it extends north to the Colorado border, with the Continental Divide pushing up the middle. Most of the county's small towns and villages lie east of the mountains. The arid land west of them is occupied principally by the Jicarilla Apache Indian Reservation (1,600 Indians on 742,000 acres, or about one Indian to each 463 acres).

The raid hadn't been a simple act of banditry, nor one of spontaneous violence, but a carefully planned, though clumsily executed, attempt to make a citizen's arrest of the district attorney of New Mexico's First Judicial District, Alfonso Sanchez, thought to be in town at that time, and to bring him to trial in a kangaroo court of *El Pueblo Republica de San Joaquin del Rio de Chama,* a municipality resurrected by Tijerina from the past to "resume all rights and authorities vested in it, August 1, 1806, by King Charles IV of Spain."

Sanchez, considered a key enemy of the land restoration movement, although himself a land grant heir, was convinced that Tijerina was exploiting the poor and ignorant, inciting them to violate the law in a hopeless cause. Anger centered on District Attorney Sanchez chiefly because of his dragnet arrest of 11 of Tijerina's leading adherents on the eve of a show-of-force rally planned for early June at a village called Coyote. Further harassment by state police at roadblocks and warnings of arrest for unlawful assembly prevented Tijerina's devotees from getting together, and the projected meeting was a dud. The police action also disrupted Tijerina's plan to discuss the land grant grievance publicly with New Mexico's sympathetic governor, David Cargo, a young liberal Republican whose wife is Spanish-American.

Trouble had been brewing between Tijerina and the law officers ever since the previous October, when a small army of his well-armed followers marched into a campground of the Echo Amphitheater Recreation Area of the Santa Fe National Forest (just west of Georgia O'Keeffe's haven of peace) and announced that they'd assumed jurisdiction over 600,000 acres of the San Joaquin Spanish land grant, in which the forest recreation site is located. They arrested two forest rangers, tried them on the spot for trespassing, then released them with a warning. The federal government's reaction was to indict Tijerina and four of his lieutenants on charges of assaulting federal officials and illegal seizure of government property. (They'd driven off in government trucks equipped with radio gear.) Tijerina flew to Washington, D.C., but failed to gain diplomatic recognition for his city-state.

Refusing to surrender membership lists of his organization, Tijerina was found guilty of contempt of court and technically became a fugitive. During the ensuing winter and spring there had been a good deal of fence-cutting and some arson in the territory of the Tierra Amarilla land grant, a traditional site of hard feelings between Anglo ranchers and Spanish villagers. The thin mountain air smelled of violence.

At the time of my visit to Tierra Amarilla in September, Tijerina and more than 30 of his henchmen—as an aftermath of the bold court-house raid in June—awaited trials on charges ranging from illegal handling of explosives to first-degree kidnapping and assault to murder. (His trial was held in December, 1968, and he was acquitted.) Tijerina had been held for 45 days in the state prison without bond, but was out again, holding rallies to raise funds for legal fees.

Many New Mexicans are convinced that Tijerina's cause is hopeless under existing American law. They point to past decisions in land grant cases, including Supreme Court rulings. At most, they hope the agitations of Tijerina may awaken the conscience of New Mexico and the nation to the plight of the state's poverty-ridden Spanish-Americans. Their frustrations have been long accumulating—rutted roads impassable in winter, village schools closed in consolidation programs, years of broken political promises.

Father Robert Garcia, the Catholic priest who heads the New Mexico Office of Economic Opportunity, characterized the courthouse raid as "a symbolic gesture of despair." Governor Cargo charged that federal War on Poverty officials spent the people's money "paying one another to make surveys."

"They keep counting the outdoor toilets," Cargo said. "We already know how many outhouses there are—one for each family, and if they're lucky they have a two-holer."

The majority of Spanish-Americans do not comprehend American politics, especially those of their home state, which is said to be among the most corrupt in America. To the commoners of Mexican or Spanish descent, politics is a big dramatic hoopla every two years—speeches, parties, excitement, gifts—a system with no meaning for them. Governors, legislatures, judges, and *politicos* come and go. Nothing changes. Promises are made and kicked under the rug. The Spanish-American masses are burdened with cynicism though they hunger for justice. Arrested or forced into a local or state court over any issue, they feel they haven't much of a chance.

Possibly the most irritating factor in the north is the U.S. Forest Service policy which aims at improving range management and developing more efficient use of national timberlands. The enforcement of rules and the making of new ones has created hardship for the Spanish-Americans by cutting down or drastically altering long-established pasturing and grazing patterns. The villagers believe that the Forest Service is deliberately trying to drive the small permit-holder off the range to make room for big operators.

The melodrama of the Tijerina affair intrigued me. I'd thought the old-time, shoot-'em-up West was long gone—especially from this state so involved with atomic research and outer-space projects.

A local service station attendant sent me to Reverend Ernest Day, head of a small Baptist mission church, Primera Iglesia Bautista, with mixed congregation of Anglos and Spanish-Americans, at Park View, a couple miles north of Tierra Amarilla.

He filled me in on the social and economic aspects of the predominantly Roman Catholic region. No abject poverty, but much welfare. No challenges for young people—"I'm gonna quit school; I already know enough to sign my name on a welfare check." No social organizations or meeting places. Corrupt school board members habitually siphon off funds from the annual federal allotment of one-half million dollars (covering 16 communities: one high school, two junior highs, two centralized elementary schools, and a few village grade schools). Nepotism is widely practiced, giving to relatives jobs as teachers' aides, secretaries, cooks, custodians, and school bus drivers.

Winter conditions up here are miserable—35 degrees below zero at times. Not many jobs, except as police or forest rangers, or on ranches. Shootings and knifings in bars. Many people pack pistols—illegally, as no permits are issued for concealed weapons. Rifles and shotguns are common in most homes. (The reverend himself had a well-stocked gun rack just inside his front door.) Crime rate low, because few complaints are made to police; scores are settled privately. A bum check in this territory can get you from two to five years in the pen.

By phone, Reverend Day arranged for me to call on a rancher named Bill Munday, who lived just down the road. I was warned that

Mr. Munday might give me only five minutes or might not see me at all, as he was displeased by what a writer for the *New York Times Sunday Magazine* had written about him recently in an article on Tijerina. As I left, the minister recommended that I read *The Memoirs of Pancho Villa* by Martín Lub Guzmán.

The rancher couldn't see me until late afternoon, so I went around to the courthouse to talk with the police. There were two on duty, pleasant young fellows, both Spanish-Americans.

"They are violating *our* civil rights," said the older and heavier one. "And what's more," he added sardonically, "they only shoot with blanks. *Oh* yeah—only blanks." He pointed to a bullet hole in the room's ceiling.

"The newspapers didn't help much," said the younger, more trim cop. "Where we had them rounded up in that sheep pasture, I saw one reporter paying them a dollar each to line up for a picture behind the barbed-wire fence to make it look like we had some sort of a concentration camp stockade there, which we didn't. It was just the regular fence to keep the sheep in—no different from any other sheep pen. We didn't put it up."

I don't recall that the news reports were especially lurid, but it was reported (truthfully) that Acting Governor E. Lee Francis had called out the National Guard—350 men armed with two M-42 tanks —and that 80 state police had fanned out into the hills to hunt down the insurrectionists.

"And that one that took the hostages," said the other lawman, "he's nothing but a habitual and violent drunk. He's been in the joint a lot— how'd ya like that? I call it a joint—I mean the courthouse."

"My grandmother," said the younger fellow, "when my grandfather died, she sold the ranch for four thousand dollars. Now you couldn't buy it for a hundred and four thousand dollars. My father got maybe a hundred bucks out of it. But we don't think we still own that land. That was a *business* deal."

"His followers are all nuts or alcoholics. You tell them to sit and they sit anywhere—like dogs," the other cop said. "And it's not just a dollar a month dues, like they say, but *five* dollars—and these people can't afford that. It was upped to twenty-five a month when his brother was arrested."

As we talked a third policeman brought in off the street a kid of about 14, skinny and scared, with an unruly mop of long black hair. Nothing was said, but from a desk drawer the young cop handed out electric clippers. The kid made no protest and tried to ignore the move, but his eyes told me that he was being threatened with an enforced and humiliating haircut. I left, not wishing to embarrass him further with my Anglo presence. From behind the bars of a window of the basement jail, another young Spanish-American called out, "Hey, mister, take my pitcher, mister, take my pitcher."

Next, I went to the home, on the edge of town, of Juan D. Martinez, the fellow who'd allegedly been sprung from jail in the raid. He wasn't there, but I was invited in by a son, Lloyd Felix—in his twenties, I judged—and met Juan's wife, mother of 12 boys and two girls. Many of her sons had served in the armed forces. Their framed pictures in uniform were proudly all displayed around the small living room.

"It wasn't a jailbreak, like they say," said Lloyd. "My father was released at eleven for pretrial investigation, and the raid wasn't until three. None of the defendants was behind bars at the time."

On that day, Lloyd said, he'd been picked up coming back home from Carlsbad, where he'd been visiting relatives. His car was confiscated by the police, and he was held in jail incommunicado for 11 days. At the time I talked with him, he said his car was still in possession of the police. The stated charge had been evidence of conspiracy, but he had yet to be arraigned. He claimed also that local ranchers had supplied the police with firearms after theirs had been taken away by the raiders, and that after the raid the police, without search warrants, had pushed into the home of every family of Tierra Amarilla that bore a Spanish surname and appropriated its guns, but hadn't taken any from Anglo homes. The guns had not yet been returned, according to Lloyd. About the land grant problem, he said, "It is for the World Court to decide or the United Nations, because the 'King of the Indies' is involved. But maybe they couldn't implement a decision because neither has any power. But it would be a good decision to show the world."

I asked if he thought the Negro civil rights movement had touched off a restlessness among deprived Spanish-Americans. Would they too adopt the tactics of protest marches, sit-ins and acts of civil disobedience?

"I can't say about that," he replied. "It's all up to Tijerina. I just know that the Negroes say, 'We're gonna stop the lootin' and start the shootin'.' And there's a lot of Negroes now knows how to shoot— they're professionals trained in Vietnam."

Before I left, Lloyd Martinez gave me Tijerina's phone number in Albuquerque in case I wanted to talk to him, but said I could see Tijerina in person the next day, Sunday, at a little place called Chili, 12 miles north of Española, where he would be speaking.

"Don't know *exactly* where," Lloyd said. "In the hall, I guess. It's only a teeny little place—maybe seventy-five people. Just look for all the cars parked."

Rancher Beleaguered

In late afternoon, with trepidation, I called on Bill Munday, the rancher I'd been told about. I found him tough, but pleasant—like a well broken-in boot. He was lean, hard-muscled, and sunbaked, with the kind of incredible sky-blue eyes often found out west. He wore his battered range hat like he never took it off. When I commented on his slim figure, he said, "You stand up every day in those stirrups dodgin' that oak brush and *that*'ll make you skinny."

Munday had come into the Tierra Amarilla area 16 years ago from southern New Mexico.

"I had twenty-five thousand dollars cash," he said, "from trading —horses, cattle, hogs, turkeys, anything and everything—eighteen hours a day on an average of seven days a week. And now I've got an acre for every dollar I brought."

Munday told me that the land he now occupies once was a private land grant to one individual, Manuel Martinez. His son, Francisco, sold it to a Senator named Catron, who peddled all the irrigated land to settlers for $2.50 an acre. When Munday got his parcel, it had been overrun by trespassers, in defiance of absentee owners, for 17 years. He'd paid $11 an acre—and everyone thought he'd been rooked.

"And now," he said, "they say we're thieves. But not one acre was public domain; it all was deeded land. And, besides, it's been a test case in the land grant problem—decided in my favor in the district court and appealed to the state supreme court and got the same decision. I've got clear, clean title to this land. I'm the one who has set precedent in land grant titles, so now you can buy title insurance for ranches up here. And you know as well as I do that title insurance is a thing that can't be bought just if you happen to need it; it has to be a lead-pipe cinch before they'll give it to you."

Before Munday took over the property, previous owners had been run off by Spanish-American squatters and poachers. There had been a good many burnings of ranch buildings and some horses destroyed. During their first summer on the land, the Mundays lived in a tent and raised broncos—had no corrals, but kept their big, salty horses hobbled and staked out.

"They were the ranker type of horse," said Munday. "Any time one got gentle we sold him."

During the first three months the new owner put off 450 trespass cattle and three bands of sheep, plus a good many trespass horsemen. Because of his firm stand against trespassers, Munday encountered considerable hostility. In the ranch yard stands a chimney and fireplace, totem reminders of his first home—burned to the ground by arsonists. Since then he has been the victim of eight other such acts: a hay barn, three open hay sheds, and four stacks have been destroyed by deliberate burnings.

"The last shed had twenty-two hundred bales of hay in it," he said. "I remember the date well. It was my son Emmett's birthday."

A good many of Munday's fences have been cut from time to time, and a prize stallion was shot. Munday takes a dim view of those Spanish-Americans whom he suspects as culprits. "Of course," he said resignedly, "I can't *prove* a thing."

He's not the only sufferer. Arsonists have burned hay sheds, stacks, and grain houses of at least six other ranchers in the area. Munday named them for me; four have Spanish names, so this isn't particularly a racial problem. More than racial bigotry, a prime fact of life in Rio Arriba is a bitter brew of pride and resentment. The poor Spanish-Americans have a strong distaste for fences. They like to graze where they please and cut wood on land that their fathers, grandfathers, great-grand-fathers freely used. They also feel keenly the scorn and detestation shown them by white Anglo-Saxons and the more prosperous of their own race. The poverty-ridden Spanish-American, bitter and distrustful, is traditionally violent.

Munday said that he'd built 56 miles of fence and in the past year there had been 14 fence cuts.

"They love to cut fences," he said. Then he told a story to illustrate the futility of bringing fence-cutters to local justice. Some neighbors, new to the area and unfamiliar with the warped outlook of the Spanish-American villagers, had a fence-cutter hauled before a justice of the peace.

"I told them it wouldn't be any use," Munday said, "but they served papers anyhow. The man and his accomplices came up before a judge who lives down here a ways in what we call a shotgun house— one room right in back the other—and conducts court in the bedroom from a desk and a swivel chair. We all crowded in as best we could— must've been nine or ten of us, maybe more, all standing up except the judge. He'd read to himself from a big lawbook, or pretend to—it was so dark in there you couldn't hardly see anything three feet away, let alone read small print—then he'd turn and ask questions. It went something like this: 'What is the charge?' 'These men cut my fence.' 'Did you cut his fence?' 'Yes, I did.' Then the judge went back to his book and pretended to read some more from it, and when he turned back this time he said, 'Case dismissed.' My friends asked on what grounds? 'On grounds of hearsay,' said the judge. 'This man say he cut the fence and I hear him say it.' My neighbors were outraged. So I asked for a recess and then outside, in Spanish, I talked to the fence-cutters. We parlayed back and forth and finally we agreed to drop our fence-cutting case if they'd drop theirs against my friend's wife for assault with a deadly weapon—she'd driven them off at gunpoint. And we agreed to pay the costs of seven dollars in each case. And then I told them it was no use for them to cut fences, that every time they did we'd just repair it and they had best decide to be good neighbors and get along or else we wouldn't get along with them at all. They knew what I meant wasn't just bringing them up before some justice who'd always decide in their favor."

The affair Tijerina has caused Munday to lock horns with Governor Cargo, who is charged by his opponents with being sympathetic to the land grant claimants for vote-getting purposes.

"Why, I heard that Cargo knew about the Tijerina raid three days before it happened," said Munday. "And nothing was done about it. It was ridiculous, too, how the state police let them hold the town for as long as they did. A couple of good men with rifles could've cleaned them out in no time at all. I offered to help, but the cops didn't want me around. They sent my son Emmett to the water tower to see who was sniping from atop the courthouse, and whoever it was shot at Emmett and he came back to the police and *they* shot over his head with his own gun. They didn't recognize him. He had to steer with his knees and come in with his hands up."

Mr. Munday suggested that I stay to dinner and sleep in my camper in the ranch yard. As an added inducement, I was offered a hot bath and Sunday breakfast. I accepted on all counts, for I had qualms about parking the camper out along the highway. My creamy behemoth no doubt had been well observed on the Munday property all afternoon by every Spanish-American who'd driven by—friendly and hostile—and I didn't remember the camper brochure saying anything about how cycolac acrylonitrile-butadiene-styrene stands up against bullets.

At breakfast, I met Munday's ranch foreman, Alberto Terrazas, and some of the ranch hands, all Spanish-Americans. Alberto's father, a nephew of Don Luis Terrazas, a famed cattle baron of Chihuahua, Mexico, has been associated with the Munday family for more than 40 years. A full-blood Spanish sheepherder, an old-timer in the neighborhood—with bushy black eyebrows, rosy cheeks, and green eyes—came by and had a breakfast drink with us, but no breakfast, a specialty of which was a seemingly endless supply of panfried tiny fish. Munday's manner with these men was free and easy; they seemed fond of each other and spoke together in both Spanish and English.

The rancher apologized to me that he had a good many morning chores to attend to, but we took time anyway for a drive in his pickup truck to see some of his holdings. He kept a loaded pistol in the glove compartment and a loaded rifle lay handy behind the seat. He said right now Tierra Amarilla was a ghost town, not on the road to anywhere, but when the new highway was finished over the Cumbres Pass, then it would be on a direct route into Colorado, and another highway would be going east through Tres Piedras to Taos and on up to Colorado Springs. "People won't have to go all the way around north, like you did, to get here from the east."

This unspoiled high country then will open up for tourists, and Munday is hoping that some of them will return to build wilderness homes on his land. He envisions a ski resort on one of his mountaintops and a fancy steakhouse cantilevered over the most beautiful of his canyons. He pointed out a wide right of way he'd granted the state through his acreage.

It looks as though communication is about to set in, and perhaps the most attractive area in New Mexico no longer will be the most depressed. With more money floating around, the embittered burghers of this place may begin to lay down their firearms and be able to afford to open their human arms and hearts to each other.

The Saviour Speaks

Chili wasn't on any of my maps. It's a scatter of houses along the highway to Española, below where the Rio Chama merges with the Rio Grande—seemed hardly big enough for Tijerina to bother with. Perhaps I'd been sent on a wild goose chase.

But he was there, already speaking to about 50 roughly dressed country people, quietly seated Spanish-style on chairs ranged against three walls of a one-story wooden meeting hall. The room's middle was completely open and empty; Tijerina and staff were along the fourth side, opposite and facing the narrow entrance doorway, which was jammed with latecomers like myself.

I sidled through and wormed to the front of the hall for my first look at the famous revolutionary. He is short and stocky, big-chested, has hazel green eyes, and nervously blinks a lot. His manner was forthright. He was speaking in Spanish—warmly, on a level with his humble audience, although he was in slick city clothes. The speech was sprinkled with barbs at public officials—District Attorney Sanchez in particular. Senator Joseph Montoya was criticized for proposing a bill which would make it illegal to enter the White House with a weapon.

"I say he should pass bills to protect citizens from police brutality," Tijerina said. "The White House has plenty of bombs, planes, and tanks to defend it. You can see how far he is from reality. He should be looking after the needs of New Mexico citizens."

The partisans were with their leader all the way, murmuring appreciatively whenever Tijerina scored a point, laughing at his sallies, nodding approvingly. He had them, no doubt about it. They willingly contributed to the cause after the speech was over in little more than an hour.

Then I was introduced to Tijerina by a pleasant plump young fellow, Gerry Noll—an adopted name, he said, chosen by his sister from a mail slot to avoid racial discrimination when once she and he were trying to rent an apartment in New York City. Gerry claims to be "a fifth-generation descendant of the Duke of Pontevedra, the Spanish Hapsburg, and successor to Ferdinand the Seventh, who abdicated June third, eighteen thirty-three." Gerry's family, he said, fled Spain then and was absent from the United States at the time of land grant registry. I asked Gerry if Tijerina's organization, now called the Federation of Free City-States (*Federacion de Pueblos Libres*), had anything to do with barn- and hay-burning.

"If it'd be us burning barns," he said, "we'd've burned down the whole state long before now. We've got enough members to do it." How many? "Do you want the real figure, the private one—or the one for publicity?" he asked, smiling. "We have thirty thousand families represented and about one hundred thousand other contributors." He wouldn't say in which of his categories the figures belonged.

Gerry reported the current rumor among the land-granters regarding the famous raid: that the sheriff himself had shot the policeman to settle a long-standing grievance, and then had thrown the gun into the Rio Grande, from where, according to Gerry, it had been retrieved by an Albuquerque detective on a fishing vacation; he'd hooked the gun, and ballistic tests had proven it to be the sheriff's—so went the story making the rounds of the underground.

Tijerina and his brother, Cristobál, came out of the hall and were surrounded by admirers. As I took photographs, a young fellow asked, "Will this be on Channel Four?" When I talked to Tijerina, I was impressed by his sincerity.

"They try to make us pink," he said, "but we laugh at that stuff. I have never been to Cuba or Russia either, like the John Birchers claim. You see today how the people respond to our meeting. We are not taking the law into our own hands, as some people say."

As much to impress a group that surrounded us, as for my benefit, Tijerina launched into a speech in English.

"The potential element is justice. We are determined to bring justice as no other people has done it before. Justice is our creed. In this land of enchantment the people are enchanted—sleeping. It takes time for a poor man to build up to something. Now that the claim is known all over the world, I think a judge would think twice before he would refuse to consider these claims. The pattern was established. We must have enough power to break that pattern."

A document supporting the land grant claimants was being prepared (for $300) to be presented to the United Nations. In October, Tijerina said, there would be a big conference in Albuquerque—the land-granters meeting with other beleagured minority groups from seven states. "We will join with Hopi Indians and Negroes," said Tijerina, "and sign a coalition treaty. We are a new breed joining forces to end the white success to divide and exploit. The whites no longer will be human beings acting like beasts fooling around with our God-given rights. The only time they pay attention to us is when we organize and rebel. We are about to change the history of our country."

I wish Tijerina well, but in my heart I feel he has about as much chance of getting the land of New Mexico back to its Spanish-American claimants as Abbie Hoffman has of being invited for a weekend at the White House.

Missileland

Fat Man City

About 20 miles southwest of Chili, on a 7,000-foot mesa, is Los Alamos, once America's most secret place, but now an open city—albeit an unconventional one. There is no "Main Street," only two centrally located shopping malls, and the community has all the earmarks of a prosperous one-industry company town.

Los Alamos is roomy and antiseptic, prim and proper. There is no flavor of the West. This could be any respectable, pleasantly wooded, upper-middle-class suburb on the outskirts of any prosperous eastern or midwestern city. The low business buildings are of functional design; sedate homes have well-manicured lawns and circumspect flower beds. There are 18 churches for 13,000 residents, mostly under 40 (including 5,887 children). There are no slums, for—as a man in Colorado Springs said—"slums are made by slummy people" and obviously no slummy person has been admitted here. An enormous library, out of all proportion to the size of the population, indicates that it serves no ordinary collection of petty bourgeois. It takes brains to be a citizen of Los Alamos.

In spring the blossoms here seem a little nicer. Summers are blessedly cool, and in fall God touches the aspen leaves with just the right shades of gold. The rainbows are never overblown. In winter snow stays clean; there is skating on thick ice; and the sledding is ultrasafe.

Everyone goes about his business—smiling, congenial, mannerly—enjoying the hedonism of a government-provided good life, not prying into the occupations of neighbors, trying to believe nothing sinister is going on behind the walls of the formidable buildings of the Atomic Energy Commission (all work performed for it by personnel of the University of California). These huge science factories don't turn up in the illustrated colored brochures promoting the city, but their presence dominates it.

Los Alamos is the main ganglion of New Mexico's network of scientific communities and those beyond the borders. Ideas germinated here are fed to laboratories and testing grounds of Albuquerque and Alamogordo, the desert flats of Nevada, and empty stretches out in the Pacific. This is where the monstrous fire balls are sparked that delight scientists and terrorize everybody else.

I did not enjoy Los Alamos. I felt a subtle, uncomfortable tension. In fact, the place gave me the creeps.

The Science Museum is the only tourist attraction the town has to offer. There in an outdoor patio are displayed the ballistic cases of the first two atomic bombs: Little Boy, exploded at 1,800 feet over Hiroshima, August 6, 1945; and Fat Man, the one that devastated Nagasaki three days later. Both are painted lily white. Also proudly present are the cases of an eight-inch, artillery-fired atomic projectile (1955); a thermonuclear bomb (1961); and a bazooka-type, rocket-launched atomic missile named Davy Crockett (1962). A sickening exhibit. Nowhere is any recognition given to the innocent civilian victims who'd been burned to cinders or altered for life by the atom bombs dropped on Japan—not even a small memorial plaque.

The museum does do a credible job of emphasizing peacetime uses of atomic energy. The intricacies of atomic principles and the development of atomic power are simplified by various demonstrations with the aid of a girl guide. I stayed prudently clear of a simulated "hot cell," which permits a visitor to write his name within it by using a mechanical hand designed for handling radioactive materials. I might have written something dreadful.

A simulated atomic reactor, using Ping-Pong balls, reminded me of a hailstorm. A camera is displayed that takes three and a half million frames per second—now obsolete, replaced by one that takes 15 million pictures per second. There is a clear plastic life-size man with every part—including plastic testicles and large penis—wired for testing atomic reaction. There are mock-ups of a critical assembly called Jezebel ("Because it gets hot in a hurry," explained the guide) and one called Godiva ("Because it is a bare critical assembly"). Who says atom bomb makers don't have a sense of humor? I wonder what cute name they bestowed on the poor people of Hiroshima and Nagasaki. Toasties?

A human touch slipped into this grim assemblage; an interoffice memo of October 18, 1943: "Mr. Oppenheimer would like a nail in his office to hang his hat on." And the follow-up: "Subject: nail for hat. While you sent him a very nice coat and hat rack this morning, he would still like a nail for his hat. Please put one up in his office."

On a wall of a hallway outside some offices I read a now-unclassified Teletype sent from Washington, D.C., headquarters to the commanding officer at Los Alamos, announcing the drop on Hiroshima. The lengthy historical message was loaded with typographical errors and there had been many confused exchanges between the operators at both ends due to malfunction of the Teletype machines. But, finally, with only two misspellings, there was an eyewitness account of the explosion of the first atom bomb on a living target: "A BALL OF FIRE CHANGED IN A FEW RECORDS TO PURPLE CLOUDS AND BOILING UPWARD SWIRLING FLAMES PD TURN JUST COMPLETED WHN FLASH WAS AXXX OBSERVED PD INTENSLY BRIGHT LIGHT CONCEALED BY ALL AND RATE OF RISE OF WHITE CLOUD FASTER THAN AT TR PD IT WAS ONE THIRD GREATER IN DIAMETER REACHING THIRTY THOUSAND FEET WITH FLATTENED TOP AT THIS LEVEL PD". (TR refers to Trinity, test site of the bomb in northern New Mexico; PD is the symbol for period punctuation.)

Inside one of the offices I heard a museum employee ask another, "Do you want a sandwich?"

"Do you know what's on the menu?"

"Corned beef today, roast beef tomorrow."

Into a telephone another museum minion was imploring, "Would it be possible for you to arrange for us to see the house again, the reason being that Lois now has all sorts of second thoughts about storage space and she thinks maybe she'd like a few more closets . . ."

As I left the museum, which is a registered national historical landmark, I noted its motto: "That the Past Shall Live."

Shadow of Billy the Kid

Driving away from the atomic city, between mile after mile of wire-mesh
fencing spotted with warning signs against trespassing, I remembered
something said by Hans Albrecht Bethe, winner in 1967 of the Nobel
Prize in Physics and the man largely responsible for the basic design of
the atomic bomb: "Everything starts with Los Alamos—with the A-bomb.
All the tragedies and all the mistakes that haunt us now begin there."
    I sought solace by driving south to Bandelier National Monument,
where I roamed among the late pre-Spanish-period cliff and pueblo ruins
in Frijoles Canyon. To see this proof of a civilization long gone only
depressed me more. Bandelier gets its odd name from Adolph F. Bandelier, a Swiss-American ethnologist, archaeologist, and author, first scientist
to make a survey of this region, between 1880 and 1886. He wrote a novel
about the people of Tyuonyi Pueblo called *The Delight Makers.*
    It is thought that Frijoles Canyon was first occupied in A.D. 1250.
During 300 years Indian farmers built 13 groups of habitations, holding
a maximum of 2,000 people. The ruins are reached easily by foot trail.
On the canyon floor are those of Tyuonyi (chew-OHN-yee), a circular
pueblo that once had 400 rooms. Along shelves of the cliff walls are talus
houses (built of rock debris fallen to the cliff base); scores of caves are
carved into the soft volcanic ash rock, called tuff.
    A mile up the canyon from the visitors' center is a ceremonial cave
140 feet above the canyon floor, accessible by steep trail and ladders.
After I'd climbed to it and back down I was so overheated and the little
stream that rollicked along the trail looked so inviting that I stripped
down to take my long-postponed bath. I'd been quite alone for some
time and didn't expect anyone to come along. I'd no sooner begun to
frolic in the chill water than I heard voices down the trail. I splashed
out and hid behind a tree—barely in time. Two couples—one middle-aged,
the other much younger—and a trio of small children hove into view.
As they passed I could hear the older woman explaining archaeology to
her grandchildren. "The Indians were wild like the deer and the bear,
and they moved out here to be far away from the city." Then the younger

woman said loudly, "We went to a real fancy restaurant in Santa Fe, Mother, and we had dungaree crab." Her husband added, "The people there were very high-class; some of them were wearing riding habitats." Good thing they didn't spot me behind the tree. I might have been jailed for indignant exposure.

From Bandelier, I went back to Santa Fe and then south through Santa Rosa to Fort Sumner, where Kit Carson brought his rounded-up Navajos on the Long Walk.

There seemed to be nothing in town commemorating the event—not even a Kit Carson Jiffy Launderette. Nor is there any monument to the first white man who opened up this part of New Mexico, Señor Álvar Núñez Cabeza de Vaca, hero of the most astounding epic in the history of exploration. But I found a bizarre roadside establishment, the Billy the Kid Museum, proclaiming "Over 10,000 Items"—everything from Billy's pistol ("Count the Notches") to petrified turtles, a restored 1920 Fordson Tractor, personal items of General Sumner, photos of Billy the Kid's pallbearers, quartoscope picture viewers of 1897, and live rattlesnakes. I felt just about numb enough for something like this. I couldn't resist.

In the souvenir store I paid my quarter, or whatever it was, to a paunchy, elderly gent.

"What have you got in there?" I asked.

"Everything." He did.

I was turned over to a skinny kid of about 13, ostensibly to guide me through the museum—though I suspect more to see that I didn't filch anything. We went out a back door and serpentined through a labyrinth of a dozen or more narrow sheds, past a tiresome hodgepodge of old tintypes, dog-eared postcards and faded photos, old coffee grinders, cash registers, kindergarten academy certificates from 1898, auto license plates from 1912, old Ford flivvers, buggies and buckboards, rotting saddles, horse collars, deteriorating wagons and coaches, a belfry bell, potbellied stoves, iron and copper kettles—but little of Billy the Kid, beyond that one notched pistol and a few rifles claimed to have been his.

"My pap's been collectin' for over forty years," said the boy, coughing, wheezing, and sneezing from the dust. "I got asthma," he apologized. A hell of a job for someone with asthma.

Eventually I was led to the prize treasures from old Fort Sumner: a post-office slot-cabinet, a tattered American flag, a moth-eaten uniform, a blanket, a sword.

Out in the yard stood a hideous replica of Billy the Kid's tombstone and grave, locked in a little enclave of wire-mesh fencing. I dutifully viewed the marker, took off my hat, held it over my heart, and then made the sign of the cross (I think I may have done it backwards), genuflected, and for good measure did that Hindu thing—whatever they call it— bowing with hands pressed together. I should have saluted, but perhaps that would have been too much. I could see the kid was impressed. On our way back to the front of the museum he pointed to a pair of double-barreled shotguns and said, "Bet them could sure blow you apart." I conceded that they probably could.

What happens, I thought, when this lad grows up and finds out that his dad's collection of marvelous relics is just a lot of old useless junk, and that his shining hero, Billy the Kid, "the Boy Bandit King, 21 Men to His Credit," was nothing but a homicidal cretin punk?

On across a high lonely mesa to Roswell, location of Walker Air Force Base, home of the 509th Composite Group that dropped the first atomic bomb and the place where Dr. Robert H. Goddard, a young physics professor from Worcester, Massachusetts, began in 1926 to conduct his now-famous experiments with primitive rockets, laying the foundation for our present astronautical program.

Many of his strange-looking, spindly skyrockets are on exhibit at the local art museum; in its rose garden stands Dr. Goddard's very first rocket-launching tower, looking like a heroic Erector-set construction in comparison with the gigantic gantries devised by modern space engineers.

On to Artesia, which boasts Abo, America's first combined elementary school and fallout shelter. "Pilot Project for the Atomic Age," says a leaflet describing it. The odd name comes from a 7,000-foot-deep geological formation in the vicinity, source of a major oil discovery; the meaning, presumably Indian, has been lost in antiquity.

Kids attend classes underground in windowless classrooms beneath an insulated 21-inch slab of concrete. Whiskers once told me that, when she was a little girl, for a while she'd had to go to classes improvised in a movie theater and how dismal it was, shut in with no windows. Nature should be allowed to flow gently through the educational process. Simply hammering facts into kids within a blank chamber isn't good enough. Deprived of outlook, their viewpoint will warp.

Advocates of this dug-in educational institution, completed in 1962, cite its advantages: low construction cost; saving on real estate, due to the roof being used as playground; no window breakage, washing, or shade maintenance; reduced maintenance cost and longer life of buildings. They fail to mention that the peepers of spring cannot be heard. Butterflies cannot flit in and out, nor delicious zephyrs ride above the chalk dust. Nor can rain be seen spattering on the panes, nor rivulets racing each other down the glass. No bird songs are heard from the meadow. The leaves of trees do not rustle and whisper, trading secrets among themselves. No wispy clouds can be seen drifting across the blue, or a storm on the horizon brewing, slate-gray and angry, flicked by fingers of lightning. God has been barred.

I'd be pretty disturbed if I had to go to a school that not only shuts out nature but also harbors a morgue.

Mirror, Mirror on the Wall . . .

The most pleasant backwater place I found in New Mexico is a tree-shaded village called La Luz, dating to 1882. Hervey Allen, the novelist, made it the last home of his swashbuckling hero, Anthony Adverse. One evening there I sat in the patio of a small adobe house lighted by candles as its owner, sister of a neighbor back home, spoke of the lovely light of New Mexico.

"It's what I like best of all," she said. "The light. Nowhere else in the world can you get this kind of pure light. How can photographers judge it? You have to have a built-in light meter in your eyes."

I knew how she felt, as I'd just driven down from the mountains to the east, facing the most gorgeous spread of sunset I've ever seen. When I spoke of it, the lady said, "We have them like that all the time. And the stars are nowhere more clear—and there seem to be more of them. I stay out here nearly every night just watching them and thinking and remembering and promising God I'll live a better life."

She thought I should call on Peter Hurd, who'd painted the controversial portrait of President Lyndon Johnson, although she didn't approve of Hurd's paintings of New Mexico.

"He paints the east side of it," she said. "There are bigger and better mountains in the west. And some of his things are like old *Saturday Evening Post* covers. He paints too many rich socialites; he's sold out."

I phoned Mr. Hurd, and late the next afternoon drove back into the mountains about 25 miles northeast of Ruidoso to San Patricio, a village on the Río Ruidoso settled about 1875, a favorite resort of Billy the Kid and his band of outlaws.

The Hurds live in a handsome Spanish ranch house of adobe, built in 1867. The painter met me wearing knee-high, soft-leather boots, a battered range Stetson, and a paint-spattered, bib-front apron. He'd been working in the studio. He is lanky, six feet tall, and has wavy sandy hair that is graying. He was then 62 years old, and his work has had enthusiastic acceptance for the past 30 years. His father-in-law, from whom he learned a great deal, was N. C. Wyeth, famous illustrator and muralist. Hurd's wife, Henriette, is a sister of popular painter Andrew Wyeth and is a very good painter herself.

I asked Mr. Hurd to tell me as much as he cared to about the Johnson assignment.

"Stanley Marcus, of Nieman-Marcus in Dallas," he began, "had written Ladybird a note suggesting me for the official portrait whenever it would be done. He didn't even bother to ask me. He knew I'd consider it an honor to do it. But from the first I knew it would be difficult. Mrs. Johnson said to me once, when we were at the White House sitting out on the Truman Balcony, 'Peter, you're going to find this the most frustrating, exasperating work you've ever undertaken.' I told her I don't frustrate easily. 'I'm sure it will be difficult' I remember saying, 'but it'll come out all right.' I've often pondered about that later.

"The next thing I knew about it, I had a letter from Lloyd Goodrich, then director of the Whitney Museum in New York, asking for photocopies of some of my portraits. I didn't bother to answer. My work is on record, and I thought it a useless request. Then one day when I was painting Mrs. Nicholas Longworth at her Georgetown residence I got a phone call from Mr. Goodrich—had to come down two flights to answer it, I remember—and I agreed to send the photos, but he wouldn't say what they were for. Then much later when I was lunching at Mrs. Longworth's with John Walker, director of the National Gallery, his wife, and daughter, the puzzle began to fall in place, and I guessed who it was was interested in my work, and the cat was out of the bag. It was all very devious. But that's the way Johnson is—there's no straight line between two points."

The painter was given little time with his subject: two hours of sitting in on an LBJ news conference at the White House with two research-reporters from *Time* magazine, during which Peter and his wife made color and physiognomy notes; a half-hour sitting during one weekend at Camp David; and a fruitless session at the Johnsons' Texas ranch while the president was conferring in the dining room with Supreme Court Justice Arthur Goldberg, who'd just been named ambassador to the United Nations.

Of the Camp David sitting, Hurd said, "I hung around and it finally was arranged, but the poor man was so dead tired—he'd gone up for a rest—and his great head nodded twice as he sat for me. I said, 'Mr. President, I'm very worried about how tired you are, and I wish you'd go and take a siesta.' He said, 'No, no. I promised Bird I'd give you half an hour and I will.' So, just under the half hour, 20 minutes, to be exact, I said, 'Time's up, Mr. President,' and he got up and lumbered off."

At the ranch session LBJ never stayed in one position long enough for Hurd to be able to sketch him. For 40 minutes the President fussed and squirmed—getting up, sitting down, pacing the floor, tugging his earlobes, rubbing his nose, wiping his brow, screwing up his face.

Hurd had been in Mr. Johnson's company twice before: once at a party given in Peter's honor by New Mexico Senator Chavez, in George-town, and once on the yacht *Sequoia* as a guest of the secretary of the navy, along with 20 Texans.

The painter realized that he'd be unable to get from the president the 25 to 30 hours of sittings he usually demands of a portrait subject, and so decided to work from eight photographs and to use, as a stand-in for the president's body and hands, a friend of Hurd's and fellow rancher, J. O. "Bud" Payne, who came to model at least a dozen times, traveling 75 miles each way to and from the Hurd ranch.

After 400 hours of work—five times longer than Hurd's usual total labor on a portrait—the painting was finished, and all the world by now knows that Mr. Johnson took one look at its unveiling and said, "That's the ugliest thing I ever saw."

I asked Mr. Hurd if he had anything to add to the mountain of comment that had already been printed about the celebrated affair.

"I'd just as soon the whole thing was forgotten," he said. "There are things I'd say that might sound waspish and I'm not that way at all. The fun far exceeded the unhappiness of the confrontation. Mrs. Johnson particularly was hospitable. We were invited to a state dinner and were overnight guests at the White House—an exciting thing, wonderful experience. We met cabinet members, and to be on the fringe of history in the making was just wonderful."

Hurd explained that some of the rash remarks attributed to him in a *New York Times* story by Howard Taubman had been made because he'd been called to a telephone interview from a sickbed with 103° fever.

"I haven't the faintest resentment toward the president," Hurd said, "for what certainly was a breach of etiquette, an act of rudeness. I enormously respect his office. In my opinion he knows nothing about fine arts and he'd probably be better off to leave his opinions unstated. This man, however, is under the damndest pressure of anyone in the world with problems absolutely so complicated and numerous that I wonder how anyone can live through one day even. He is a very complex individual and just about the vainest man I've ever met who wasn't a professional actor. Egotistical. Obviously, you have to have great ego to run for the office of President. Men are more vain than women; a man will always say, 'Paint me as I am.'

"Had I forseen the lampooning that President Johnson has gotten, the damage caused, I hope I would have had strength of character to overlook it and drop the whole thing," Hurd added.

Mrs. Johnson was terribly upset by the uproar her husband's inconsiderate remark had caused. She'd phoned Mr. Hurd and said, "Peter, I hope never to go through another weekend like this if I live to be a thousand, which you know I won't. Everything went wrong. Everything happened, except the government of Vietnam didn't fall." She had objected mildly to the lighted capitol dome which Peter had painted in the background of the portrait. "Couldn't you make it kind of hazy?" she'd requested.

In consoling Mrs. Johnson about the painting, Peter had told her by telephone that it wasn't as bad as she thought it was, and that he'd already had several offers to buy it—and not from the John Birch Society to use as a dart board either. "I couldn't believe I was saying this," he told me. "Neither one has a sense of humor, as you and I know it. Oh, he has a kind of backhouse wit, but at the ranch everyone sits around the big table and watches for him to guffaw before they laugh."

Hurd was stopped one day by a New Mexico highway patrolman and asked to show his driver's license, which in this state carries a photo of the holder.

"How are you and L.B.J. getting along?" asked the officer.

"I think that's the ugliest thing I ever saw," said Peter jocularly, as he handed the officer his license.

"I'll just bet it is, Pete," replied the cop. "Because your license has expired and I'll have to cite you, but I'll do it in your own district so the local JP can decide the case."

As I was leaving, Hurd's ranch foreman came into the office and marked Peter's birthday on the calendar, so his driver's license could be kept in order. While Peter spoke with his foreman, a teen-age girl sidled in and left two stamped letters on the desk to be mailed. "It's my tie to the outside world," she said to me softly.

Mountain Talk

It's ironic that in this land where Indians still court their rain gods with ancient dusty ritual and where Spanish villages cling to medieval ways, the atom bomb was born—an event that drastically altered the character of New Mexico. The native population is a blend of three races: Anglo, Spanish-American, and Indian, each remaining true to its own culture in harmony, not without a few sour notes. Onto it now has been superimposed a conglomerate of scientists, engineers, and military professionals, inhabiting an autonomous aerospace and missile community that dominates the state's southwest.

Some natives resent the invasion of their beautiful territory by the merchants of outer-space hardware, but most regard it as the best thing that ever happened to New Mexico, for it has raised not only the economic level, but the intellectual one as well. Brainpower has become a commodity much in demand and well paid. An intelligent hierarchy has been gathered in, and through it a golden flow from the United States Treasury filters down to all levels.

The newest New Mexicans are spread over an area of more than two and a half million acres, lying largely in the high country of the Tularosa Basin west of the Sacramento Mountains. In those highlands are charming places named Cloudcroft, Mountain Park, High Rolls, Mescalero, Ruidoso, Hondo, and Lincoln—scenic havens of strongly opinionated old-time residents. I drove there to learn how the changing face of New Mexico looks to these particular High Westerners.

I found the native highlanders proud that their state is the only one which welcomed Mexicans, and fond of the so-called "salad dressing" overtones Latins have given the local speech.

Nobody up there talked much about Indians except to sympathize with those who leave their own tribal and reservation culture and then, unable to adjust to that of the white man, become hopelessly lost on both counts.

The lack of communication between pueblos was cited as a factor in causing the Indians' backwardness.

Texans were largely disliked and distrusted. Referred to as "them damn Texans," they've never been forgiven for trying to invade New Mexico during the Civil War.

The mountaineers found hard to comprehend the aims of the liberated longhair generation, although one woman told me, "Instead of getting so worked up by the unwashed, people over thirty ought to be bothered by the unfed—there's more of them." She believed that older folks are inclined to be neurotically blind to violations of human dignity and aware only of things that violate conventionality. "They get upset by four-letter sex words," she added, "but don't give a hoot about those that say bomb, hate, kill, hurt, burn, maim, and guns. Sargent Shriver once said that and I admire him for it."

Dismay was expressed over the congenital backwardness of the state's educational system. (Not until 1891 was there a substantial law for state-supported education; total expenditure for public schools then was less than $50,000, and the illiteracy rate was 45 percent.)

People who lack an enthusiastic appreciation of nature came in for some lumps. Regarding ranchers: "They're all business. The rain is business to them. The sun is business. Animals are just business. These men have no heart; they're no fun even to themselves." Space and missile people: "They aren't really part of us. We go about our business mostly on land. They never touch the earth; they fly in and fly out—don't really see the beauty at all. Why, do you know, them astronauts, when they was up in space, none of them even bothered to look at the stars at all?"

Folks who neglect their children were castigated. "There's none of us spends near enough time with our kids. Too often they're bought off. We see them coming up the road here with an expensive new rifle and a lot of shells, and they'll sit and plunk them all into the water, when they'd much rather be out with their folks along, even with just a little old BB gun."

It was generally acknowledged that the state needs more tourism. "Tourists are big business everywhere out west but here," said a modern Apache in the coffee shop of the motel and gas station run by that tribe at Mescalero. "Even so, only the government spends more money in this state than tourists. If only we could get them to stay longer—if we just had Grand Canyon or Yellowstone, for instance, or Monument Valley, like the Navajos. Something big we could blow about. I like it this way best, myself, but you can't eat trees, mountains, white sands, and ruins."

The very factors that have kept New Mexico backward—aridity, remoteness, and immense distances—have allowed it to retain its natural beauty, and have also been just right for missile development. Many of the mountain people do not consider this one of God's blessings.

"When they was working on the A-bomb," said a groom at one of the stables of the Ruidoso Downs Racetrack, "my old grandmaw knew some devil's work was going on out in the desert. She felt it in her bones, she said. Boy, I'm sure glad she's not alive to see what they're up to today. Her bones'd really be jumping. I sure get a little uneasy living even this close to what's going on down there."

Wild Blue Yonder

What's mainly going on down there is that one hell of a lot of the citizens' money is being spent. Nine minutes from Alamogordo (fat cottonwood) is the Missile Development Center at Holloman Air Force Base, a spread of over 50,000 acres, containing 1,247 buildings, a technical fantasyland community removed from ordinary everyday realities. The people there even speak a different language, understandable only to computers and the initiated. To be one of the latter requires high military rank or a retinue of educated initials bringing up the rear.

The center's purpose is "to conduct and support the test and evaluation of airborne missiles, target drones, aircraft reconnaissance systems, and missile reentry vehicles and aids, and to operate the Central Inertial Guidance Test Facility, the Air Force Systems Command highspeed track facilities, and the Radar Target Scatter Site."

According to a fact sheet handed out at the base, funds invested by the Department of Defense in guidance control and navigation research development and hardware—in one fiscal year—"would purchase over 235,000 Cadillacs at $5,000 each." (The public relations people like to bring things down to the common level.)

Many of the installations here for conducting tests and measurements are uncommonly expensive. For instance, facilities of the Radar Target Scatter Division (condensed to Ratscat)—whose job it is to collect characteristic radar signatures which are reflected from weapons systems, nose cones, decoys, and aerospace craft—use approximately $8 million worth of electronic equipment. To replace the laboratory gear of the Central Inertial Guidance Test Facility would require $16 million.

The captain assigned to me when I visited Holloman pointed out the long building occupied by computer memory banks. He spoke of a balloon 300 feet higher than the Washington Monument, and ventured the thought that inertial guidance is a subject more suited to a priest of God than to a scientist. "It's almost a spiritual thing," he said, "to be able to figure out how to guide a vehicle through outer space by an inertial system. Those fellows are really way out. But then everyone on the base is spiritually motivated. We have Ph.D.s here who are only lieutenants."

While there is a remarkable gathering of high domes among the 7,000 people who toil at Holloman, there's also the regular GI Joe, who doesn't know an azimuth angle from his left foot. I read, in a guide to the base, under "Some Rules To Remember," that "switch-blade knives, blackjacks, saps, loaded hoses, brass knuckles and other similar items are prohibited," and that BB and pellet guns are considered weapons.

Because of my interest in animals I was taken to see work being done with chimps at the Aeromedical Research Laboratory, where I met Harald J. von Beckh, M.D. (University of Vienna, 1940, and in 1941 on the staff of the Aeromedical Academy in Berlin, Germany, where he lectured for student flight-surgeons, according to his published bio.) After World War II Dr. von Beckh went to Buenos Aires, Argentina, and in 1957 came to Holloman. His present position is chief scientist.

Before being escorted to see the apes I was pinned down in the office of Dr. von Beckh, who gave me at great length, in a methodical manner, the justification for using the chimps as precursors of human astronauts, the main point being that these primates are the most similar to man—anatomically, psychologically, and intellectually.

Chimps have been conditioned to count, to match symbols, to

operate push buttons and levers, to respond to light and sound signals, and even to handle the simulated stick of an aircraft.

There are 200 of these animals in Dr. von Beckh's colony. The oldest and biggest is Samson, at 13 the equivalent in age of a 26-year-old human. I was told that one fully trained chimp is worth $25,000—and I'll bet he can't even walk a tightwire or hold a potty over his head and go *Skreeek! skreeek! skreeek!*

Dr. von Beckh took the captain and me to see the subjects of his peroration—first to the Consortorium, a 30-acre circular, treeless enclosure, fenced and bounded by a moat, and then to the Vivarium, going warily past cages of heavy wire mesh, each containing a fairly large chimpanzee.

"Be careful," the doctor warned. "They like to spit on us. Watch that big one does not grab you. He is powerful."

Inside, everything was white and antiseptic—like the establishment of a prosperous veterinarian—and seemingly better equipped than some hospitals I've been to. Off the long corridors were small windowless cubicles in which various experiments were in progress. Well secured in high chairs of plastic and metal sat chimpanzees of different sizes, their old-man faces framed by flap ears, their liquid brown eyes looking appealingly at us. The animals yawned and some dozed, but they couldn't do much else because of the way they were enclosed in thick plastic collars and bibs, as well as arm, leg, and hand holds.

"They have pedals, you see," said Dr. von Beckh, "that work automatically, so that they must get exercise whether they want it or not."

Some of the skulls were shaven and wore little metal caps from which wires trailed off to various instruments and mechanical devices. Some had no wires leading off. I was told that those caps were fitted with transistorized radio transmitters sending out electroencephalographs.

Behind the chimps were high metal frameworks hung with exposed spaghettilike wiring, relays, timers, switches, and all kinds of electronic junk, looking like the innards of a telephone switchboard. Suddenly the sound of a band playing the "Star-Spangled Banner" came over the public-address system. How weird, I thought. Everyone is standing already —everyone but the chimps and they *can't* stand up, no matter how patriotic they are. *Shades of Dr. Strangelove!* Then I realized it was only the radio; the music marked the opening game of the World Series.

"How long can a chimp be kept like that?" I asked Dr. von Beckh.

"For hours," he said, "days, weeks, months, years, forever—until he dies."

Then I was told that by means of an electrode in a chimp's brain, pain, hunger, or aggression could be provoked.

"We can effect very strong control on behavior," said Dr. von Beckh. Might be a good idea for the circus. Dial a trick. I'll pass it along to Ringling Bros.

"Can such electrodes be put in the brain of man?" I asked, and received an affirmative answer. So get ready, boys, for the new electronic army. Not only will there be bombing by push button, but push-button infantry as well. I doubt, however, that chimps, at $25,000 a head, will ever be used in the front lines—men are much cheaper.

Dr. von Beckh left us with a young lady who was conducting a "little mother-love project." A rhesus monkey was being reared by a pair of surrogate mothers. Both were constructed of terry cloth, but one had a pair of staring knobs like the eyes of a totem, making it look like something Picasso might dream up out of old scrap. The project was being constantly monitored by closed-circuit television, so that the scientist could observe and record, without being seen, which substitute mother the monkey preferred. To the surprise of everyone involved, it cared most for the horrible-looking one with the two knobs. The lady scientist, a neurophrenologist, was at a loss to understand this.

"Simple," I told her. "Those knobs look like teats to the baby monkey, and not like scary eyes, as you think."

"I think you hit it right," exclaimed the captain, a normal, healthy, unprogrammed American boy.

But the lady scientist didn't take kindly to my theory. To accept it would mean the end of the experiment—and that would never do. Ah, science. Ah, motherhood. Ah, wilderness.

I left Alamogordo with its Rocket Motel, Missile Motors, and Rocket Pawn Shop, and drove on west 50 miles to the White Sands Missile Range, our nation's largest military reservation, 4,000 square miles. It is one of five such test ranges; the others are in Florida, California, and on Kwajalein Atoll, in the Pacific. White Sands base employs 19,708 persons, including about 3,000 civilians, mostly from nearby Las Cruces. The annual payroll, including contractor employees, is approximately $85 million. The range is considered "the best instrumented test center in the free world." Under constant test and development here are the army's Pershing, Sergeant, and Nike Zeus missiles; the air force's Falcon; the navy's Talos; the National Aaeronautic and Space Administration's Apollo vehicles.

The most impressive and terrifying sight on the White Sands Missile Range, and the only one casual visitors are permitted to see, is what the brass there calls "the Missile Park"—a broad, paved esplanade on which a dozen full-scale models of various missiles stand on display—great loveless erections of destruction—with smaller, winged missiles poised like hateful insects among them.

At the information office in the headquarters building, which faces this callous show of force, I was greeted by a man from back east named Gabriel J. Brillante. What a wonderful name for a public relations officer at a missile range! I was tempted to ask if he played a horn.

Mr. Brillante, relaxed and ebullient as befits his calling, turned out to be avidly interested in the historical background of the missile range, a large part of which once was the Saint Augustine Ranch, named for the 7,030-foot San Augustín Peak and its pass, between which the highway goes just east of Las Cruces.

On a large wall map I was shown the location of the McDonald Ranch, just west of Oscura Peak, where, at a spot 80 miles uprange, the first atom bomb was set off on July 16, 1945. Other famous ranches were pointed out, as well as several valuable mines in the San Andres. Victoria Mountain was pinpointed for me. A cache of Spanish treasure—gold bars, early parchments, swords, and religious relics—is thought to be hidden there in a deeply buried cavern. The story goes back to a half-breed Indian who allegedly stumbled on the gold bullion—said to be worth $22 million—while on a hunting trip. The discoverer lost the loot, he said, when a cave-in buried it after a dynamiting attempt to enlarge the cave's entrance. The Indian was shot and killed shortly thereafter, and the legend goes on. The army does not encourage gold seekers, but did once permit a private mining company a 60-day exploratory period, which uncovered nothing.

North of the main missile range on the map I noted a supplemental range, about one-third as big, and asked about it. It is 40 miles square and used about 20 times a year to allow longer flight tests of supersonic missiles. In the area, called FIX (firing in extension) live some 90 families —about 175 people. They hold contracts with the government, agreeing to evacuation at missile-firing times upon notification of at least ten days.

The families move out through four established checkpoints, where strict tabs are kept on the evacuees. Maximum evacuation time is 12 hours. Upon completion of the firing, radio stations in the area announce permission for return to homes.

"Everyone is always very cooperative," said Mr. Brillante, "except one old lady up there, who always gives the boys a hard time. Usually she hangs back and refuses to budge until the very last moment, and then they have to go in and take her out—sometimes by helicopter if the time gets really short."

She sounded like someone I ought to talk to—a defier of the space age. Despite the fact that Mr. Brillante didn't know the lady's name or where she lived, I set out to find her. I'd wanted to go up that way anyhow to have a look at atom-bomb country.

Place of Nativity

The place where the world's first atomic bomb was exploded is known as Trinity Site. It is only about 15 miles south of the road that more or less divides the two missile-range areas, and is not open to the public except on one Sunday in October, when a motorcade of several hundred people is conducted there by the Alamagordo Chamber of Commerce. The annual trek is made in the autumn because on the actual anniversary day this part of the desert is too blazing hot. After all, who wants to risk sunstroke just to make a pilgrimage to some godforsaken place nearly everyone has forgotten about?

A small pyramidal monument of black lava rock marks the historic spot. Affixed to the front is a plaque identifying the bomb as a "nuclear device." Five lines of the plaque's 11-line inscription are devoted to crediting the monument's erection in 1965 "by the White Sands Missile Range," with the name of its commanding major general prominently displayed.

There isn't much else to see here in the naked, glaring, dusty desert. Only stubs remain of the four concrete piers that supported the steel tower from which the bomb was detonated; the tower itself was vaporized. Three mounds of sand, fenced off from the main blast site, indicate locations of instrument bunkers—concrete dugouts about 6 by 12 feet. Sometimes there still can be found shards of trinite—a cloudy, greenish, glass-like substance made by the fusing of the sand by the bomb's tremendous heat. A wide but shallow scoop in the center of the blast area is all there is of the bomb's crater. An atom bomb doesn't have to go very deep to accomplish its end. In comparison with Grand Canyon, the hole left by the original atom bomb is nothing. It can't even compare with the saucer of the bullring at Cuidad Juárez, across the border from El Paso, where White Sands and Holloman personnel spend many a carefree Sunday afternoon rooting—in the tradition of American good sportsmanship—for the bull against the matador.

My drive north took me through Carrizozo, where I made some inquiries of the postmaster, in several offices of the county courthouse across the street, and at the local weekly newspaper, and finally came up with the name and location of the woman I was seeking. I found her out raking stones in front of her house, a casually shingled frame affair of one story, standing back somewhat from the highway. The only other habitation in sight was the gas station-general store-post office far down the road, where I'd just gotten final confirmation of the location. A large, home-painted sign stood in the woman's barren yard: "DEATH Was Created By GOD. Caused by MAN it is MURDER."

The woman was very old, slightly hunched over, emaciated, and carelessly dressed. Her face, sunk in agony, was deeply wrinkled, its skin marked by brown blotches. The veins stood out on her thin bony hands. I was received without a smile, but invited into the house.

I felt uneasy and became more so as the woman locked the outside door behind us. I became very much on edge as the doors leading from one small room to another were locked behind me as we made our way through the unkempt place. It was a mess—nothing in its proper place, only a few miserable sticks of furniture and the floors littered. Garbage and dirty dishes were stacked in the kitchen sink. On the floor of every room was either an old dirty mattress or a rude pallet of rags and torn blankets.

Finally we came to the other side of the long, narrow house, to the last room. On shelves and benches around the walls were piled hundreds of mineral specimens. More of them covered a long table extending down the room's middle, and still more were in boxes on the floor—beautiful rocks, iridescent and sparkling, wonderfully colored. Apparently, the woman was, or had been, a professional rock hound. She bade me sign a register and then a printed form, which I gathered absolved her of any responsibility for my safety when I visited her mine. Undoubtedly, she thought I'd come to search for rocks. The dust made me cough.

"Why do you cough?" she asked sharply, then almost immediately answered her own question, "It's the rays. They're getting you, too."

I never did get the chance to ask her how she felt about the missile range or about what she was doing on that day in July when the world's first atom bomb was set off. The poor thing was suffering from a delusion that the postmaster down the road was trying to kill her with infrared rays.

"That's why I have to change beds every night," she said. "So he'll not know where I'm sleeping, where to direct the infer-red rays. They're killing me and no one is doing anything about it. *You* don't do anything."

"What can I do?" I asked.

"You can do nothing," she said sourly. "You'll just go and leave me like all the rest and tonight the infer-red rays, they'll come again."

There seemed to be nothing more to say, nothing to do, but to back off edgily, get to my camper, slide in, and drive away. She sagged by the corner of her dilapidated house and silently, accusingly, watched me go. She stayed in my rearview mirror until I got up the rise and over.

It was damned chilly that night, so I stayed in a motel in Alamogordo instead of in the camper. The room clerk was a white-thatched Pickwickian who'd been a tent-show repertory actor and a contortionist, and he was familiar with my circus career and my present work. I told him about my unhappy visit to the old lady up north.

"Peculiar things are happening out here," he said. "There's a whole new atomic folklore being built up."

Then he told me of some high-country people who'd kept a dead young woman above ground on an altar in their barn for weeks, because they believed she'd merely gone off in a spaceship and would be back. I was shown a news clipping concerning an Appaloosa horse that had been found dead in a remote mountain valley near Alamosa, Colorado, just northeast of Tierra Amarilla, after allegedly tangling with a flying saucer. The flesh had disappeared from neck and head, and the bones of those parts had been bleached white, while the rest of the horse's body remained intact. "Lightning don't do things like that," the horse's owner was reported to have said. "It sure as hell don't boil all the meat off the bones and take it away and never leave a speck." A forest ranger had checked the area with a Geiger counter and recorded extremely high radioactive readings. Over a 500-square-yard area, about 100 yards from the carcass, was found black material like that from an automobile exhaust, in about 15 irregularly shaped patches, each about 18 inches in diameter.

When we'd begun this trip into the High West I'd no idea it would end on such a macabre note. I bedded down for the last time before turning back east. At 4:00 A.M. I was awakened by a nightmare in which all the people were naked and headless and running around on all fours.

Shortly after dawn, I took off to return the truck-camper that had been our summer home. Then I'd be winging back to Whiskers and the kids.

I hadn't realized how attached I'd become to the camper, how poignant the leave-taking would be. We'd been through a lot together. I felt I'd lost a dear friend, and when I walked away I didn't dare look back. Please omit flowers.

Of course it's impossible, in a few months of gypsying about—even in a trek of over 12,000 miles—to cover completely so large a geographical section as our nation's mountain states. Therefore, I haven't tried to present the definitive picture of these highlands, their inhabitants, and their tourist visitors, but simply to set down what we ourselves saw and heard from people encountered as we rolled along. I don't even claim that these persons are typical, and from their words and actions you may draw your own conclusions.

In the High West we'd expected the avariciousness of eastern population centers to be missing. Mostly, it is, but not entirely. We knew from our circus-traveling days that more than a few western mountaineers we'd meet would be penurious, bigoted, and spiteful, living as miserably here as they would anywhere else. We weren't disappointed in that respect. A notable instance of locals preying on trusting tourists occurred when we were passing through Utah. There was a public scandal, widely reported in the newspapers of Salt Lake City, over service station attendants covertly puncturing tires in order to sell new ones, and of frightening out-of-state motorists into unnecessarily replacing batteries and brake shoes.

In dealing with mountain westerners it is wise to bear in mind that not all those who ventured across the Mississippi were strong and noble. Failures also came—those unable to earn a living back east, wastrels and discriminated-against younger sons. Many headed west, not because they were especially daring and enterprising, but simply because they got squeezed out.

However, Whiskers and I concluded that those who make their homes in the High West are mostly admirable Americans. Fiercely independent, their behavior is exemplary more often than not. They are largely primitive in their desires, conservative politically. They embrace each other fondly; they respect the land and each man's right to it, his individuality, privacy, creative potential, and his ideas because they are his alone.

We'd been anxious to observe the impact on High Westerners of their hordes of tourist visitors—demanding, critical, impatient, often unappreciative, and greatly fatigued travelers. We found that highland residents are able to survive the annual peregrinations of that mob of ingrates because the native-born out this way have something of the jut-jaw optimism of their ancestors and, like those earliest settlers, are mostly openhearted and openhanded. Out here, the frontier is a living reality. As recently as 1946, a High Westerner still lived who'd assisted in the burial of Sitting Bull—not his bones, but the old bronze medicine man himself.

The mountaineer is more at peace with nature, seems more capable of enjoying simple things. Men among the peaks are hearty, genuine in social exchange. Mountain westerners will stop unsolicited to help a stranger change a tire, to puzzle over a balky automobile engine, to fetch gas when the stranger has foolishly run out, to find him when he is lost. They'll share a meal with folks they've never before laid eyes on and expect to never again. They'll go out of their way proudly to show a visitor a favorite place or view, to find a spot for him to bed down or take a much needed bath. They'll recount an adventure, re-create for him snatches of the tumultuous past. To a casual acquaintance, most westerners will gladly lend their own belongings—such personal and expensive things as a camera, a portable typewriter, hiking boots, or a rod and reel. Once in Cheyenne a man who'd known me less than an hour turned over the keys to his family's second car and I drove it freely for a week. (Granted, neither of us was stone-cold sober.)

In Wyoming, there is a saying: "A stranger is a friend you haven't met"—quaint, but the natives take it seriously. Out west in general a man really is considered an honest brother until proven otherwise.

Some of this good fellowship undoubtedly stems from the High Westerner's isolation. In many parts of this cloud-scraped land denizens are few and far between. In Wyoming, for instance, some dots on the map cover as few as five people. Westerners believe, as did Thomas Jefferson in 1786, that a population density of ten is uncomfortably close to saturation. But, few or many, most mountaineers are bluff, proud, and fearless, bearing a welcome as refreshing as the crisp air they breathe. The true westerner usually is damned glad to see anyone from beyond the wide horizons that rim his special world.

A neighbor of mine who hails from Vermont once explained the chief difference between a New Englander and a westerner in relations with outsiders: the downeaster won't talk to a stranger at all until he gets to know something about the interloper and what he is up to, whereas the outwester will talk readily to a stranger—but only up to a point. As soon as the westerner finds out what's going on, he clams up, and from then on the stranger must prove himself.

In the High West are strains of almost every European nationality. Italians, Greeks, Poles, Finns, Welsh, and Scots came to work the mines. Scandinavians drifted to logging camps. Russians and Germans specialized in beet farming. Basques became sheep herders. Orientals and the Irish came west with the railroads, to bend their backs spiking tracks over the mountains. French joined Indians as fur trappers. In Wyoming's Big Horns, remittance men from Britain prospered by selling range horses for cannon fodder during the Boer War.

All religions are represented, including Jewish and Hindu. In addition there are such unusual ones as the Church of Jesus Christ of Latter-day Saints (Mormons) and the Native American Church, an Indian sect whose sacrament is a psychotomimetic drug derived from cactus buttons.

Indians are firmly woven through High West fabric—ever present to remind us that in our ancestral hearts we are a race of ruffians. To a lesser degree there are Mexicans—some proud to be called that, others who'd rather be known as Spaniards or Spanish-Americans. The Negro is present, but not yet in numbers great enough to cloud the clear blue eyes of the purebred High Westerner. To him, some men will always be more equal than others, and "darkies" are something that southerners and easterners have to deal with—not him, no siree. Not yet.

In the mountain West there is less desperate bustle. A man doesn't risk a nervous breakdown getting to and from work. Few cities and towns are noisome frantic hives. People have more time for each other and enjoy such a kinship with nature that anyone who shuns hunting, fishing, and boating is looked on as subversive.

Our trip through the High West opened my eyes wider and gave all of us a greater understanding and love for this beautiful high country and its energetic people. Perhaps small regional truths which we'd encountered and uncovered will help clarify larger ones that concern America today.

I was glad to get home, but it wouldn't take much urging to get us back into the High West—with or without a cycolac acrylonitrile-butadiene-styrene plastic camper named *Malgré Tout*.

About The Author

BILL BALLANTINE has been a free-lance writer and graphics artist for more than 20 years. His three previous books are: *Wild Tigers & Tame Fleas* (1958), *Horses & Their Bosses* (1963) and *Nobody Loves a Cockroach* (1968). More than 200 articles by him have appeared in major national magazines, including *Reader's Digest, The Saturday Evening Post, True,* and *Holiday,* where his Shunpike Tours were very popular. He is an insatiable traveler. For seven years he toured America coast-to-coast with the Ringling Bros. and Barnum & Bailey Circus—first as a clown, and later as special representative of the Executive Director. As a writer, Ballantine has visited Canada, Mexico, South America, Europe, many Caribbean islands, India, Turkey, and the Soviet Union. Mr. Ballantine lives in the Hudson Valley near New York City with his wife —poetess and potter Charlotte Russell—five teen-aged children, two hound dogs, one Labrador retriever, three Persian and two Siamese cats.

Printed in the U.S.A.